I0123708

Through the Years with Romany

Eunice Evens

*Annotated and with
Appreciations of Romany*

Lamorna Publications

i

The last known photograph of Romany

Lamorna Publications

Yew Tree Studio, Marshwood, Dorset DT6 5QF
www.lamornapublications.co.uk

First published 1946

This new annotated edition published 2023

Original Text and Photographs © The Evens Family 2023

*Appreciations © Terry Waite, CBE 2023,
Eric Robson, OBE 2023   Simon Bain 2023
respectively*

Annotations/editorial material © Leonard Hollands 2023

ISBN: 978-0-9933898-7-0

Set in 12pt New Times Roman

Contents

List of Illustrations

Introduction

This book, written by Romany's widow, Eunice Evens, was originally published in 1946 and is the definitive biography of Romany of the BBC, Reverend George Bramwell Evens – Bram.

Gratifyingly, eighty years on from his death, interest in Romany continues, but copies of this book are becoming difficult to source. That, plus the opportunity to add snippets of information, and, I hope, interest, as well as the odd correction, is the justification for republishing this book.

It has been pointed that the 'magic' of Romany is to be found in the reading of his books, but, once 'hooked' on that magic, it is so rewarding to be able to learn more of the man who created (and creates) that magic. Also, this book is the only significant source of information about Romany's ministry and his Gypsy ancestry, both of which are of interest to many of his devotees.

I am grateful to Terry Wait, CBE, Eric Robson, OBE and Simon Bain for their contributions to this edition, and to John Thorpe, Phil Shelley, Les Horton, Jonathan Briggs, Des and Edith Potter and Peter Wilson who have contributed valuable information for the chapter notes.

I am, of course, additionally grateful to Simon Bain, Romany's grandson, for enthusiastically consenting, on behalf of the family, to this republication.

It is my hope that there is no breach of copyright with regard to the photographs and poetry quotations used as most of these should be out of copyright by now and, as they were approved for inclusion in the original publication, it is hoped that such approval applies to this edition also.

The quality of some of the images leaves much to be desired, but I thought that their interest was sufficient reason for them to be included none the less.

It has been an especial honour and joy to work on the re-publication of this book; a small thank-you for all that Romany has meant to me. My Romany 'journey' began when I was eight and borrowed *Out with Romany by Moor and Dale* from the school library. As a 'townie' I had no idea what moors or dales were.....but I soon learned! And O what pleasure! The Countryside, Wildlife, Wildlife Art (thanks to Reg Gammon, Romany's illustrator) and Fishing all became an enduring part of my life. And, above all, in my teenage years, Romany's influence brought me to the Church. More than any other, Romany has influenced who I am – and my gratitude knows no bounds.

Rev Dr Leonard Hollands – Editor

Dorset 2023

PART 1

His Family

Had it been possible to convey to the young, swarthy, dark-eyed Gypsy who was driving his caravan along the Hertfordshire lanes that the death of his grandson should be considered of sufficient importance to be announced in the BBC News Bulletin, he would have been surprised.

But Cornelius Smith, the owner of the gaily-painted caravan, knew nothing of wireless in that far-off year of 1865. All that concerned him at the moment was that Emily, his eldest daughter, was ill, and that he must get her to the doctor in Baldock as quickly as possible. Even his old mare seemed to sense that something was amiss, for why was her master using the whip? The normal pace of a Gypsy caravan, or wagon,[1] as they call it, is leisurely, and she had been accustomed to amble along, stopping now and then to nibble at the nearest hedge. The lurcher dog, Boz, who spent most of his time tied to a hook on the chassis, also found the pace unusual, though he prided himself on his speed.

With the usual prejudice against Gypsies in those days, the doctor, instead of going to her bedside, summoned Emily to the wagon door and, to their dismay, pronounced the dread word smallpox. The child must be isolated from the family at once.

Though it was late in the month of March, snow was falling heavily when Cornelius reached Norton Lane, a mile and a half away. Turning a bend on the left-hand side of the lane, he pulled up, and pitched a tent for his wife and the other four children under an overhanging hawthorn tree. He then took Emily into the wagon, two hundred yards farther up the lane, and placed it on the right-hand side near an old chalk pit, so that he would be within easy call, and could be seen by his family.

Meanwhile his wife Polly was in great distress. Though only a young woman, just under thirty, she was expecting her sixth child. Her natural desire was to be with Emily, but her duty was to look after the children and leave Cornelius to nurse the sick

1

child. Emily, aged twelve, was the eldest, then, came Lovinia, Rodney and Matilda, known as Tilly, who afterwards became Romany's mother.

A few days later Ezekiel complained that he was unwell, and when the doctor arrived he ordered the boy to join his sister in the wagon. In order to avoid infection, they had arranged that Polly should prepare their food and leave it on a stone half-way between the wagon and the tent. But this was only a small part of her burden; for a whole month she trudged backwards and forwards through the snow to Baldock, a mile and a half each way, to buy the necessary provisions.

One day when she took the food to the appointed place, she was surprised to receive no answer to her call. Where was Cornelius? Could the children have taken a turn for the worse? In desperation she threw discretion to the winds and ran to them. Though satisfied that her fears were unfounded, her action brought further disaster to her family, for, within a few days she herself sickened and had to be moved to the wagon.

Poor Cornelius was almost distracted. Not only had he another patient to nurse, but who was to look after the children in the tent? Never was he in such need of a friend. He had no alternative but to take a chance and bring them into the wagon. One trouble followed another. Within a short time, the new baby was born, but, alas, Polly only lived a few hours after its arrival. Meanwhile, Emily and Ezekiel having recovered, Cornelius cleared all the infected clothes out of the wagon into the tent. Unfortunately, however, the kettle overturned, and the tent burst into flames, a grim sight for the already frightened children. Owing to the infection this was a good thing, though they could ill-afford to lose their tent. It was a Gypsy custom to burn the caravan as well as all the belongings of any member of the family who had died; perhaps it was this disaster that made him ignore this burial rite.

The Health Authorities ordered the funeral to take place after dark, and a heavy farm cart was sent to take Polly away. It must have been pathetic to see Cornelius's solitary figure, carrying a storm-lamp in the darkness, as he followed the rumbling cart down the lane.

His troubles were not at an end, for the Vicar of Baldock refused to bury a Gypsy even in the un-consecrated part of his churchyard, and Polly's remains were relegated to a dust heap on the fringe of the cemetery.

Added to this, the baby did not long survive its mother, and was later buried in the same grave. This indignity was remedied some years later by the younger son, Rodney, and the grave now bears a headstone as imposing as any in Baldock Cemetery.

Romany's Grandparents' Gravestone at Baldock

Little eleven-year-old Emily now becomes the heroine of the story, for it was she who did most to fill the gap left by her mother. She cooked, cleaned, and washed for the family, and mothered young Rodney and Tilly for many years until they were able to look after themselves. Even with her help, Cornelius's problem was not an easy one, for it was his wife who had sold all the goods that he made. And so, Emily took her mother's *kipsi*[2] and went off early each morning to peddle her wares, and her children, who are living today, tell sad stories of the miles she trudged, arriving home exhausted and footsore.

These children were remarkable. Not only were they unusually alert and quick-witted for their age, but each possessed an unusual share of personality. They were dark-eyed, good-looking, arresting in appearance, and had such persuasive powers that, as they grew older, they found it easy to sell their wares to housewives who did not need them, and to induce simple servant girls to believe that they could tell fortunes.[3]

They had none of the advantages of other children – no education, no books, no tradition to live up to, and no religious background. True, the School Attendance Officer did track them down in one village, but these undisciplined children of the wild so disturbed the class that they were dismissed from the school when they were still learning to do 'pothooks'[4] in their copybooks. That they should have made their way in the world without these advantages shows how gifted they were. In later years, three of them, Rodney being the outstanding example, held audiences spellbound, and few who listened to them could tell that they had not received the education of the average child.

It is interesting to conjecture what might have become of them had their lives been shaped differently. Had Rodney and Tilly, in particular, come across a travelling theatrical company at an impressionable age, there is no doubt that they would have become outstanding on the stage, for not only had they strong exhibitionist tendencies, but they possessed all the necessary qualifications –speaking voices of depth and charm, singing voices of quality and wide range, grace of movement, and that fascination of a stage personality which holds an audience enthralled. Conversely, had they come under the influence of thieves and rogues, they would probably have become a power for evil in the world, for they had the natural craftiness and acquisitiveness of their race. But we must return to their father to find out in what. channels their gifts were to be directed.

After his wife's death, Cornelius packed up his belongings and made his way through Cambridge. Soon after leaving the town he was delighted to see two familiar Gypsy wagons approaching him, which belonged to Bartholomew and Woodlock, his brothers. Greetings were exchanged between the families, and after Cornelius had told his sad tale and received their sympathy, one of the brothers suggested that they should turn their horses towards London, for he had heard that wonderful religious Revival Meetings were taking place at a Mission Hall in Notting Hill.

The journey took; about a week, and the three brothers eventually reached the Mission. Their appearance when they pushed their way in must have caused concern, for they were tall, strapping fellows, and the idea that Gypsies were as much in need of Christianity as other people had never occurred to anyone. During this meeting the three brothers became 'converted,' and one can imagine the surprise of their families when they eventually returned home to their wagons singing hymns.

It is an arresting thought that had Cornelius's family been born a hundred years later, nothing might have been heard of them, but this was the nineteenth century when religious revivals were an accepted part of the national life. The words 'Evangelistic Mission' and 'Religious Revival' convey nothing to the young person of today, but it was a common thing in those days to see the Albert Hall crowded for weeks on end for the meetings of Moody and Sankey, Torrey and Alexander, and others. Today many of us scoff at the methods they used, and some of us can remember the embarrassment we suffered when we were buttonholed in our seats and asked if our souls were saved. But the fact remains that thousands of both educated and uneducated people owe all that religion has meant to them to such Missions.

Cornelius was one of five brothers, the others being known as Christopher and 'Pizzler' Jimmy. All of them were badly in need of 'conversion,' for they were known to be exceptionally lawless; deer-stealing in Epping Forest was one of the least of their 'crimes.' Cornelius, too, had been by no means a model husband and father. Being a clever musician, he used violin not only for dances on the village greens, but to provide entertainment at the various public-houses he passed on his way home. He then returned home not only with full purse, but so full of drink that his behaviour scared his young children. He also pilfered the wood he needed to make his wares, and pulled up the potatoes and turnips for the family meals from the fields they passed.

It is difficult to make excuses for him, but it can be said that the genuine Gypsies in those days had much to contend with.[5] As a race they were naturally simple and trustful, and a recent writer, who has spent many years getting to know them intimately, sums them up as "a gentle and courteous people." He also says, "I have yet to meet a man or woman who is not proud of the possession of Gypsy blood." Just as today few can discriminate between the true Gypsies, the *tatcho Romani foki*,[6] and the sham fortune-tellers, so in those days all were classed together as thieves and vagabonds. Landlords refused to allow them to camp anywhere near their property, and they were even debarred from common grazing land. The worry of never knowing where they could encamp the following night was seldom absent from their minds, for a villager had only to catch sight of a caravan to inform the police immediately. Is it any wonder that they became secretive and vindictive and retaliated in their own way?

But Cornelius's conversion was the real thing, so real that his children were at first perplexed. No longer did he pilfer the wood he needed, nor curse them when they displeased him. In order that the temptation of the public-house should not prove too strong for him, he actually burnt his beloved violin. It was indeed a change of life, especially as he was desperately poor at the time.

One incident to prove this is worth recording. One night when the wagons of the three brothers were standing in a lane and they were asleep in their tents, they were rudely awakened by a gruff voice, "Get up, and come with me. You're trespassing here." In the ordinary way this would have caused these three big stalwarts no concern. They had their own methods of dealing with either a policeman or gamekeeper, and their caravans would have been miles away before their victim was in a fit condition to call for help. But the brothers were now converted and must show no resistance, so they quietly submitted to being handcuffed. It must have been a strange sight to see these big fellows being taken away, singing hymns as they went. They spent the night in gaol, but sang so lustily that it was more than their gaoler and his wife could stand, and they were released early the following morning.

So great was their joy in their new-found religion that they felt compelled to tell other Gypsies about it, and during the next few years they visited the various encampments in the Eastern counties and converted many of their race to Christianity. After that, they took up their stand on the village greens which they passed and achieved remarkable success. All this, naturally, had a good effect on Cornelius's children, and when they went round the villages to sell their wares, they no longer told fortunes, but spoke of the religion that had so changed their home life.

As Rodney grew older he not only helped his father by singing solos at his meetings, but tried his hand at public speaking and became so popular that people flocked from miles around to hear him.

The month of June 1877 was an epoch-making one in his life. One day his Uncle Bartholomew took him and Emily to London to attend a meeting at the headquarters of the Christian Mission run by the Rev William Booth, who afterwards became General Booth of the Salvation Army. Knowing Bartholomew already by sight, he soon recognised Rodney as the famous boy preacher, and called him up onto the platform to take part in the meeting. So well was he received that Mr Booth then asked him if he would join his staff of evangelists. There was great consternation in the caravan when they returned home late that night and woke the family to tell them what had happened.

And so, when the great day of his departure arrived, this simple unsophisticated Gypsy boy of seventeen discarded his pearl-buttoned velvet jacket, corduroys and coloured neckerchief for a black frock coat, striped trousers, stiff starched collar and cuffs, tied his half-filled new tin trunk with rope, tearfully bade farewell to his family, and, leaving behind the freedom and irresponsibility of open-air life, set out for the grime and sordidness of Whitechapel Road in the East End of London.

Old Meg she was a gypsy
And lived upon the moors,
Her bed it was the brown heath turf
And her house was out of doors

No breakfast had she many a morn,
No dinner many a noon,
And 'stead of supper she would stare
Full hard against the Moon.

Keats

Chapter 1 Notes

1 The Romani word for caravan is actually *vardo,* but in English gypsies use the word waggon (or wagon) for a horse drawn caravan, and trailer for a motor towed caravan, the latter beginning to replace the former from the 1950s.

2 Here Eunice uses the Romani word for basket. (She renders it *kipsic.*)

3 Gypsy fortune telling is a vexed question. I have known some Romanies personally who have admitted that they have earned money by 'telling fortunes' (*dukkering*), but it has been shrewd guesswork and crafty manipulation of the sitter's own words, rather any clairvoyance, but one lady tells of many occasions when she really has been able to predict events.

4 Pothooks are cursive shapes used in forming letters. It was once the custom to teach children to write by learning these shapes.

5 Eunice seems here to imply that discrimination against gypsies was a thing of the past. The truth is that the situation in the twenty-first century is worse. Not only is public distrust, even hatred, rampant, but legislation is making it ever more impossible for the Romani people to live their traditional nomadic way of life.

6 Another of the few occasions where Eunice uses words from the Romani language. Here she wrote *tachino Romani chals*, but as *chals* is the word for boys or lads, *foki*, meaning people, is more appropriate. *Tatcho* or *tatchi* means true/real. *Romani* is essentially a spoken language, not a written language. Consequently, words are often spelt in various ways to indicate the word phonetically, eg *Romany rye* or *Romani rai* – a Romani gentleman or scholar.

Chapter 2

Childhood

During all the years of their childhood the two youngest children had been close companions, and when Rodney had left the family circle Tilly used all her wiles to induce her father to let her go and help him with his work. She was only fifteen at the time, so his refusal proved a blessing in disguise, for she was then sent to live with an aunt who did her best to improve her education. But it was not long after this that she, too, left her caravan life and joined her brother, who, to his pride, was now called Captain Rodney Smith of the newly formed Salvation Army. Education was not an essential in a preacher of the gospel in those days, but the fact that they were Gypsies, their sincerity, their ability to make their audiences laugh or cry at will, and, above all, their conviction that their mission in life was, as they put it, to save souls, brought great crowds to their meetings.

Tilly was only seventeen when she was sent to conduct open-air meetings in Carlisle, and several photographs of her at that time show her to be very striking-looking, with her black hair, oval face and compelling dark eyes. The Salvation Army was anything but popular in those days, and it was a common thing for her meetings in the Market Square to be broken up by the rougher element of the crowds that gathered to listen to her as she spoke and sang her gospel songs. But because of her attractiveness she could always rely on a certain small band of well-dressed, educated young men in her audience who were not only ready to be converted by her each night, but clamoured to be the first to rescue her from the mob. Among the many proposals of marriage she received in this town alone, was one from a member of a well-known family who afterwards became Mayor of Carlisle.

It is not surprising, therefore, to learn that when she met the young Salvation Army Lieutenant who was stationed at the Icehouse in Hull, he at once fell in love with her and proposed to her. He was good-looking, dark complexioned, and had curly

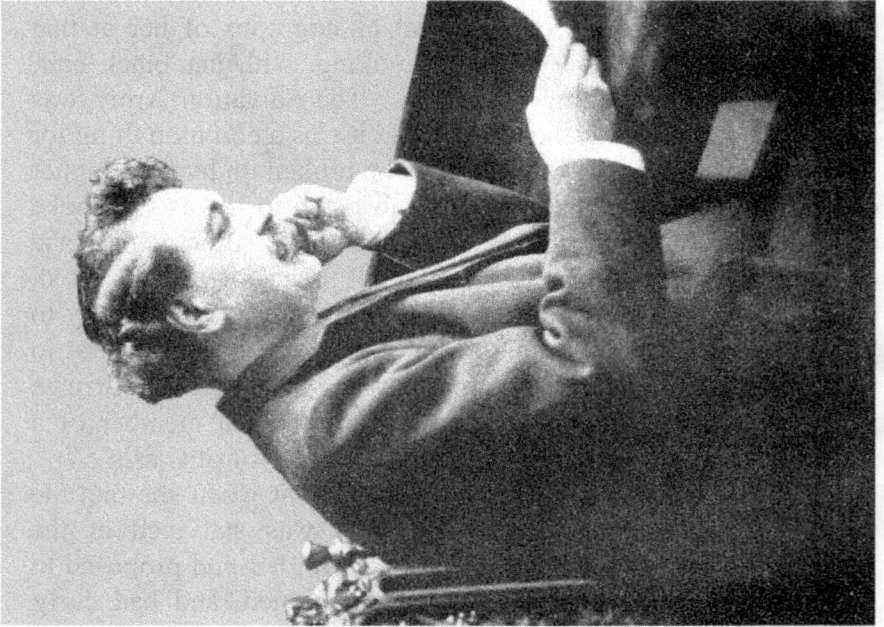

Romany's Parents

11

black hair, and whether the fact that he was very like Rodney weighed with her in her decision or not, I do not know, but in 1883 she became Mrs George Evens, and the following year their only child, whom they christened George Bramwell,[1] was born at 3 Argyll Street,[2] Anlaby Road.

He began attending Church at an early age for, until his mother managed to secure a woman named Ada Ablett to look after him, he was taken to their meetings from one month old, and deposited in the church vestry. The new arrangement worked well until he was a year old, when they decided to sever their connection with the Salvation Army and tour the country, holding ten-day Missions in various towns. And so, for the next few years, this small boy spent a good deal of his time in railway trains travelling from one part of the country to another and staying in homes where the presence of so young a child was not always welcome. Though the presence of both parents was essential to the success of their work, his mother's was the greater personality, and so, more often than not, he had to be put to bed before the evening meetings and left in the care of strangers. I have often heard them tell how, when a meeting was over, they would run home anxiously and, long before they reached the house, they would hear his lusty cries. But it was not long before he was to share their triumphs, for, at the age of four, he made his first appearance on a public platform as a singer. So sweet was his voice that the audiences were usually reduced to tears when he stood up in his black velvet suit and broad lace collar and sang his solos. Much to his pride, these were actually printed under his name in the book of his mother's songs. In later years he used to recall with some amusement the words of the most popular of these, which began: 'Come home, my boy, come home. Why break your mother's heart?'

But though he must have missed the companionship of other children, these Missions had their compensations. There was always Monday to which he could look forward, for that was the day on which all their admirers flocked to the station to see them off by train, and he was sure of armfuls of toys, pockets bulging with sweets and pennies to relieve the tediousness of the journey.

Neither this publicity nor this roaming life was ideal for a boy of his age. Even when they rented a small house in Frizinghall, Bradford, his parents were still obliged to take him with them on their journeys, and it was not until he was seven, when his father became a Missioner in the Wesleyan Church at the old Cranmer Street Chapel, Liverpool, that he began to lead a normal life.

During one of their earlier Missions in Cornwall a young girl named Polly Furzland had been 'converted' by them, and the day she arrived at Errol Street to take up her duties as their maid proved a memorable one for them.

Unlike Cornelius, Polly was not in need of conversion, for she was a kind, unselfish creature, and I could write much of her self-sacrifice and fidelity during the twenty-seven years she was with them. She not only did all the cooking and housework, but nursed them when ill and mothered Bram when his parents were away. She herself was at fault for the way she waited on them hand and foot, for when Bram returned from school and dropped his coat and cap on the nearest chair, she was there to pick it up, and in later years he used to blame her affectionately for the fact that he became an incorrigibly untidy, helpless man in the house.

Meanwhile, having missed much of his early education, he was now attending the nearest elementary. school. This brought with it a new problem. Until then his world had been one of Evangelistic Missions, and the fact that his mother was a Gypsy had seemed, to his childish mind, to be a distinct advantage. How proud he had always been of the admiring crowds which his Gypsy mother, in her gaily coloured shawls and vivid necklaces, had attracted to their meetings. Why, so great had been the crowds at High Park Street Church on one occasion that the gallery almost collapsed and, had it not been for her presence of mind in starting to sing when the people screamed, there might have been a serious disaster.

But the boys at school saw no romance in his ancestry, and when he boasted about it he was bewildered to hear the scorn that they put into the word 'Gypsy.' This was something new to him, something that he would have to fight alone, for he no longer had the protection of his parents or Polly.

Later, he was transferred to a higher-grade school in Aspeen Grove, Lodge Lane, where the conditions were such as would not be tolerated today. Not only had each master a class of at least sixty boys, but two classes were held in the same room. While one master conducted a singing lesson at one end, another shouted himself hoarse trying to teach arithmetic at the other end.

"Now then, Black-eyes, bring me what you have in your desk," the master would shout, and Bram would produce a couple of caterpillars for his inspection. From then onwards he was always known to his schoolfellows as 'Black-eyes.' The teachers did their best, but even if they did possess imagination, they had no chance of expressing it, for the education in those days was dull and uninteresting. In later years, he could not recall having learnt very much at this school, but he did remember the noise of the scratchy pencils on the greasy slates, and how he would look forward to cleaning his, for he then had the joy of spitting profusely on the top of it and watching the interesting patterns it made running up and down.

In those days caning was the punishment for every fault, and in spite of the fact that he always kept his trousers well padded, he seems to have received his fair share. But these canings were soon forgotten when the boys were let out of school, for there was always a rush to 'Mother Brown's' next door, for it was here that the whole of his penny a week was spent. He could buy a farthing bag of pink popcorns, and a half-yard strip of wide shiny liquorice called Spanish ribbon, which he could tear into innumerable pieces, and still have two farthings left for another day to spend on 'All Sorts' and aniseed balls. These not only lasted a long time, but changed colour in a most inexplicable way each time he took them out of his mouth.

On the way home from school the boys played the usual boys' pranks – tying string across the narrow street from one door-knocker to another, and then listening to the abuse of the angry housewives as they faced one another and hunted for the culprits; or waiting until the lamp-lighter with his hooked pole had turned a corner and then climbing the lamp-posts and turning out the incandescent gas burners.

It was during these early schooldays that he remembered having the first of the many headaches which were to trouble him so much in later life; so severe were they at times that he had to sit on the kerbstone on his way home until he felt better.

When very young, he had shown an aptitude for music, for he always seemed drawn towards the organs and pianos in the various churches and halls they visited. In fact, his parents usually put him in the care of the organist, because they knew that he could be relied on to behave well when seated on the organ stool. His love of music was inherited from his Gypsy grandfather, but his father was not without musical ability. As I am a tidy, methodical person, I am both blessed and cursed with the habit of throwing things away. In an old trunk in the box-room labelled by Bram 'Not to be thrown away' there lies today the old concertina which his father used in his early days to accompany the hymns at their open-air meetings. In this same box is a faded old book entitled 'Animals of the World' which he kept by his bedside for many years when a boy. His books in those days were few, but the well-thumbed pages of this one show that he was never tired of reading it.

It happened about this time that his parents were invited to conduct an eight-month Mission Tour in America, under the auspices of the Moody Institute. It was a sad day for this small boy when he stood with Polly on the quayside, watching the huge steamer which was taking away his beloved parents, although he little knew what a wonderful mother Polly would prove to be to him during the months that followed.

When they returned, his excitement knew no bounds, for they had brought with them a mountain goat almost as big as a donkey, and an American buck-board in which, to the envy of all the boys of the district, he and his father drove round the streets and parks of Liverpool. One day, when he came home from school, he found a small crowd of boys in the back-yard teasing Dan, as they called him. When the goat saw him he gave a bleat of delight, but there was a knowing look in his eyes which assured Bram that he was well able to deal with the matter himself. The moment that he was waiting for then came; one of the boys inadvertently turned his back on him. Putting his head down Dan butted him with his horns and catapulted him over the wall of the yard.

Great was Bram's grief when he had to part with him, because he would persist in leaping from the roof of one house to another, and in disturbing the neighbours as he pulled the mangle, to which he was tied, round and round the back-yard. Complaints, too, came from the bill-posters when he ate all the newly pasted bills off the hoardings.

In spite of the fact that they succeeded in finding him a good home, Bram was inconsolable for many months afterwards. Some years later, Bostock and Wombwell's Circus came to Liverpool, and he and his father went to see it. As they were walking round they saw a goat in the distance which looked very much like theirs. Bram ran up to him and called him by name. They were right. It was Dan, and when he recognised them he bleated and nosed them both all over. with, affection. They went off immediately to the proprietor to ask if they could buy him back again, but he would not hear of it.

In spite of this disappointment, Bram's life was full of interest and happiness, to which his parents added later by bringing back with them from their second visit to America a wonderful big sleigh. Again, he was the envy of all the boys in his neighbourhood, for he and his father would carry it to Sefton Park and, surrounded by a crowd of admirers, they would dash down the snowy slopes at such speed that all the other sleighs were left far behind.

Thus, his childhood slipped by until, when he was ten years old, his parents were transferred to Hutchinson Hall, where they remained until they joined the staff of the newly opened Wesleyan Central Hall in 1906. One of the most important events of each week was their large adult Bible Class, which he and Polly usually attended. It is not to be wondered at that he found this at times extremely dull, for it was the custom for each person to give what was called his religious 'experience.' As the class consisted mostly of reclaimed characters, such as drunkards and gaol-birds, their powers of expressing what they felt were very limited, and so each week they would recite the same monotonous phrases with such regularity that he was able to repeat many of them word by word years afterwards. One of them, however, never failed to interest him. A certain man would get up, take out his watch and always begin in the same way, "It is now exactly two years, six months, twelve days, eight hours, forty minutes and six seconds since I became converted," and he was then relieved of the boredom of listening to the rest of the experiences as he checked up the figures on his own watch and compared them with those of last week in the hope that he might find a flaw in the man's calculations.

It was at this Bible Class that he suffered an undeserved rebuke from his father. Being fond of singing, he naturally looked forward eagerly to the hymn intervals, but when on one occasion his father, in between the verses of one of them, stopped and said to him in front of everyone, "Don't sing so loudly, son," he was very embarrassed. On the way home he protested that he had not been singing loudly, and his father replied, "No, I know you weren't, but the man sitting next to you was!"

But he had lots of fun to make up for the sober atmosphere of the Mission, for he was never without pets of some sort – white mice, pigeons, rabbits and, best of all, his beloved dog, Floss. His father, too, being a native of Plymouth, had a great love of the sea, and in the evenings would take him down to the docks where the big ships were berthed. Even in those early days he must have been storing up knowledge of the habits of wild creatures, for he was far more interested in watching the myriad rats as they left the holds of the ships, cleverly balancing themselves on the mooring ropes, than in the ships themselves.

Best of all were his long country walks with Floss, for they were now living in Ashbourne Road, Aigburth, and in those days the outer belt of Liverpool was mostly green fields and leafy lanes.

A 'Road Under Repair' sign always thrilled him, for he knew that it meant that a night watchman would be on duty when dusk fell. Potatoes and chestnuts eaten at home never had quite the same flavour as those roasted on a glowing coke fire under the starlit sky.

His pleasures were simple compared with those of the modern child. There were no cinemas, and his only indoor excitements were Band of Hope magic-lantern shows, concerts at the Mission Hall, or the arrival of a travelling circus.

It was fortunate that his parents and Polly proved such companions to him, for he was solitary by nature and had few intimate friends. But he made up for this by often going with his parents on their various Mission tours and sharing in the hospitality shown to them.

In spite of the abnormal religious atmosphere of his early days, and considering that he was an only child and spent much of his time in the company of older people, he had, on the whole, a very happy childhood.

"Where are you going this nice fine day?"
(I said to the puppy as he went by.)

"Up in the hills to roll and play."
"I'll come with you, Puppy," said I.

A A Milne

Chapter 2 Notes

1 It would be interesting to know why they chose the name Bramwell, and also why it was his second name they used. His father's second name was Moysey. Bramwell is not a name used by Romanies.

2 Now Argyle Street

At the Age of Seven

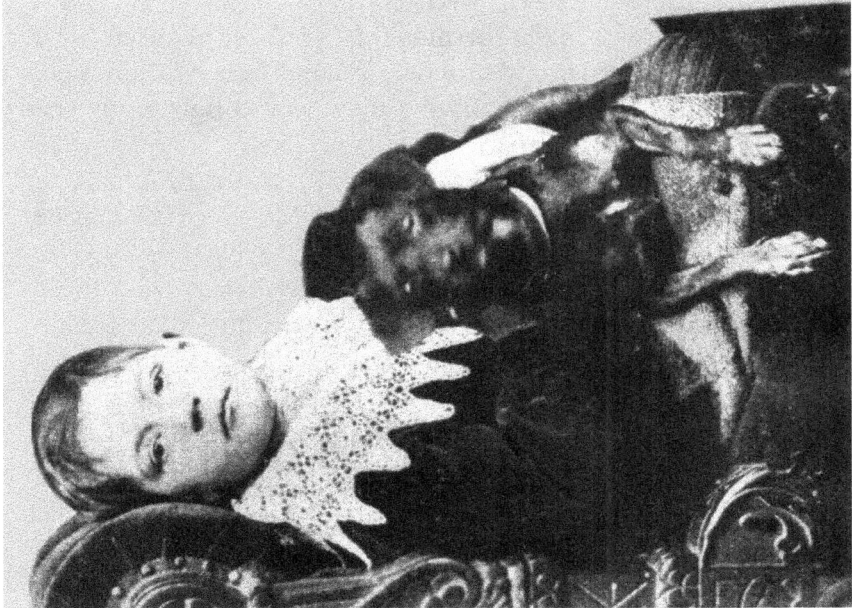

His First Dog

Chapter 3

Youth

Bram was now thirteen, and though he had made some progress at the local school, neither the discipline nor the teaching was adequate for an intelligent boy of that age. His parents, therefore, decided to send him to boarding-school, and arranged with J G Beattie, the headmaster of Epworth College, Rhyl, to send him there the following term.

He had two vivid recollections of the day he arrived – of his father rolling marbles along the gutter to distract his attention from the sad parting ahead of them, and of being kissed by the motherly wife of the headmaster.

Thus began four of the happiest years of his life. This discerning headmaster saw at once that this was no ordinary boy and that he was not cut out of any conventional schoolboy pattern. He knew the boy's ancestry, his love of outdoor life, and the fact that he had led a different kind of life from other children. He had it in his power either to make or mar this sensitive undisciplined child. Being a wise man, he proved a second father to him and, during the whole of his life, Bram's eyes would light up at the mention of Mr Beattie's name.

This decision of his parents was to mean a great deal more to him than improved education. The type of Mission Hall that he had been attending had made up in fervour what it lacked in reverence, and an ordinary quiet church service was an entirely new experience for him. The over-emotionalism of the Mission Meetings, though none too healthy an atmosphere for him as a small boy, was less likely to appeal to him in his adolescence. In later years he used to amuse me by telling me that he had been converted weekly, for instead of waiting about for his parents at the close of their Sunday evening meetings, for lack of anything better to do, he would sometimes follow the band of prospective converts into the 'enquiry room,' as it was called, and kneel down with the rest. On one occasion he was kneeling down when a small boy named Bertie Sugden, with whom he was not on friendly terms, appeared in the doorway. Jumping up, he ran over to him and punched him on the nose, saying, "Go away. Can't you see that I'm being converted?"

To his parents, however, the Mission atmosphere must have seemed the right; one, for, reprehensible as it may seem to modern parents and to psychologists, they had already chosen his career for him – he was to be a Wesleyan Minister. In later years I often heard his mother, when on a public platform, say of him, "I gave him to the Church before he was born." Not only did I feel embarrassed, but it astonished me to think that, in deciding his career for him, she might have diverted him from the wider life which I felt he was meant to lead. That he, of all people, should have had his career chosen for him filled me with dismay. It seems curious, with his love of nature, that they did not decide on an outdoor life, for had he been put to work on a farm, for instance, he would have had ample scope for developing his natural instincts. On the other hand, whether he would have acquired the academic knowledge that afterwards proved of such value to him is doubtful, for he would probably have left school at an earlier age. If, as some people think, a successful life means a happy one, he would have been supremely happy in some outdoor occupation; but if it means benefiting one's fellow-men, he certainly eventually achieved this. Then again, had he devoted his time entirely to the study of nature, he could not have made a living by it,[1] for in those days comparatively little was known of the subject and few books written, and even those who took it up as a hobby were considered to be cranks. Even today a naturalist cannot make a living unless he has the gift of imparting his knowledge to others.

As luck would have it, his parents' choice proved to be the right one, and here again it was Mr Beattie, with his broad religious outlook, who was responsible for making it so. He had such a unique way of interpreting the Bible, especially some of the Old Testament stories, which he knew would appeal to boys, that Bram began to look forward to the Scripture lessons, and to him, as well as to many of the others, the Bible became a new book.

Mr Beattie had more influence for good on him than any man he ever met, and so when the time came for him to leave school, it was his own wish as well as that of his parents that he should become a Wesleyan Minister. Thus was he enabled to open people's eyes both to the beauty of religion and of the world around them. Had it not been for the deep and lasting impression that his headmaster made on him, he would probably have drifted half-heartedly towards the type of evangelistic work his parents were doing. Knowing the aesthetic side of his nature, I feel sure that he would have been most unhappy.

But I must return to Epworth and show the impression that he was making two terms later on his school friend, Ding Hilton, which is best described in his own words. "I was very shy and nervous when I arrived at Epworth, and it was a great help to me to find in Dick, as Bram was called, one friendly soul in a strange world. He was a very good-looking, well-set-up chap, and he breathed self-confidence. Even in those days he was an individualist and did not get on too well with some of the boys, having to submit to a good deal of bullying from the older ones."

Poor Bram. Of course he was self-confident, for his mode of life had made him so. Had he not stood on public platforms for years in front of admiring crowds and shared in the flattery his parents received everywhere they went? And yet these boys did not seem a bit anxious to hear all he had to say. And why did they show their disapproval of his bragging in such a cruel manner? But he was too happy-natured a boy to let all this depress him; life was so full of interest, and he especially loved the walks in the country around Dyserth and Rhuddlan.

To go into further details of his schooldays, which were similar to those of most boys, would be boring, but Ding's letter tells me that he was a good all-round athlete. Before he left, he was captain of the school football and cricket teams, and when Epworth played against other schools he was always one of the recognised bowlers.

He was an average boxer, and seemed to be involved in many of the fights that took place out of school, but so far as I could make out, like most boys, he seemed to fight for the sake of fighting rather than because he was unfriendly with his opponent.

Most proud of all was he of the silver cup awarded him for the half-mile handicap,[2] for not only had he got up early each morning for months while in training for the race, but had denied himself many visits to the tuck-shop.

Practising the piano was never a trial to him, and when, at the age of fifteen, he passed the Advanced Senior of the London College of Music, his music master was full of praise. Ding writes, "Music was born in him and he could play anything from memory or improvise whenever entertainment was needed. At the school concerts his name was always included in the programmes for pianoforte and mandolin solos, and I think he could have mastered the technique of any instrument without much trouble."

He had the natural indolence of the artist, but the fact that his parents were not finding it easy to pay his school fees goaded him on; he worked hard during the four years he was there, finally taking his London Matriculation when he was seventeen – not a bad achievement for a boy who had missed so much of his earlier education.

In later years, when he became well known, Mr Beattie invited him to lecture in the Town Hall at Rhyl. Commenting on this in the school magazine, Ding wrote: "Dick's lecture reminds me of some pleasant rambles we had together by field and hedgerow, sometimes I fear out-of-bounds, when he tried rather vainly to impart to my townsman's intellect some of the secrets of wildlife. He was always a child of nature."

On another occasion he was asked back to present the school prizes on Speech Day, and had the boys howling with laughter as he recalled his early escapades. Mr Beattie's son, the present headmaster, when writing to me, says, "On no occasion were we treated to a more delightfully spontaneous talk than he gave the boys on that day."

At this time his parents were occasionally conducting their own Missions in different parts of the country, and it was during one of these, held at Frodsham, that they came to know the Booth family. When Bram, in his Eton suit and mortar-board, sadly left home at the beginning of each school term, he always broke his journey at Frodsham to pick up the tuck-box they had generously provided for him. He had originality, even in these early days, for instead of sending his parents the usual postcard on arrival, he would take with him one of his homing pigeons, and when he reached the school grounds, he would release it. As soon as the pigeon arrived in its loft his parents knew that he had reached school safely.

Those who attended his lectures in later years may remember a story he used to tell which concerned Frodsham. He and two of the small boys of the Booth family went out one afternoon egg-collecting on the neighbouring hills. Whether they felt guilty of having robbed the nests I do not know, but as they returned, they put the eggs under their caps. Down the village street came an old man who, recognising Bram, placed his hand in patriarchal manner on his head and said, "God bless you, my son." In later years Bram's sense of the dramatic alone could describe his appearance at that moment, and I have seen many an audience rocking with laughter as he stood on the platform wiping the imaginary sticky mess from his eyes, ears and face.

His visits to Frodsham meant much to him, for, to quote a tribute paid to him recently in the local paper, "He came to know the Weaver Valley, the bird life of the Marshes, and the forest hinterlands of Delamere."

Delamere Forest, Bickerton Hill, Malpas, Egerton – what memories these names revive. Most of that district belongs to the Cholmondeley estate, and it was there that Bram, his parents, Polly, the dog and the parrot spent their summer holidays for several years with the Ruscoes at Oak Tree Farm. He and his father usually cycled there from Liverpool, and it is to be hoped that by then his father had discarded the solid-tyred cycle that Bram used to tell me about, and had bought one of the new pneumatic ones, for the lanes were rough and stony around Bickerton.

He looked forward all the year to these holidays. For an only child to have the companionship of a family of ten children would seem sufficient reason for this, but he was a solitary boy, and to him Ruscoe's farm meant freedom to wander alone through the woods and fields and to sit on his favourite fallen tree-trunk as he lured the roach and tench from the Cholmondeley Mere. From the many stories he has told me, I gather that he lost many a fish because he was more interested in watching the wild creatures around him. He would disappear after breakfast, and they would not expect him home until dusk fell. He was never lonely, never bored. The days were all too short to get in the things he wanted to do – fishing, watching and, what will come as a surprise to many, shooting, for he was now seventeen and had the natural desire of a boy to handle a gun. When Mr Ruscoe took one of them down from the rack and told him to have a pot at the rabbits which swarmed the fields, he did not need much persuading, for there were seventeen mouths to be fed each day.

One day, however, he shot a hare, and its pathetic wail of pain haunted him for months afterwards. From then onwards he used the gun less and less, and the more intimate he became with wild creatures the more he regretted ever having used one.

If at times they were short of meat and game, of one thing they were never short, and that was cheese, for this was a Cheshire cheese-making farm. He loved watching Mrs Ruscoe making them, especially when she tested the curd with a red-hot poker. He would drink pints of the sweet-tasting whey, and when his 'baggin' sandwiches were packed up each morning, so huge were the chunks of cheese put between the bread that it was always spoken of as cheese and bread, not bread and cheese.

What a contrast their evenings were! The farmer and his big family would gather in the stone-flagged kitchen, and after the big paraffin lamp had been lit, the gossip of the day would be exchanged over the meal. Then Bram would put one of the old-fashioned barrel-shaped records on his phonograph, and the lads and lasses would dance till bedtime.

One evening one of the girls returned from the pantry in a state of great fright. She had seen a ghost standing by the edge of the pond. Bram did not take this very seriously, because superstition was rife in those parts, and every neighbouring hall had its own ghost. But when he reached the pantry window he too was scared. There, by the full light of the moon, could be seen a tall white figure with wide outstretched arms. With manly bravery he fetched the farmer's gun, and, watched anxiously by the rest of the party, he crawled through the garden into the field beyond.   Just as he got into position and was ready to fire, it slowly raised its arms several times and was lifted gently into the air. The ghost was none other than a heron. How relieved he was that he had not shot this beautiful bird.

Some evenings they would sit round the friendly open fireside whilst Mr Ruscoe told tales of the strange prophecies of Nixon, the farm labourer, whose foretellings had brought him to such a sad end.   One of them was, that any member of the Cholmondeley family who rode a white horse would be killed. One evening Bram returned to the farm to find excitement running high. Lord Cholmondeley had been killed when riding his white horse through the wood. From then onwards a white horse was never seen on the estate.

Amongst other prophecies which came true were that a miller should be born in that district without a thumb, that Ridley Pool would be sown and mown, and that a wall on the Bickerton hills would fall upwards. Lily Ruscoe, now Mrs Walley, tells me that proof of the two latter can be seen within a few miles of Oak Tree Farm today. Unfortunately for the farm labourer, he lived in the days of witchcraft, and after being locked up in a barn because of his eccentricities, his persecutors forgot his existence, and when he was discovered, he was found to be dead.

The women-folk would then talk of the doings up at Broxton Lower Hall, or of the latest pranks of Robin, the son of Lord and Lady Arthur Grosvenor. Lady Arthur was especially interested in Bram's family, because she herself had leanings towards a roaming life. Dressing herself up in coloured Gypsy shawls, she would travel about the countryside in her own caravan, selling baskets. She would recount her experiences to Bram's mother, and was never tired of hearing of the early life of the Smith family. When, in later years, I asked what Broxton Lower Hall was like, all Bram could remember was that Lady Arthur had a pet donkey which used to follow her all over the house, even up and down stairs!

One hot morning, he was sitting on his favourite tree-trunk by the mere when Robin arrived, accompanied by a footman with his fishing paraphernalia and an imposing luncheon basket. Robin invited Bram to join him in the boat and then handed him the oars. For some time he rowed round the mere, but being a very independent boy and seeing that Robin was having all the fun, he said, "It's your turn now." For the rest of the morning, as he was so often fond of telling, he fished for pike and roach, while a future Duke of Westminster sweated with the oars. This was but one of many happy days spent with Robin during his holidays there.

These outings encouraged Mr Ruscoe to tell the story of the footman who had been drowned in Cholmondeley Mere, and of how the diver who was sent to recover his body refused to go down a second time because he had been attacked by a pike as big as a shark!

Each year that Bram went to Oak Tree Farm his inseparable companion was a black spaniel called Raq, and they used to tell how, when he returned to Liverpool, the dog was always found in the same place, lying on his old breeches on his bedroom floor. Raq would lie there for days, so inconsolable that no member of the family dare touch the breeches or try to persuade him to leave them.

When I visited the Broxton Hills with him a year or two ago, he took me to Cholmondeley, and when we reached the mere guarded by tall pine trees, he was strangely moved to find that the old fallen tree-trunk on which he had sat for countless hours when a boy was still there. He sat quiet and intent for quite a long time, and he seemed to forget my presence as past memories came surging over him.

The childhood shows the man as morning shows the day.

Milton

Chapter 3 Notes

1 Without access to the family's bank account one can't be certain, but it is likely that Romany's income from lecturing and writing, then broadcasting would have made earning a living as a Naturalist feasible. Eunice effectively implies this on page 232 when she almost persuaded him to retire. However, one accepts Eunice's point that it would have been a difficult field to break into as a young man starting out on a career.

2 Bram was also awarded a 'Special Subject' prize:

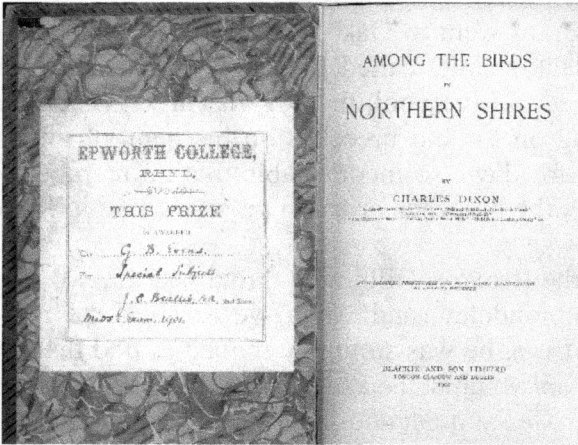

Cholmondeley Lake Today

Chapter 4

College Days

The next eighteen months of his life were spent at Queen's College, Taunton, where he arrived for the summer term of 1902. He entered as a Divinity Student, having gained a scholarship of £30 per annum towards his fees. Here again his games, musical ability and love of outdoor life loomed large. H J Ghannon, who was in the sixth form with him and is now a master at Queen's, tells me that when 'GB,' as Bram was then called, could not be found on the premises, "they were fairly certain that he was out observing bird-life in the beautiful well-wooded villages of Trull and Pitminster," and that he also contributed articles on bird-life to the school magazine.

I should love to have heard the first sermon he preached in one of the neighbouring village chapels, for the Divinity Students were all on the 'plan' of the local Methodist Circuit. I can remember little of what he told me of those experiences, except that on one occasion he missed his train home on the Sunday night. The old couple who had entertained him for tea in their tiny cottage took it quite philosophically and invited him to stay with them. Eventually he retired to what he thought was his bedroom, and one can imagine his surprise when he woke the next morning to find the old man and woman lying by his side in the one and only bed!

He did not get on very well with the headmaster. It may have been that, after the privileges he had enjoyed as head boy at Epworth, he found the restrictions irksome. How could anyone come up to Mr Beattie in his estimation? Perhaps if he had been a little less indulgent, for Bram was always a favourite of his, it might have been easier for him in later years to submit to discipline with better grace.

When he left Queen's, he was still too young to be accepted as a candidate for the Wesleyan Ministry, so had to find something to occupy his time for the next six months. He therefore applied for a post as a master at a school in Lytham, Lancashire, under a headmaster whose name, I believe, was Waterhouse. Here he was most unhappy, for he taught general subjects to one of the lower forms, and not being interested in what he was teaching, he lacked the necessary patience. In later years, of course, he was in his element when addressing audiences of children on his own subject, and never failed to hold their attention.

Before entering College, each candidate for the Wesleyan Ministry had to spend a year on probation in ordinary Church work, and the town chosen for him was Colchester in Essex. Soon after his arrival there in September 1904 to take charge of a newly built church in Wimpole Road,[1] he was presented with a photograph of himself standing proudly outside the building. The caption beneath it read: 'The Church's first Minister and the Minister's first Church.' He had cause for pride, for he was only twenty at the time, and was now earning the large salary of £90 a year which, after paying for his board and lodging, left him with a small fortune. His landlady must have gained considerably on whatever she charged, for he practically lived at the home of a family called Nash, and for years afterwards, when writing to Mrs Nash, he always called her "Other-mother."

A W Nightingale, who also showed him great kindness during his stay in Colchester, writes: "He was a most gifted preacher and certainly left his mark in this circuit. He was beloved by all, chiefly because he was so natural." And in a letter from Bernard Nash, who is now Editor of the *Essex County Telegraph*, he tells me that Bram was exceedingly popular with the young people of the church. He describes, too, how he loved to get out into the country, and before his week-evening appointments visited the various farms, and in one in particular spent much of his time riding bareback on a favourite horse. Bernard Nash adds significantly that he had good reason to know that he was more keen on these outings than in dealing with the business side of his church work. His 'good reason' for knowing may be due to the fact that he afterwards married the daughter of the Minister who had superintended Bram's work. Be that as it may, he was supremely happy at Colchester, so I imagine that he was not taken to task for any of his omissions.

The only other recollections I have of his Colchester days are that he owned a dog of unknown breed, and that he constantly referred to Colchester natives, which, in my ignorance, I thought referred to the people living there. He was an epicure where oysters were concerned. When he attended the Annual Feast, he was bitterly disappointed that he was only able to swallow a couple of dozen, for those invited were allowed to eat as many as they wished, and he had heard that it was possible to dispose of eight dozen at a sitting.

Leaving Colchester, he was looking forward to his coming three years at College when he received a sad blow, for at his medical examination he was rejected on the grounds that his heart was not normal. In vain he protested that the idea was absurd, for how otherwise could he have taken such a prominent part in the games at Epworth and Taunton? He went home in the depths of depression, and I can remember his telling me later that the train journey was the most miserable one he ever experienced. However, he visited a famous heart Specialist, who soon reassured him that he had not the least cause for worry, for the heart murmur, a common symptom, was not only normal in his case, but would in no way detract from his leading an active life. And so, September 1905 found him at the Wesleyan Theological College, Handsworth, Birmingham.

On arrival, the new men, or 'rams,' as they were called, had the ordeal of standing on a platform known as Killiecrankie, and either singing or performing in some way. As he had been accustomed to publicity as a boy, this held no terrors for him, and Stainton Marris, another new arrival, writes of the occasion, "I was very impressed by the way Bram turned Killiecrankie, which to me was a humiliation, into the scene of a real triumph for himself."

Letters from his fellow-students show, too, his individuality during those years. Frank Boynton writes: "He was a great personality in the College, and I should say that he had the most original mind of any of us." Albany Renton writes: "He was the only man of his year who left any impression on me, and his practical jokes have become legendary." R T Morrison, an assistant tutor, whose friendship, like that of Albany Renton's, he valued in later life, writes: "He always impressed me by his extraordinary susceptibility to beauty of any kind. He was famed, too, for his brilliant and often crushing repartees. His chief fame was as a composer of various College songs, which were always roared out with immense gusto by the men. Some years later I was present when he took over the organ at a Gateshead church. on some informal occasion, and as members of the audience started fresh tunes, he picked up the music in the various keys without hesitation. There are hosts of quite experienced organists who would never have been able to do this." Were the countless hours he had spent sitting on organ-stools, as a small boy, partly responsible for this, I. wonder? He certainly never had an organ lesson.

In all the College 'rags' and escapades he seems to have been the leader, and wherever there was fun he was in the midst of it. The night when he dressed up as Mephistopheles must have been an outstanding event, for all the letters I have received mention it. He went to enormous trouble to rig himself out in a skin-tight red costume, complete with horns and a long tail, and then glued red spangles on his eyelids. With his normal dark skin and piercing eyes, the whole effect gave him a most frightening appearance. When he had completed his toilet, he crept down the badly lit staircase to be met by the elderly Governor, who was on his way up to bed. So terrified was he, some of the men say, that he turned tail and ran for his life. This caused much merriment amongst the men when the 'Devil' entered the Common Room and described what had happened.

As College Precentor, it was his duty to start the tunes for grace at meals, and these he varied from the most solemn hymn-tunes to the most jazz-like choruses which, at one time, disgraced the old Methodist Hymn-book. The Governor was inclined to spend rather too long over College prayers, and knowing exactly how long they would last, Bram would lead a procession of the men on their hands and knees along under the tables, arriving at their seats just in time to utter a solemn "Amen."

Although he was usually hard-up, he and a friend once returned to College and announced to their incredulous friends that they had been abroad. The fact was that they had seen advertised a cheap twenty-four-hour trip to Paris, had crossed the Channel in utmost misery, for Bram, in particular, was always a bad sailor, and their only view of Paris had been what could be seen from a seat in the *Bois de Boulogne* from which they felt too exhausted to move.

In spite of all this fun and adventure he was often lonely, for, as is often the case with an individualist of his type, he had no very intimate friends. His inherited exhibitionist tendencies, which had rarely been curbed, needed little egging on by the other men to make him break rules and regulations which, later, made him unpopular with the newly appointed Governor. I rather imagine from what Bram told me, that, having generations of culture and tradition behind him, the Governor found it difficult to make allowances for his unusual background, as Mr Beattie had done.

Outside College, however, he was never lonely, for he had wonderful friends in the Halliwell family at Handsworth Wood and the Bucklers at Sutton Coldfield, and spent much of his spare time with them.

Then, too, there was the interest of his games, and it is not surprising to find that he not only became the College Soccer captain, but, because of his long stride and reach, was elected goalkeeper.

Meanwhile, he had, by careful saving, collected a small library together. This he added to on one occasion in a very unusual way. One Saturday afternoon on his way down New Street to the station for his week-end appointment, he happened to notice that there had been a fire at a bookseller's shop which the men frequented. Going inside, he found it in a state of great confusion, for, though the books were not destroyed, most of them were saturated with water. Knowing how keen his fellow-students were to add to their own collections, he took a risk. After choosing several hundred which he wanted himself, he said to the bookseller, "If I tell the men at College about this when I get back on Monday, may I have these books on account?" In those days, books did not sell as well as they are doing today, and the thought of the College men swarming down and helping him out of the awkward predicament in which he found himself appealed to the bookseller. Although he knew that most of them would only be able to pay him a few shillings weekly, he agreed, and the men eventually arrived and cleared most of his stock.

Though Bram deprived himself of many necessities, it was not until two years later that he became free of debt, and, thanks to the action of this bookseller, his shelves were filled with costly leather-bound editions that he would never have been able to purchase in the ordinary way. He was reading more widely at this time than he did in later years, and Stainton Marris tells me that "he brought bits of Swinburne to table, lovingly turning over the sensuous phrases on his tongue." His desert-island books at that time would, I think, have included 'Amiel's Journal,' the poems of Walt Whitman and his English Dictionary, for he made a point of adding new words to his vocabulary each day. In later years I think his choice would have been mainly those on wildlife.

When, during his college vacation, he was asked to preach in the Liverpool Central Hall which seated several thousand people, he was filled with importance, especially as he now possessed the regulation black frock-coat and high silk hat. There must have been something arresting about his preaching even at the age of twenty-three, for, glancing through the Annual Reports of the Central Hall, I came across an interesting account written by a young man of his first introduction to the Hall. He tells how he was spending the weekend at an hotel in Liverpool with the idea of getting thoroughly drunk. He was in a state of intoxication when he went to bed, and on the Sunday visited one public-house after another until he was quite incapable. Following the strains of a band along Renshaw Street, he reached the fringe of an open-air meeting, conducted by Bram's parents, and finally found himself inside the Central Hall in which he had never been before. He writes: "I was so drunk that I knew little about the Service, but I was able to take in an illustration which the preacher, the Rev G Bramwell Evens, used about Achilles being dipped in the stream by his mother to make him invulnerable, and I caught the words 'everyone has an Achilles heel – a weak spot somewhere.'" He went on to say that he felt the enormity of his failing more acutely than he had done before, and that, though he had a hard fight to keep sober, the next day being Bank Holiday, in time he overcame his desires and eventually became a worker at the Hall.

Had Bram known of this it might have been an encouragement to him, for at that time his loyalties were divided between the excessively emotional Evangelistic Meetings of his youth and his natural preference for the ordinary conventional methods of conducting Church Services. Owing to the influences of School and College too, he had gradually been growing away from much of the showmanship he had seen manifested in his early days, and disliked the idea of using his Gypsy ancestry as a means, of attracting people to public worship. This was the first rift that had come between him and his parents, and he felt it acutely; but as he was rarely at home, it did not mar the happiness of their family life.

He was ordained at the Wesleyan Methodist Conference held at Roath Road, Cardiff, in July, 1908.

Give me music, give me rapture,
Youth that's fled can none recapture.

Margaret L Woods

Chapter 4 Notes

1   The Wimpole Street Methodist church, completed in
1904 at a cost of £4500.00,
stands proudly still and has a
flourishing congregation. It
was quite outstanding when
built, being in contrast to the
little chapels in the surround-
ding villages.

The present Steward says that
there were still people in the
1960s who spoke of Romany
but not as their first minister
but rather as the famous
broadcaster!

Queen's College, Taunton

Wesleyan Theological College, Handsworth

Chapter 5

London

After the freedom of school and college life it would be hard for any young man to find himself sent to an East London church, but for a man of Bram's temperament it was more than unfortunate. His description of his arrival in Dalston was a poignant one. For this lover of green fields to have found himself amongst rows of dingy tenemented houses, with scarcely a blade of grass to be seen, must have been heart-breaking. Dissatisfied with his first dreary lodgings, he spent the rest of the week tramping the dismal streets in the rain and, although he eventually took the place of their son in the home of two dear elderly souls, his arrival in London in September 1908 was not a happy one. But he was young, and it needed more than sordid surroundings to damp the ardour of one so full of the joy of living. He looked forward to his preaching each Sunday and, in addition to all his other work, much of his time was occupied in studying for his Intermediate BD, which he passed before leaving London.

One of his first jobs, of course, was to buy a dog and, after searching the Leadenhall Market, he arrived home with a wire-haired terrier called Jack. He had missed the companionship of a dog during his college days, the only period in his life when he was without one.

It is difficult for me to convey in words my first meeting with him. As my father was the Minister of a neighbouring Congregational Church, we had heard from time to time of the crowds that were flocking to hear the young minister at Mayfield Road. I had been studying singing at the Guildhall School of Music for several years, and often sang at concerts in the district. When I accepted an invitation to sing at his church one Saturday evening in November 1910, I little knew that it was going to change the whole course of my life. During my first song I had the uncomfortable feeling that someone sitting in the front row was fixing his dark, penetrating eyes upon me, and I felt relieved when the song was over. During the interval in the artistes' room, he came in and made a bee-line for me through the crowd, and it was not long before I fell under his spell.

The following day I received a letter from him asking me to join a Costume Concert Party which he was forming, with the idea of giving entertainments at the various local churches. He also asked if I would help him with the canvassing for his election on the Hackney Borough Council. Of all the things he ever did, this venture of his was the most inexplicable. Why he, of all people, who disliked any kind of business meeting, should have allowed his name to go forward was a mystery. It may have been that he felt his inability give expression to all that lay within him and needed an outlet for his restlessness and repression, but he overlooked the fact that he would make the world's worst councillor. Of course, he won his election, for who could have resisted his persuasiveness at the election meetings? Fortunately for the Council, he did not remain in London long after this, so it is unlikely that his numerous absences from Committee Meetings were noticed.

The more I saw of him the more I realised what an attractive man he was, so brimful of life and fun, so gay[1] and witty, so wild and free, and yet so kind and gentle, with that childlike simplicity of nature that in later life endeared him to everyone he met. There was a helplessness, too, about him which I soon discovered was due to the fact that he was a dreamer and an artist rather than a practical man. So striking was he in appearance that people turned in the street to look at him. He had unusually broad shoulders, and had he held them back he could have added considerably to his height, which was well over six feet, but he was loose-limbed and inclined to adopt an easy gait, probably because he was more interested in his own thoughts than in the people around him.

He had a head of raven-black hair, thick and glossy, worn rather long and inclined to curl. His dark hazel eyes were deep-set and sparkling, and changed with every mood. He had heavy eyebrows, a dark moustache, a strong nose and chin and the high cheek-bones typical of the Gypsy race. Oddly enough, he was not naturally dark-skinned, but tanned very easily. When we went swimming the contrast between the colour of his face and hands and the rest of him was very marked. If there is any truth in the science of phrenology, his powers of observation were far greater than that of most people, for these bumps protruded above his eyes so far that in later life it almost gave the impression of a receding forehead. He could not have been called handsome in the usual sense of the word, but when he smiled, he was irresistible. Was it any wonder that when he proposed to me a month after the concert and asked me to marry him before he left for Yorkshire the following August, I accepted him.

A friend of mine once remarked that proposals made in the fault-finding glare of the sunshine were more likely to be genuine than those made in the hazy, romantic light of the moon. If this is true, our happiness was assured, because when he proposed to me we were in an Oxford Street café eating liver and bacon.

It is quite impossible to put on paper the next idyllic months, but I must tell something of our walks in Epping Forest, for this was the only place within easy reach of Dalston where he could get away from the din of traffic to the quiet of the woods and fields. When his surroundings were too much for him, he spent a good deal of his salary on these train fares. London Fields and Downs were, of course, nearby, but what murky fields and downs they were!

Epping Forest Today

42

I soon discovered much that was unusual about him as a lover, for as we sauntered through the woods he would break off in the middle of an interesting conversation and wander off by himself to watch some bird or climb a tree to explore a nest. Like many Londoners, I hardly knew the difference between a sparrow and a starling, and these things seemed to me far less important than our few precious hours together. I was to learn later that our walks were of double interest to him, for, although we were unaware of it, he was storing up knowledge for the future. I shall never forget the look of pleasure on his face when we paused to listen to the first nightingale I had heard. As it stood on a branch only a few yards away and the pure liquid notes, half fear, half rapture, floated through the wood, his eyes filled with tears.

One other recollection of Epping Forest is of interest. Either his grandfather, or one of the other Gypsy brothers, when camping there, buried a box containing his savings under a certain tree, and would return from his journeyings from time to time to add to them. "I wonder if this is the tree," he would say as we walked along. The habit of burying their money was very common among Gypsies, for they not only distrusted banks but were inclined to be secretive over money matters. One member of the older generation of the Smith family – alive today – is known to have hidden his money in a place known only to himself. Nothing will persuade him to tell his family where it is, and it does not seem to have occurred to him that some builder, rather than his own family, may be the future beneficiary!

Though I had lived in London practically all my life, I went to the various Art Galleries and to the Zoo more often during the next six months than I had done before, and if we could secure a front seat on the top of a Regent's Park bus, and he could sit and chat to the top-hatted driver about his horse, he was content. Visiting the Zoo was to him a mixed pleasure, for though there were countless other things of interest, it pained him to see magnificent eagles and vultures imprisoned, and he had a great pity for the tigers and panthers as, with noiseless tread, they paced restlessly to and fro in their cramped cages. To him there seemed something particularly pathetic about the far-away look in their eyes, those eyes made for peering into the shadows of dark forests and for scanning long distances of sun-baked sand.

It was about this time that he had the good luck to meet Gregory Brown, the well-known impressionist artist, whose posters at that time were to be seen on the Underground Railways. This brought him in contact with other artists, and he had the pleasure of going with them on several of their sketching expeditions. Though he had inherited a talent for drawing and painting from his father and had learnt a good deal from Gregory, he was always conscious of the inferiority of his own work. He was too impatient to devote the hours that great artists spend on the preliminary accuracies of their drawings, and was anxious to splash on his colours too soon. But the effect was often quite pleasing and, had it been possible to reproduce one of his paintings in its original bold colourings, I should have liked to include it in this book.[2] Gregory showed him, too, how to paint theatrical scenery, which proved very useful later for the many sketches which he produced. He also had a gift for poster-lettering, and saved his various churches many a pound for printing expenses. Above all, this background was responsible in later years for his skill in being able to illustrate his lectures with charcoal drawings.

His musical ability was soon recognised, for he could sit at the piano and play by ear almost any well-known tune suggested. In those days it was considered the thing to take music when invited out for an evening, and to need much persuasion when asked to play or sing – the music was hidden under one's coat in the hall. Unless the accompaniments produced were very difficult, he could play them with ease and, though he had not a good voice, his old College songs proved one of the most popular items of the evening.

The people with whom he lived in Evering Road were members of a nearby Congregational Church, and it was not long before he was choosing his personal friends from the people who visited the house. At the first rehearsal of the Concert Party, I was concerned to find that it consisted entirely of these young people and not those of his own church. Although I thought it odd, when my parents suggested that his officials might have reason for complaint, I resented their criticism, for, in my eyes, he could do no wrong.

Looking back, I feel that if he had been wisely guided at this time, he would readily have given up his outside activities and devoted the time to his own work. Having sole charge of his own church, he saw little of his Superintendent Minister – as far as I could gather, they rarely met, except on Lord's cricket ground.

With all the preparations for our wedding, the months passed quickly. I can see him now as he stood waiting for me on the edge of the pavements in Regent Street whilst I did my shopping. He looked so out-of-place, somehow, in a city crowd. I was perhaps disappointed that he did not come into the shops to help me choose the necessary fallals. To the clothes, as such, he was indifferent, but his keen sense of colour would have been of value to me. I was soon to discover that it was a mistake to expect a man of his temperament to show interest in such trivialities.

London streets are gold – ah, give me leaves a-glinting
Midst grey dykes and hedges in the Autumn sun.
London water's wine, poured out for all unstinting
God! for the little brooks that tumble as they run.

Ada Smith

Chapter 5 Notes

1   Gay did not then have the homosexual overtones it does today,
    which sadly so often now precludes the use of the word in its true
    sense and context.

2   This edition of the book includes one of his watercolours,
    Penton Bridge (page 66), and the front cover design is based
    on another of his watercolours.   These watercolours had
    been given to John 'Rubb' (Graham) whose daughter kindly
    allowed the editor to photograph them.

Our Wedding

Chapter 6

Goole and Early Carlisle Days

Bram was twenty-seven and I was 'twenty-four when we were married by my father, the Rev Owen Thomas, at our Congregational Church in Middleton Road on the first of August, 1911, and our combined congregations filled it to overflowing. The best man was G H Hilton, or Ding, of Epworth College days, and the only flaw to mar the day was that Bram's beloved Polly was not present. However, when we reached the tiny cottage in North Wales which we had chosen for our honeymoon, she was there to welcome us.

The word Yorkshire had conjured up visions of fertile dales, running streams and breezy moorlands, but when we arrived at Goole in September, I saw at once that my husband was disappointed, for the town and its surroundings were flat and uninteresting.

Reaching the manse, we received another set-back. I had naturally been disappointed when he had told me that Wesleyan ministers were provided with furnished houses, for, with his artistic leanings, it would have been a joy to have been able to express our ideas of art and beauty in the furnishing of our own home. But I had not pictured it as a house in which countless families had been living, and it came as a shock to us both to find that the furnishings showed both the care and neglect of a succession of ministers' families, and the good and bad taste of a succession of the stewards who had chosen them.

However, our happiness in each other and the kindness we received from the congregation soon dwarfed our feelings of frustration, and we settled down and began to unpack our belongings. Before leaving London, he had surprised me by saying, "I've engaged a maid for you," and though I did not see Bella, who had been a member of his congregation, until we arrived in Goole, his unerring instinct for character-reading proved right.

At first I discouraged my relatives from visiting us, for I was none too proud of my new home. With his help, however, I banished a few of the more aggressive pieces of furniture up to the attic, and when he had arranged the lighting effects and put the finishing touches to the rooms they looked almost attractive. He was peculiarly sensitive to inartistic surroundings, and when he needed inspiration to write, he would arrange his armchair so that the light from the rose-coloured shade of his reading-lamp cast the shadows of the tall fern-like plants on the wall, or showed up the vivid tones of his favourite watercolours.

After several of my relatives had come and gone, I waited expectantly for my in-laws to follow suit, but except for his parents, none ever came near. When I questioned him about them, he laughed, and said that he knew very little about any of them. On his father's side, he mentioned vaguely an Uncle Phil, but seemed more interested in a nameless uncle who was a diver, and who had nearly lost his life when he was knocked off the propeller of a ship by a shark. Of the rest of that side of the family, which included various cousins, he did not even know their names.

On his mother's side he knew a little more. His Aunt Emily had been at our wedding, he could not tell me if Uncle Ezekiel was married or not, but he had occasionally met his Uncle Rodney at Methodist functions. This was all very strange to me, for mine had always been a clannish family.

Meanwhile we settled down to our work and anticipated eagerly the appointments in the surrounding villages. We would start off early on our bicycles and picnic in the picturesque village of Airmyn where the quaint red-roofed cottages line the river-bank. Or we would have tea at some farmhouse, and he would chat to the farmer about his stock and his crops and stroll round the fields with him until it was time for the evening preaching service.

Sometimes on Sundays, if there was a seat to spare, he would take me with him in the antiquated high dogcart which took the various preachers to their village appointments. We had to make an early start, for we were always sure of being provided with the oldest worn-out mare the ostler had in his stables, and not even

Bram's experienced handling of her would make her change her sabbatic walk to a trot. She knew every inch of the road and would stop at the various chapels of her own accord. It was always a tricky business to arrange the sliding seat to balance each other's weight, and I either found myself perched up on the back seat with my feet in the air, or leaning forward at such an angle that a bump on the road nearly threw me out on my head. In winter weather there was no protection except for the big green dilapidated umbrella stowed away under the seat. One very windy night a sudden gale blew up as we crossed the marshland; up went the umbrella like a balloon, and we never saw it again.

We loved those outings, in spite of the fact that at some of the smaller chapels his congregation often numbered less than a dozen people. On one occasion we cycled out ten miles to the tiny village of Adlingfleet to find a congregation of only one, but he preached with as much vigour and sincerity as though the chapel had been full. When the service was over, and he had shaken hands with the old man, he turned to me and said, "I hope you were listening, for he's stone deaf."

It was the old Vicar of Adlingfleet lack of convention Bram often admired, who frequently prefaced his sermons by saying to his congregation, "Would you like me to read you a good sermon by Charles Spurgeon, or give you a poor one by myself?"

During our first year in Goole my husband had been studying for his final BD, but whether it was due to our preoccupation in each other, or the fact that our son was born in the August of 1912, I do not know, but he unfortunately failed to obtain his degree.

I shall never forget what happened at the Christening Service. It was to take place at the close of the Sunday morning service at our church opposite the house. Bella and I had spent the whole morning dressing baby Glyn, and I felt very proud of him in the smart embroidered christening gown which I had bought for the occasion. As I stood alone with him at the window, waiting impatiently for the important moment, to my surprise the church door opened and the congregation began to file out. Presently my husband appeared, laughing and chatting to a circle of friends. By this time I was almost in tears. He had forgotten all about the christening. Meanwhile, the congregation had almost dwindled away and, had it not been that the Minister who was to conduct the ceremony then arrived on his bicycle, he would probably have sauntered home. The christening took place in the presence of the caretaker, the organist, and two or three other people who had stayed behind chatting longer than usual. Penitent as he was, I do not think he understood my disappointment, for, to him, the number of the onlookers was unimportant.

The arrival of Glyn must have been responsible for the fact that I can remember little else of what happened at Goole, except that it was during those years that I first discovered my husband's intense appreciation of beauty.

We spent pleasant afternoons on the banks of the Ouse, when I hovered between him and the pram, as he used his water-colours to portray the ferryman plying his boat from one bank to the other. On our way home he would point out to me things that I had never noticed before – the grace of movement and poise of a passing girl, the delicate petals of a wild flower, the graceful flight of a bird, the softening effect of the shadows on a building, the beauty of the lines of character on an old man's face, or of the green weathered tiles on the roof of some farmstead.

I discovered, too, that what I often thought was lack of interest in my chatter was due to his absorption in these things, and I soon learned to forgive his absent-mindedness and dreamy vagueness, for I realised that he was living in a world of his own of which I knew nothing.

But this was not always understood by other people, and in Church Committee Meetings matters would sometimes become complicated when he did not listen to the views expressed by other people. His naturalness and charm of manner appealed to the young people of the church, but his disregard of convention, his obstinacy and his youthful enthusiasm often brought him up against the older and more conservative members, who were quite satisfied with things as they were. They naturally resented drastic changes, and were not afraid of telling him so.

This lack of convention occasionally caused me concern. He had very little interest in his appearance, and I can remember, to my dismay, as I walked up Boothferry Road in Goole one afternoon, seeing a tall, brown-tweed-coated, conspicuous figure towering above the black coats of his fellow clergy and ministers as a Civic procession passed by. But once I had pointed out to him that his appearance might have given offence, he was always afterwards easily persuaded to wear clothes to suit the occasion.

It was not long before we were welcome guests in a great many homes, for not only was he good company but his musical ability helped to enliven many an evening. In his church work, too, it came in useful, for if the. organist failed to turn up at any chapel, down he would come from the pulpit to play the hymns. Whether it was a stately organ, a piano or a wheezy harmonium, he could always step into the breach. One glance round his congregation was enough to tell him that few of them would be able to reach the high notes of some of the hymns, and he would transpose them to a lower key.

These gifts brought him into contact with the musical people of the town, and he was soon both accompanying and writing songs for another concert party unconnected with his own church. All this was great fun for both of us, but, again, his officials naturally disapproved of his devoting so much time to outside interests. Perhaps I should have discouraged him but at the time it was unthinkable that he should not be perfect. In later years, as I looked back, I came to the conclusion that he must have been conscious of a certain limitation in the work that he thought was expected of him in these early appointments.

I know that my husband was no usual man, and that he would not fit into any conventional mould, but I always felt that he was at a disadvantage when he started his career. Having been brought up in a small Mission, he knew nothing of normal church life, and less still of the business side of his work. If his college training provided the latter, I can only imagine that he made persistent efforts not to learn anything, for he had no idea how to conduct business meetings, keep a methodical visiting book or plan his work from day to day. I was, of course, not conscious of this at the time; in fact, I thought him worthy of one of the biggest congregations in Methodism, and could not understand why he had been sent to Goole.

September 1914 found us on our way to an equally un-important church in Carlisle. That journey was a memorable one because our train followed the course of the river Eden and he saw the Cumberland Hills for the first time. He was as excited as a child – as though he felt that these hills were to have an influence on him throughout the whole of his life.

On arrival at a manse, it is usual to find a generous meal prepared, which is often shared by the stewards and their wives who provide it. This is somewhat of an ordeal, especially after a tiring journey, and it was not to be wondered at that Glyn should have spoilt the good impression we were trying to make on our new friends by doing something that necessitated his being sent to have his tea in the kitchen. When the meal was over, I found Bram preparing to go down to explore the river, and was only just in time to prevent our making a second bad impression. As they went out of the front door, he slipped out at the back, quite oblivious of the fact that his assistance would be needed to carry upstairs all the luggage which littered the hall. But when I saw his face on his return from his explorations, nothing else seemed to matter. I knew that he would find happiness in Carlisle.

As at Goole, he enjoyed his village work, especially when he could exchange country lore over tea with Jimmy Hodgson, the Hesket village postman, or learn wisdom from old John Huggon, as he sat in his cobbler's shop at Monkhill. He would often afterwards tell of the influence of the old village cobbler, and contrast the badly attended funeral which he conducted in memory of some so-called personage in Carlisle with the huge multitude of people who turned out the same afternoon to pay their homage to the memory of this fine old man.

We received such wonderful hospitality during our stay in Carlisle that I must mention the Collins, the Grahams and the Curreys. We just walked into their houses at any hour, and long after we left the border city, we retained fond memories of their kindness. We, too, loved entertaining, and our Sunday night supper parties strained the manse crockery to its limit.

Life was very pleasant; Bram was like a wild bird released from its cage, and the days were not long enough to get in all the walks we had with the dog in the glorious country of Wetheral and The Lynns. This part of the Eden Valley enchanted him. His terrier, Jack, having died, he had now bought a cocker-spaniel called Raq, who became his inseparable companion.

But outside all this peace and happiness the world was in a tumult. We knew that there was a war on, of course, for we had seen the garrison regiment leave Carlisle Castle; but it was to feel keenly about it, for neither conscription nor food rationing was then in existence. In any case, Carlisle was not dependent on the outside world for much of its food, and as long as the Cumberland farmers' wives brought their delicious butter, eggs, fruit and vegetables into the market each week, we were all right.

But Bram, being of military age, felt that it was his duty to volunteer, and in due course he joined the new recruits in Carlisle Castle. Though the language of the sergeant-major rather took him aback when he was told to take off his clothes for a medical inspection, it was nothing to his surprise when he found that he had failed his medical on the grounds of his heart murmur. Later, this was found to be such a common symptom among recruits that it was no longer regarded as a disqualification. The idea that he was not in perfect health was unthinkable, for we went long walks, climbed the fells and played games strenuously.

When we went for a ramble, he always walked a few paces ahead of me. I thought this strange. I wanted to take hold of his arm and talk to him, but I soon found that to him, a country walk meant not only going in single file, but in silence if one was not to disturb the wild creatures that might be about. He would turn off the main road at the first lane, saunter up the side of a field, exploring the hedge for nests. Then he would settle himself on a stile, his eyes roving in every direction.

His natural walking pace seemed leisurely, but with his long stride he was usually so far ahead that I was left to flounder through streams and push my way through prickly hedges alone. At first, I thought this ungallant, but I soon learnt wisdom. He was so absorbed in what he was seeing that he was hardly aware of my presence.

He had a great gift for adapting himself to the various types of people he met. The humblest person was never embarrassed in his company, and I often envied him this trait. On one occasion, when preaching in a colliery village, he was taken home by a miner to dinner. The first thing he noticed was that the womenfolk did not join the men at table. They waited on them, and had their meal afterwards. He then saw that the men looked ill at ease. It suddenly occurred to him that they were not accustomed to wearing their Sunday jackets at meals. Getting up, he pulled off his own, saying, "My word, it's warm." He had broken the ice; off came theirs, and he at once became one of the family.

And so it was with everyone he came across. When we met country folk in the lanes, I, in my conventional way, was inclined to say, "Good afternoon," and then comment on the weather, but he, without any introductory remarks, would ask a gamekeeper, "Any foxes about?" or "Is the fly bothering them?" to a shepherd. One sentence was sufficient to show them that he knew something of their work, and the rest was then easy. Poacher, rabbit-catcher, blacksmith, mole-catcher, it was all the same; he immediately became friends with them all.

He liked best of all to chat with an intelligent gamekeeper who knew the habits of birds, not only those which were harmless to his pheasants and partridges, but those which fed on insect pests harmful to agriculture. It worried him that such men were few, and that he so often saw useful birds such as kestrel-hawks[1] strung up on gamekeepers' gibbets.

But these ordinary pleasures were nothing compared with the discovery that I was making that he was a most thrilling person to live with. Not only did he make ordinary commonplace things interesting but he opened my eyes to a new world of form and colour. To me, a country walk had just meant fresh air, good exercise and a chat with a friend. I had never noticed the iridescent sheen on the plumage of a common starling, the perfection of an insignificant wild flower or the dignity of a fine tree. As we sat on the river bank, he showed me the deep pools where the salmon lay, and how the trout darted under the bank when we went near. I had never before seen any beauty in a field of wheat swaying in the breeze, or in a flock of gulls fluttering like moths as they followed the plough up a freshly furrowed field.

The effect that some things had on him bewildered me at times. I can see now the lane where he stood for several minutes with head thrown back and eyes closed as he drank in the intoxicating scent of a field of bean-blossom. I can see, too, the hedge-bank on which we were sitting as, with face transfigured, he listened to the rustle of the breeze as it combed through a field of wheat. For him these things had a deep meaning. He rarely spoke to me when out of doors and never consciously taught me anything, but his own joy in every miracle of Nature made him want me to share it.

Sometimes I wouldn't speak, you see,
Or answer, when you spoke to me,
Because in the long still dusks of Spring
You can hear the whole world whispering...
The pebbles pushing in the silver streams,
The rushes talking in their dreams."

Charlotte Mew

Chapter 6 Notes

1   Kestrel-hawk was a term once used for the Kestrel, but it is incorrect since the kestrel is a falcon, not a hawk. It also has the old country name of windhover.

Romany and his Parents

Chapter 7

On the Banks of the Eden

Until he went to Carlisle, my husband had always considered himself an angler, but when he met Joseph Fidler and John Graham (or John Rubb, as he called him later in his books and press articles) he soon realised that he was only a novice, and that his education in the art of angling had only just begun. I well remember John Rubb's pitying look as Bram described to him his adventures trolling for pike on the Cheshire meres, or sitting with float and worm on the banks of the Dee. This might be called fishing, thought John, but it certainly wasn't angling.

John Rubb was the proprietor of a small shop in Lowther Street, very well stocked with sporting equipment of every description. Here farmers came for their stack covers and mackintoshes, and anglers for their fishing waders and rubber boots. A glance at the heterogeneous muddle in John's shop window gave an entirely wrong impression of the large stock of goods in his back premises. To my artistic husband, the arrangement of the window was an offence, and he made several attempts to improve it, but though John smilingly allowed him to do it, he knew well that most of his customers fought shy of outward show, and felt more at home in his unpretentious shop than in the modern plate-glass-windowed shops of English Street.

Even John's appearance helped him. He was short, spare, with thin, tousled, nondescript-coloured hair, which gave an impression of oddness, but the most kindly, childlike, blue-grey eyes gleamed through his spectacles, gave one a feeling of trust and confidence. But what a clever salesman he was. Bram would sit in the shop and chuckle as one customer followed another. When a farmer came in for a mackintosh and was about to leave after trying on several of the kind he wanted, John would lower his voice and, in the most confidential tone would say, "One moment. I've got the very thing you want for farm work." Disappearing into the back premises, he would soon reappear with something quite different from what the man had in mind and, within a few minutes, he would be walking out of the shop with it on, thoroughly convinced that it was what he really needed.

John was a most un-punctual and irritatingly indecisive man. He always arrived late at Church Committee Meetings, and when a decision had to be made on any matter, he always sat on the fence much longer than anyone else. But if Bram slipped into the shop and whispered, "The salmon are up," without hesitation John would reply, "Penton Bridge at four o'clock," and, ignoring a shopful of customers, he would be there on the dot.

John 'Rubb'

Joseph Fidler was a very different type. He was tall, dignified, very correct in manner and deportment, inclined to be somewhat slow of speech, but a very staunch and firm friend to those he liked.

It was from these two friends of his that my husband learnt the art of fly-fishing, and of casting his gossamer line with such accuracy across the river that his fly would alight on the water as daintily as the blue dun itself. He needed few lessons on the habits of fish and the flies they fed on, for he had spent many hours watching them, but they taught him in which pools and quiet backwaters the fish usually lay, either in crystal-clear water or in flood. He learnt which artificial fly to use as 'bait' and when to use it, how to cast against the wind and how to judge the speed of the water. Above all, they told him that infinite patience was necessary, but he had no need to acquire that virtue when engaged in any outdoor pursuit.

In spite of all this tuition, it seemed to me a long time before he came home with even a tiny trout in his creel. Indeed, I often felt sorry for him as I sat with Raq on the river bank watching him patiently fishing hour after hour with no result. Enticed away from his known pools by the ever-widening rings of a rising trout, he would sometimes move farther down-stream only to get his cast entangled in a reed bed or submerged tree-trunk and lose his tackle altogether. Sometimes I proved useful, for, even after he had passed the kindergarten stage, the wind would catch his rod as he cast his fly and he would call me to disentangle the hook from the sleeve of his tweed jacket – such a difficult task that, in his impatience, we nearly always finished up by cutting out a piece of the cloth.

Sometimes, after several hours' fishing, John Rubb would appear from a stretch of water down the river, and, as he stood on the bank with the water oozing through his rubber boots, he would call out, "Any luck?" and Bram would reply, "Not a bite." John would then open his creel and show us a dozen lovely trout. I felt annoyed, for, though he certainly had an instinct for fishing, I had learnt something of the craftiness of anglers and was sure that he had chosen the best pools for himself, partly, of course, because he feared that a novice would only scare the fish that he knew were lying there.

But Bram rarely complained, and as we walked home in the darkness and he told me of the otter he had seen under Eden Bridge, or the mallards flying high over Rickerby Park, I knew that to him an empty creel was as nothing compared with a night under the stars watching the creatures that he loved.

Anglers, on the whole, are very secretive, and even when my husband had become an expert, he found it very difficult to extract from John the name of the artificial fly with which he had caught some big sea-trout, or, if they went off for the day to some river with which he was not familiar, John would not tell him of the special pools where the salmon were lying until he had fished them himself.

My memories of Carlisle are a bit disjointed, but I think it was about two years before we left there that my husband had his most thrilling fishing experience. He was out early one morning in the stretch of the Eden that lies below the railway yards, when he felt a terrific pull on his line. He struck and, oh joy! he had hooked a big salmon. He knew well that hooking a salmon is a very different matter from landing one, and that the way in which a big fish is landed soon betrays the novice.

He turned its head down-stream[1] and, after playing it up and down the river for quite half an hour, he at last got it to within ten yards of the bank. He also knew that it takes a very experienced angler to hold the enormous weight of a salmon with one hand and net it at the critical moment with the other. He looked around, but not a soul was to be seen at that early hour. Then suddenly he heard a voice, "Come on, boys. The parson's hooked a b*** fish!" Looking up, he saw dozens of heads peering over the fence of the railway yard. Down they swarmed and, amidst general jubilation, the salmon, weighing eighteen pounds, was landed. So that none of his fellow-anglers should ever dispute its weight, Bram weighed it, nailed it on the cellar door, and then photographed it. We spent the day taking huge chunks of it round to all our friends and then ate fresh salmon until we were sick of it.

The wife of an angler is not in an enviable position. The long waders which are worn when walking in the water reach up to the waist, and a false step taken in the darkness means certain death by drowning. A sudden flood often entirely changes the contours of the bed of the river, and what before was known to the angler as fiat shingle may have become a deep treacherous pool. What made it worse for me was that I had heard the gruesome story of an angler who took an inadvertent step which caused his waders to fill with water and, like a stone, he had dropped to the bottom[2]. Perhaps this was one of the reasons why I spent so much of my time on the riverbank watching Bram night-fishing, for nothing was more nerve-racking than lying in bed waiting for him when he promised to return at two o'clock and arrived at half-past three!

One morning he came home in a very nervy state. It appeared that, as it was getting dark, he had cast his line across the river and hooked something soft. With a quaking heart he went nearer and discovered it to be the body of a drowned man! He was so scared that he nearly turned tail and ran home, but he knew that had he done so he would never have the nerve to fish at night again. On the bank he found the man's hat and coat neatly folded up and a paper with his name and address. Not wanting all the bother of police-court formalities, he moved farther down the river and went on fishing. Half an hour later a river-watcher arrived and discovered the tragedy. The newspaper reports told the usual story of domestic trouble. Alas, the river Eden was a favourite spot for suicides.

As he was spending a good deal of his time both reading and writing, these fishing expeditions meant a good deal to my husband. Sometimes he left the breakfast table with every intention of settling down to his books for the morning. After about half an hour the study door would open and he would wander restlessly from room to room. There was no cure for it but that he should get out-of-doors. Though the stretches of the river that run through Carlisle are not as beautiful as those farther South, it was a boon to him that they were within five minutes of our house. But whether it was an hour with his rod on the river bank, or farther afield in the singularly beautiful district of Armathwaite, the result was always the same – he came back soothed in body and mind.

A different kind of restlessness always seized him during the month of February, for trout fishing begins on March the first. "Where are my rods?" "Where are my waders?" "Where is my fly-book?" he would keep asking, for he never could find anything he wanted, and he seemed quite surprised when I discovered some of his missing flies stuck in the band of his old tweed hat. When he produced his best rod, I noticed that he handled it with real affection, and it was an understood thing that no member of the family was allowed to touch it.

He would come into the kitchen and ask, "Where do you keep the raw mutton fat?" as though I always kept a supply of it in the house. This he used for waxing his silken line.[3] Then, for hours he would become engrossed in the most delicate operation

63

of all – varnishing his rod. This always amused me because, so important was it not to put the varnish on too thickly, that he would rub his finger on the scalp of his head in order to give it a coating of natural oil before dipping it into the varnish; but in his enthusiasm he would keep using the wrong finger, and when he had finished the job his hair was one sticky mess.

For hours he would sit completely happy while he tested his lines and sorted out his flies and various gadgets. Then off he would go to Robert Strong's for replenishments in readiness for the great day.

I objected strongly to one kind of fishing bait – maggots! I shiver now as I recall the number of times I found a handful of them loose when I cleaned out his pockets, and it was quite a common thing for him to find one or two in his pipe when he wanted a smoke.

"They can't get out of there," he would say with a smile as he shut down the lid of the tin on their repulsive, fat, bodies. Then, with his penknife, he would haphazardly punch a few tiny breathing holes in the lid, and the next morning I would find them squirming about amongst the papers on his study desk or slithering along the sideboard. What was worse, he would sometimes breed them himself, and if there was a particularly foul odour about, I would often trace it to the dead carcase of some bird or animal in his workshop.

One evening I was sitting on the bank of the river opposite the Scaur,[4] when I heard him shouting. He was always so silent when fishing that I ran along the bank to see if he was in difficulties. I discovered that, whilst wading he had trodden on something unfamiliar which turned out to be a large initialled silver salver. He continued his search, and we returned home that night with two salvers and two large Sheffield-plate cups. The next morning he reported his find at the police station and was informed that, years before, a mansion outside Carlisle had been robbed, and from the initials they gathered that this was the 'swag.' As, however, the owner had long since died and no relative came forward to claim them, the salvers and cups adorned our sideboard for many years.

It was John Rubb who first took us to Penton, a border beauty spot and a paradise for anglers. The name of the place may sound more attractive if I explain that the accent falls on the second syllable – Pen*ton*. Some days stand out above others in my memory. I remember the day of our arrival very clearly. With our heavy suitcases we went through a little wicket gate out of the station and found ourselves on a grassy slope which led through a wood. I was too burdened at the time to admire the beauty around me, and felt peeved that my husband had chosen this narrow, difficult path rather than the road. Down a steep bank we slid, across a trickle of a stream and up the other side we clambered, until finally we caught sight of Kilnholm, a lonely, whitewashed house, almost surrounded by the river. I suppose at one time there must have been some sort of a road down to it, or the house could not have been built, but I never saw any signs of one.

It was here, during our first years in Carlisle, that my husband did much of his fishing and bird-observing. Sometimes we went alone, sometimes John Rubb and Joseph Fidler came too. We arrived at all hours of the day and night according to the state of the river, and if Mrs Mitchell was out or in bed, we knew where to find the key. She understood the vagaries of anglers, for her husband had been one, and though there was no shop for miles she always seemed able to produce delicious hot girdle cakes or crisp oatmeal-covered fried trout at a moment's notice.

The great charm of the place, as Bram used to put it, was that we were not under the tyranny of the clock. We fished when other people were in bed, and we had meals at any hour of the day that suited us. There was a carefree, happy-go-lucky atmosphere about the place that suited him well.

The narrow, swiftly running, boulder-strewn rivers of the North seemed to appeal to him more than the broader, placid, sluggish rivers in other parts of the country, and I soon learnt the names of the deep pools where the salmon lurked. "Where shall I find you to-night?" I would ask, and even the names of the pools he mentioned seemed to have a fascination for him. The Loop, near Penton Bridge, beloved of poachers who always appeared to be admiring the scenery when we crossed the bridge; the Caul, dark and silent; Blaney, smooth and tranquil; and the Dormant, the deep, menacing, bottomless pool which I feared most of all.

As I have said, my husband was a man of few words when out-of-doors, and it was a long time before I learnt that I could be both happy and silent when out with him. "You can't both watch

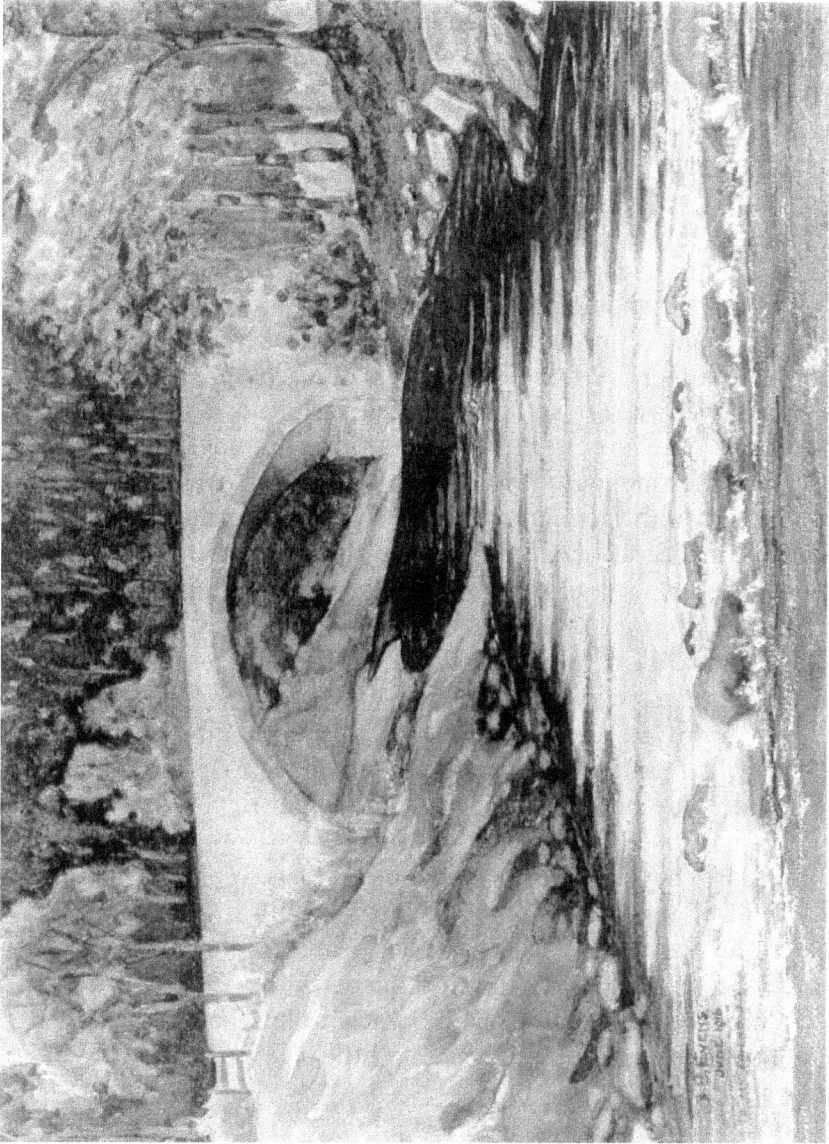

Romany's Watercolour of Penton Bridge. 1916

and chatter," he would say, and when he was fishing, hours would pass without a word between us. When we first went to Penton I thought I might make up for this by getting an innings at mealtimes, but I had reckoned without John Rubb. Not only did fishing entirely monopolise the conversation, but most of their language was quite unintelligible to me. They would talk of the salmon seen leaping up the Loop, of the monstrous sea-trout almost landed, of the pain it gave them to have to throw the tiny parr back into the river. They would talk of March Brown, Blue Dun, Stone Fly, Wickham's Fancy and Greenwell's Glory, which I later discovered were some of the names of the artificial flies[5] they used.

If the river was too low for them to fish, they would spend hours in the front garden doing odd jobs, and arguments would take place as to whether Bram's Greenheart rod was better than John's split bamboo cane; whether 3x gut was better than 4x, and the respective merits of dry-fly and wet-fly fishing, All the time their hands were never still as John cleverly put a patch on his rubber waders, while Bram produced from his pocket the most wonderful assortment of feathers which he had picked up here and there, and with them dressed a fly so deftly that I could hardly tell it from a natural one. John would then perhaps fettle up his rod, while Bram sat mumbling away as he sucked one of his old gut casts to soften it, for he hated to throw one away if there was the least chance of it holding. This cost him the loss of many a fish in his inexperienced days.

Then followed the inevitable stories of their fishing experiences which, in time, as they were recounted to other people, I came to know by heart, except that the weight of the fish caught seemed to increase in the telling.

Then off they would go to examine the river, and as John went ahead of us through the wicket gate with his rod over his shoulder, he would call, "Tight lines," and Bram would reply "Tight lines." Then it was that my husband would talk to me of the sandpipers, the herons and the water voles that he had seen during the morning, for John knew little of the ways of wild creatures.

I was especially privileged to be allowed to stay at Penton, for Mrs Mitchell's visitors were mainly anglers and women guests were rare. I often wondered if John resented my presence. If he did, he certainly never showed it. I think he knew that Bram and I shared all our pleasures and that we were not happy when apart. But I myself had one grudge against John, for it was he who had enticed my husband away from the cricket and tennis we both enjoyed together. Fishing, like golf, had always seemed to me a sport for older men. It had been such fun playing tennis together, and I had revelled in sitting on the grassy bank of the Edenside playing fields on hot summer evenings as I watched his cricket score slowly mounting up on the board. However, John was soon forgiven, for had it not been for him we should never have known Penton.

Packing up their rods in preparation for departure was always a sad business, but there was one unfortunate occasion when I was instrumental in prolonging our stay there. The night before we were due to leave I was taken ill. The nearest doctor was five or six miles away, and Bram had no means of reaching him except on foot. Stumbling through the wood to the station at two o'clock one pitch-black night, he knocked up a villager and borrowed a motor-cycle. It was a mercy I did not know what was happening, for he had only ridden one once before. Whether the motor-cycle had no lamps or whether they were forbidden at that time (for it was 1916 and during the last war[6]) I do not know, but he dashed off through the darkness, and as he crossed over Penton Bridge he was cursed by the poachers, one of whom he nearly killed.

However, my illness proved a blessing in disguise, for our holiday was extended, and those next few weeks alone with him stand out amongst my happiest memories.

Lord, suffer me to catch a fish
So large that even I,
When talking of it afterwards,
Shall have no need to lie.

Trad

Chapter 7 Notes

1   It is the salmon which dictates the direction it goes. The angler follows as best he can!

2   Such tales are still told, but extremely unlikely to be true. Waders fill with water very slowly, and even with water in them the waders actually give great buoyancy to the legs and feet.

3   How Romany would have enjoyed today's PVC coated lines!

4   The Scaur (old Scots word for scar) is an area on the outer side of a bow in the river Eden at Carlisle where the ground falls steeply to the river – a scar in the landscape. Today the area is known as Etterby Scaur where there is a row of impressive houses. At one point John 'Rubb' lived in one of those houses.

3

Etterby Scaur

5   The flies Eunice recalls are classic day-time (brown) trout flies still in use, but when Romany went night fishing it would have been for sea-trout when he would have used flies such as Peter Ross, Bloody Butcher or Lady of the Lake (Alexandra).

6   Eunice was writing in 1945-46, just as, and after, WW2 was ending, so reference to 'the last war' is to WW1 (1914-18).

Romany Trout Fishing

Photo: R. Nicholson

Chapter 8

Church Activities

In spite of the fact that his congregations recognised his pulpit ability, my husband was not a good all-round minister from the Methodist point of view. He was ever ready to help those in trouble, and did not neglect to visit the sick, but he hated making lists of any kind, and the rest of his congregation were either over-visited or he never saw them at all. The business side of the work, too, was distasteful to him, and the only time when he did not mind attending one of the district meetings, or Synods as they are called, was when it was held at Appleby-on-the-Eden,[1] and he could take his fishing-rod with him.

It was the war, however, which gave him an opportunity of using his gifts, and as it may be of special interest to my Methodist readers, I must tell of some of his ventures in detail. It was about this time that our peaceful cathedral city received a rude shock. Rumour had been prevalent that huge munition works were being built, stretching for miles around Gretna, and sleepy Carlisle woke up one morning to find an army of strangers in possession. And what an army they were – mostly navvies[2] of the roughest type, who had come to make the miles of road needed for the new works. They poured out of the trains on to the streets to find their own accommodation, and were sleeping in rows on the floors of some houses. One woman told us that her beds never had time to cool; the men worked in three shifts and three men used each bed. Those who failed to find lodgings slept in the huge drain pipes that lined the new roads.

The scenes at night were indescribable. They besieged the public-houses in the narrow alleys, and it was a common occurrence to see scores lying on the pavement. Incidentally, as a result of all this, the Government eventually made Carlisle its first experiment in State control of the drink traffic.[3]

Things then calmed down. These men departed, and their place was taken by electricians and joiners, who had nowhere to spend their leisure except in the public-houses and picture-houses. This presented Bram with a challenge, and it was not long before he had secured premises and organised a club for them. His was the persuasive power that rallied the workers, and induced tradesmen to give him the furnishings, and mine the task of putting it into shipshape. This gave many of these men the first taste of home comfort they had received; and though today, when clubs for the Forces abound everywhere, it may seem unworthy of record, little work of this kind was done in the early part of the first world war.

His next move was a more audacious one. In spite of the increase in population, the various congregations of the city churches showed little increase, and so, with the backing of his officials, he rented one of the cinemas[4] with the idea of holding a more popular type of service after the usual evening one. Only those who have lived in quiet cathedral cities can appreciate the reaction of many people to such an innovation and the many discouragements which he received.

We went through an agony of apprehension before the opening service. As we neared the cinema our hearts fell. It was a quarter to eight, the place was in darkness, and only a couple of hundred people[5] were queued up outside. "Why haven't they put on the lights?" he exclaimed impatiently. When we reached the entrance, we were met by excited perspiring stewards. The building was packed to the doors, and they had put the lights out to discourage new arrivals. Though the attendance varied according to the number of munition workers who came and went, there were rarely vacant seats during the six years that my husband conducted these services.

When. he had applied for the cinema, the manager, a tall, good-looking man, was inclined to be somewhat cynical and critical of the venture. The first Sunday he walked in and out occasionally in his smart tail-coat, as cinema managers do, to see if the rules and regulations were being observed. The second Sunday he stayed longer, for the naturalness and simplicity of my husband's talk held him longer than he intended.: After that, he rarely missed a service, and many an evening he joined our late supper parties at the manse. He joined up the next year, and within a month was killed at Mons, much to our distress.

To appreciate fully the following incident, one must be able to visualise John Rubb as I have tried to describe him. One Sunday night, he and my husband were leaving the cinema. when they met a party of six smart, well-dressed girls in the entrance hall, who turned out to be ballet girls belonging to a theatrical touring company. They were disappointed to find that there was not a picture show on, which meant that they would have to wander round the streets for several hours until their train was due to leave Carlisle. Bram at once asked them if they would like to come to our house. They hesitated for a moment, but, probably being reassured by his clerical collar and John's homely appearance, they accepted. Several of our friends who passed them as they all walked down Botchergate raised their eyebrows expressively. I already had the usual crowd of Sunday evening visitors in the house when the girls trooped in, and how to produce supper for so many people bothered me not a little. However, I opened all the tins I could find in the larder, and made sure that they were served first.

What charming girls they were – so very young and pretty, so grateful for our hospitality, so pathetically happy at being in a home after living in different theatrical lodgings each week. "A real home," they kept saying.

As the train was not due to leave until after two o'clock, and they seemed tired, I suggested that they might like to rest upstairs. I well remember their exclamations of delight when they tiptoed into the bedroom and saw Glyn asleep in his cot, blissfully unaware of the excitement he was causing.

Meanwhile, our other friends had left, but John Rubb was still downstairs – he meant to see the business through to the end. When the girls reached the station and met the rest of the company, the manager looked somewhat askance at the two men who accompanied them, but the girls soon dispelled their fears. John had quite a long way to walk home, and it must have been nearly three o'clock when he arrived. We laughed a lot as we pictured his attempts to explain to his wife where he had been. As it was Sunday night, he could not give the usual fishing excuse. We afterwards received delightful letters from these girls, and, when they next visited Carlisle, we went to see their show.

My husband then persuaded the Government authorities to put up a building in the munition area that could be used for religious services and as a week-day club with a billiard table.[6] This necessitated his buying a car, for it was essential that he should be on the spot to superintend its erection; but when he arrived home one day and asked me if we had £20 to buy a second-hand Trumball which he had seen, I was naturally concerned, because he was most unmechanically-minded, and driving lessons were not compulsory in those days. All he finally did was to get the garage proprietor to point out the various levers and then drive home in it.

Those next months were a nightmare, and though he afterwards became a good driver, experience proved that he was right when he said that he had not the least idea what went on under the bonnet. As with most cars in those days, it was constantly breaking down, obliging him to leave it on the roadside and walk home.

A Trumball of that Era

To save the daily journeys to and from the munition area he then suggested that we should go and live there and take Glyn with us. So, despite the fact that it was winter and snow was falling heavily, we packed our camp-beds and belongings into the old car and arrived at Dornock without a breakdown. To me, our new home looked very uninviting, for it stood in a rough, desolate spot far removed from human habitation and, though I found that one small room was fairly habitable, he had omitted to tell me that the building was only half-finished, that there was neither heating nor lighting and that the windows had not been put in. How we existed those next few weeks I do not know. We woke the next morning to find a blizzard raging and spent most of the day shovelling a path through the five-foot drifts. We were isolated for days and thoroughly cold and miserable. Fortunately, the joiners had left plenty of wood about, and Bram was able to make a fire in an outhouse. Finally, the weather improved, the workmen returned, and I sallied forth to find a woman to clean the hut. I walked miles with no success; they were earning high wages at the munition works. And so, each night when the men downed tools, Bram would take the only sweeping-brush, and I would take my bucket and scrubbing-brush, and we would toil until bedtime. Glyn was the one entirely happy person, for he played with Raq amongst the bricks and rubble, climbed the ladders, and made mud pies out of the mortar. However, it was not long before it became known in the munition works that a club was being built, and some of the men came to our aid each evening.

When the late King and Queen[7] visited the munition works and Bram was included in the invitation to meet them, I had great difficulty in persuading him that the dirty old suit he was wearing would not do. To have to motor to Carlisle for his best one seemed to him absurd. Finally he went, but forgot his best shoes; whether anyone noticed his plaster-covered ones I do not know.

We were more than compensated for the extreme discomfort and hard work of those months by the gratitude of the men, who presented my husband with a gold watch before we left. One of them wrote to me recently, telling what the comfort of Wesley Hut and the friendship of my husband meant to him and his friends.

Owing partly to the initiative shown in these efforts, he was invited to remain in Carlisle to take charge of the main church in Fisher Street, but, unfortunately, at the end of his first year, dry rot was found in the beams of the roof and the building was condemned as unsafe. The congregation was anything but wealthy, and to build a new church worthy of the traditions of the old one would cost thousands of pounds. Where was the money to come from? Methodism, at that time, had a millionaire benefactor in Joseph Rank, the well-known flour miller. He had, however, a curious trait, in that, he would give most generously to the building of mission halls, but not to the building of churches, and the idea of replacing the old church with a mission hall filled Bram and his officials with horror. But, after much deliberation there seemed no alternative but to accept Mr Rank's magnificent offer of £10,000 and compromise over the building of the hall. At the time my husband was friendly with H E Ayris, a clever Carlisle architect, and together they visualised a hall so beautiful that it would create the right atmosphere for church worship. In conjunction with another firm of architects, plans were eventually submitted for a hall which would cost £26,000.

When, excavations were made beneath the church, interesting Roman pottery and other relics were found, which my husband gave into the keeping of the Carlisle Museum. This upheaval meant that we, too, had to be excavated out of our manse which adjoined the church, but it proved our happiest removal, for it was the only time that I was not obliged to leave the house and furniture spotlessly clean for my successor. Raq and the family were able to tramp in and out to their hearts' content without fear of harming my reputation. I had known a case where carpets left soiled by a minister's wife had obliterated years of devoted church work.

Meanwhile, it was left to my husband to devise ways and means of raising the remaining £16,000. Organising huge bazaars gave him great scope for his artistic ability, and though his impressionistic ideas baffled some of his congregation, could Gregory Brown have seen his pupil's scenic effects he would have, been proud. By the time that he had used his persuasive powers on various outside generous Methodists, and our Carlisle congregation had given to the point of sacrifice, the sum needed was reduced to £1,000 and the opening day upon us.

April 12th, 1923, was a red-letter day for him, for the Central Hall was officially opened by Joseph Rank who had generously promised to double the collections taken on the day. Whilst sitting on the platform Bram had an inspiration. After announcing the subscriptions received during the previous month, he turned to Mr Rank and said, "May I add these to today's: collection?" The audience roared with laughter, and then cheered when the chairman smiled and nodded his approval. My husband's dream was realised. The Central Hall was opened free of debt.

It may not be known that Arthur Rank, who owns a large proportion of the cinema companies in this country, is a son of the late Joseph Rank, and a much-respected Methodist. My husband often felt that, though his ideas of using his wealth were vastly different from his father's, with his wide vision and ideals for the future of the cinema industry, he would eventually do as much good as his father had done.

The following winter we inaugurated Celebrity Lectures in the Central Hall, and one of the most popular of these was given by Sir Walford Davies, who won my husband's heart as soon as he arrived. Instead of treating him as other lecturers had done, merely as the organiser, Sir Walford took him on one side and asked him about his work. Before he began his talk, he stood a moment looking around the building, and then said, "Allow me to congratulate you on this beautiful hall which is a church, and this beautiful church which is a hall." Coming from one with his aesthetic taste, this was a high tribute.

When arranging the list of celebrities, the Committee had been greatly encouraged by the help given by a member of the congregation, whom I will call Palmer. He had arrived in Carlisle a year previously and was such a pleasant, generous man, and appeared to be so interested in the work done at the Central Hall, that it was not long before he was received into the homes of the congregation and eventually became Sunday School Super-intendent. He gave the impression of being on such intimate terms with so many well-known people that when he mentioned

Norman Allin, among others, and offered to arrange for him to give a recital, we were delighted.

At this time, we spent our holidays camping, and when he came to stay with us, he brought with him so many cases of provisions from the stores in English Street, of which he was the manager, that we were more than embarrassed. He slept in one of the tents, and talked at such length of his famous friends that Bram's only hope of rest was to pretend to be asleep.

The night before Norman Allin was due to arrive we heard, quite by chance, that Palmer had left the town. This struck us both as odd, because he had all the arrangements in hand for the recital. Early next morning Bram went to his shop to make enquiries. There he found a great commotion. Two police inspectors were in possession. They had been wanting him for years for bigamy, embezzlement and numerous other crimes both in Carlisle and elsewhere. To identify him my husband went to the police station, and it gave him a weird feeling to see the man's photograph unearthed from a pile of other 'wanted' men. He afterwards had the disagreeable task of breaking the news to his so-called wife, who had not the least idea that he was a criminal.

But what about the large audience that would be assembled in the Central Hall that evening to welcome Norman Allin? How was Bram going to explain the matter, and who would fill the bill? Without hesitation he took the next train to Glasgow. Telling the manager of the chief concert agency of his predicament, he was told that there were no artistes of repute disengaged, but being very persistent, he refused to leave the office until the manager had rung up every name on his books. He arrived back in Carlisle barely an hour before the concert was due to commence, bringing with him a very indifferent concert party. The audience was none too pleased, but was never told the real story behind it all. We often wondered afterwards if Norman Allin ever knew that his name had appeared on our list of celebrities that season without his permission.

The matter was hushed up, and when Palmer was caught some months later and given seven years, few in Carlisle connected him with the very plausible, generous Palmer of the Central Hall. We were not very proud to think that he had been connected with our church, but I believe that he had walked into the Picture House one Sunday night mistaking it for a cinema show, and had thought us easy game. He had been a frequent guest both in our home and at camp and, horrid thought, we had eaten his stolen goods.

The Committee, more as a compliment to my husband than anything else, asked him to give the final lecture of the season, and as, at the time, he had only lectured in a small way, he nervously consented. When the time came, we were worried lest the Hall should be half empty, but the subscribers, even those not connected with our work, turned out well. They felt that they owed it to him, even if it meant an evening's boredom. I shall always remember that night because it was the first time that I realised that he had in him unexplored possibilities, and also because it was the prelude to the many hundreds of lectures that he gave afterwards. For the first time he illustrated his talk with blackboard sketches, and his happiness in talking of the birds and animals that he loved became infectious. It was by no means the finished performance of later years, but he had made a start, and I pondered over it a great deal during the following months. Had he mistaken his vocation? Famous lecturers had described their wonderful nature slides, but none of them appeared to have his deep love of wildlife. But what was the use of thinking such things? He was too fond of preaching to give it up. Perhaps some day he might be relieved of the week-day routine of church organisation which had never appealed to him.

Returning to Carlisle recently, I found the door of the Central Hall open, and as I passed through the vestibule, I saw for the first time the tablet erected by the congregation, which read: "During the ministry of the Rev. G. Bramwell Evens, 1914-1926, this Hall was built."

When I walked inside I was prouder than ever of his achievement. What an artistic building it is – beautiful in design, chaste in decoration – with its dull, unpolished woodwork, its dignified, shapely rostrum, its stained-glass windows, rich in colour, and its spacious gallery so supported that not a pillar obstructs one's view.[8]

As I sat in the seat that I had occupied so often, many memories of those dear distant days came back to me. What hours he spent planning every detail, and what enormous pleasure it gave him. From the day the first brick was laid, to the day when the huge stained-glass electric bowl, which he had chosen, was hoisted up with a crane to the centre of the domed ceiling, he never seemed to be off the premises. How particular he had been to get the curtains the subdued shade of purple that he wanted, so that they should contrast with the silver grey of the organ pipes. There was the day when the pattern of the material arrived. To me the shade seemed right, but not so to him, and he actually made a special journey down to the Yorkshire dye works about it. So dumfounded was the proprietor that a parson should have travelled so far to make sure of getting the exact shade he wanted, that he left his work and went with him into the dyeing rooms to experiment with the material.

At times I have felt resentful that he spent so many years on the business side of church life, and had so few left in which to open people's eyes to the world of nature, but as I sat there I realised that in the Central Hall he had left behind him something of himself, some tangible expression of his ideas of beauty, which remained as a memorial to him.[9]

The dream that fires man's heart to make,
To build, to do, to sing or say
A beauty Death can never take,
An Adam from the crumbled clay.

John Masefield

Chapter 8 Notes

1 Now Appleby-in-Westmorland.

2 The term 'navvy' is now rather derogatory but from the mid 1700s until the beginning of the twentieth century it was used as an abbreviation for navigator – what we would now call civil engineers – tasked with establishing navigation systems. In time the workmen who carried out the excavations for canals, or railways became known as navvies. Eventually the term came to apply to any workman.

3 Since 1872 it had been an offence to be drunk while in charge of carriages, horses, cattle and steam engines, but it wasn't until 1925 that it became an offence to be drunk in charge of *any* mechanically propelled vehicle. It was 1967 before specific alcohol limits were introduced.

4 A document on the Gretna Munitions factories refers to the Stanley Hall picture house in Botchergate, Carlisle – probably, then, this would be the cinema Eunice is referring to. Apparently, it had a wooden balcony with comfortable seats while downstairs there were less comfortable wooden chairs.

5 '*Only* a couple of hundred people' tells us something of the expectation of churches in the early to mid twentieth century. Today most clergyman would consider that an unbelievably high number.

6 Surprisingly, Eunice makes no mention of the fact that a Wesleyan deaconess, Sister Lillie (Elizabeth Davis), was sent to assist in the ministry to the munitions workers. She was part of the Temperance movement and through her a thousand girls at the munitions depot signed the pledge. She stayed on after the war and embarked on a programme of work to help thousands of underprivileged children for which, in 1933, she was awarded the MBE.

Sister Lillie

7 King George V and Queen Mary.

8   This illustration certainly shows the spaciousness achieved by the use of cantilevered support for the balcony thus avoiding the columns which so often impact on vision. The photograph also shows how much light pours into the hall. Indeed an achievement of which to be proud.

Central Hall Interior

9   Sadly, in 2005 the Central Hall was closed and ceased to be a place of worship. In 2015 it was put up for sale for redevelopment. As of 2022 the building stands unused. Several artefacts, including Romany's chair, were rescued by the Romany Society. The building displays a plaque commemorating Romany. This was unveiled by Terry Waite, CBE, in 2003.

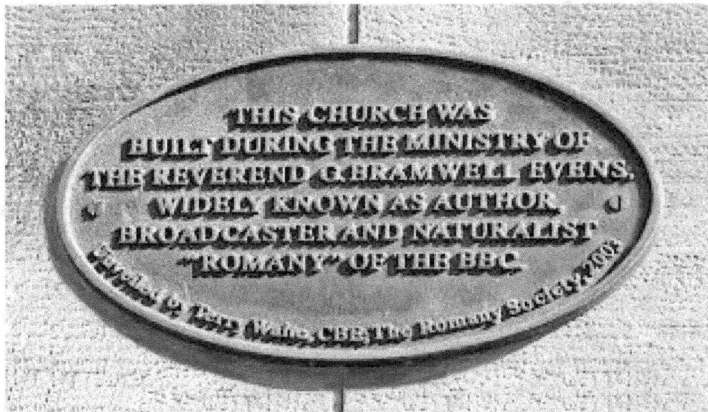

Plaque at Central Hall

Methodist Central Hall, Carlisle

Chapter 9

The Farm

The farm! What magic words. Though Bram was a welcome guest at many farms all over the country, there was none that appealed to him as Old Parks did. Arthur Gibson, the County Land Agent, a cousin of the Potters, first took him there and, for twenty-two years, it was an open house whenever he needed rest and solitude.

How excited he always was when he turned the car off the Penrith road and caught his first glimpse of the Cumberland hills.[1] He used to say that the jagged peaks of the Lake District were mere upstarts[2] compared with these mighty rounded heights which had been worn down by countless centuries of storm and frost. The very sight of them seemed to give him an inner serenity.

As we came down the steep hill from Glassonby, and he saw Old Parks among the trees on the slopes beyond, he would laugh aloud for sheer joy. However quickly I opened the gate of the Park field, we could not get there soon enough, and even the scores of rabbits that scuttled along the cart track in front of the car ran into their burrows far too slowly for him. And there was Joe, waving to us as he opened the gate into the farmyard, and Sallie, rubbing her flour-covered hands on her apron before hugging us, while Raq showed his lack of good manners by chasing the numerous cats across the cobbled yard.

The very moment we walked through the stone-flagged back-kitchen into the warm yeasty baking smell of the big kitchen, we became part of the family. There were no formalities – Sallie went on with her baking, Joe returned to the fields and, before I could get unpacked, Bram had torn off his collar and tie and, in corduroys and gum-boots, he too was out in the fields with Raq.

What was there about this farm that attracted him so much? Like most farms it had the leisureliness that was a part of his very being. Everyone was working, and working longer hours than most people, but there was none of the hurry and bustle of town life. He liked, too, the honesty and reticence of speech that marks the true countryman – no fulsomeness, no superlatives, no exaggerations, no striving for effect.

Being a Methodist home, it had the accepted traditions of hospitality. For generations it had been taken for granted that the visiting preachers always stayed there. But the hospitality of Old Parks was something far deeper than this.

The first time I went there Bram pointed out to me an old-fashioned gilt-lettered motto card which hung on the kitchen wall. One of the texts on it read: 'The glory of the home is hospitality.' If ever a family lived up to this ideal, the Potter family did. Not only were countless friends always arriving, but the postman must have his drink and buttered square each morning, as he told them the gossip of the neighbouring farms. Travellers and tradesmen called daily, having postponed their thirst until they reached Old Parks, and some of them actually brought their children to spend the day at the farm, returning with their cars in time to have their supper with them at night. Any old scrounging tramp within ten miles knew that he was sure of free meals and a bed on the hay in the barn if he only reached Old Parks before nightfall. I remember one old tramp called Tot staying there on and off for months on end. What tales the huge black kettle on the kitchen fire could tell of all the over-time it has worked! Never was it allowed to go off the boil, so that it should be ready for the casual caller. Lest I have given a wrong impression of the quiet of the farm, let me add that most of these callers came and went after delivering their goods, or filling their lorries with Joe's sheep or cattle.

I must go into details of the family, because Bram's earlier books include so many of the characters. In our early days, when Mrs Potter was alive, the family consisted of Alan, Joe, Hannah and Charlotte. Alan, who is now an Alderman of Cumberland, and his wife Margaret, live at Fog Close, an adjoining farm. Hannah and Charlotte have a cottage of their own nearby, and Joe and Sallie live in the old home.

I am sitting in my bedroom window at Old Parks as I write, and my utter incapacity to describe the scene of surpassing loveliness before me makes me wonder if I should ever have attempted to write this book.

The garden leads down to the grassy slopes of the orchard. It is May, and the fruit trees are in full blossom. Stephen [Relph]ed is busy with his scythe, waging war on the nettles and thistles on the steep grassy banks, which are carpeted with blue speedwell and pale-yellow starwort. From the woods on each side comes the soft cooing of wood pigeons, and the swallows almost graze the treetops as they fly to and from the barn. Below the orchard is a steep grassy dell, and through the massive trees I can just see the glint of the waters of Daleraven beck as it hurries along between the alders and willows to the Eden. On the opposite side of the lush valley the ground rises again steeply towards undulating fields and woods, and it gives me a pang to feel that Bram is not here with me, for yesterday a buzzard was discovered nesting in one of the trees – the first to nest on the farm within local memory. What a thrill it would have given him! Guarding it all, in the far distance, are Saddleback,[3] Skiddaw, Cross Fell[4] and the mighty hills of the Lake District wrapped in a soft mist. Willow-warblers, blackbirds and thrushes are vying with each other in song; but to me the most affecting of all is the tremulous, lonesome call of the curlew, as he keeps watch over his mate on her nest below in the marshes. This, of all sounds in the world, Bram loved best.

These islands of ours are rich in such scenery, but it is to the old motto card on the kitchen wall that I must turn again to discover the real secret of his tranquillity at the farm – 'In this place I will give peace.' It was indeed true peace and solitude that he found. He could roam over eight hundred acres of God's own country, without ever meeting a soul. Alas, that in his later journeyings all over England he found so few places unmarred by 'Trespassers will be prosecuted,' or 'Teas served here.'

So isolated is the farm that Methodists may be interested to know that when our Church authorities wanted to find a safe area from enemy action for the valuable paintings of their founder, John Wesley, they asked Joe to house them. The manner of their arrival caused some amusement. While Sallie was clearing a small space in the attic for them, Joe rang up the station to say that he was bringing his car down to fetch them. "Car, man!" gasped the station-master. "That's no use, you'll need your big lorry." When the huge packing-case arrived, it flatly refused to go through the door of any room or up either staircase, and it now occupies nearly the whole of one side of the front hall. As we went up to bed last night, I said to Sallie, "The front door is still open." She laughed. "We never bother in these parts," she replied, and I smiled to think that these valuable pictures, insured for six thousand pounds, were safer in this isolated farm amongst the Cumberland fells, even with the doors wide open, than padlocked in any town repository. Well they knew that their very remoteness is their safety, and that night-prowlers would rather unpick a dozen locks than face a couple of farm dogs.

When we were at the farm together I never dreamed of asking Bram his plans for the day. Timetables had been left behind in the town. He knew well that meals at Old Parks were non-stop, and if he were not back in time for lunch, the kettle was always on the boil and something would be found for him.

Pottering about was one of his chief joys. He would spend hours exploring the farm buildings for nests, or the oak rafters of the barn for bats or owls. He loved what he called "the musty smell of the granary," the scent of the hay in the barn, the leathery odour of the cobwebby stable; and when the horses came in after their day's work in the fields, he would sit and watch them, and listen to their contented crunching as they enjoyed their well-earned meal. No other farm buildings ever had quite the same fascination for him.

Sometimes I would follow a few paces behind him as he crept quietly through his favourite bluebell wood, searching the trees for nests, scaling them while I held my breath; or we would climb the heights of High Barn and he would sit with his chin cupped in his hands for what seemed to me hours, as he drank in the sights and sounds around him. His whole self seemed lost in the beauty of it all, and I could see from the expression of his eyes that he was far away in a world of his own.

Sometimes we would go down to the beck together, and while he fished for trout, I would sit on the bank and wonder at his infinite patience as he tried one favourite pool after another.

Unlike most anglers, his real interest was in watching the moorhens as they sought the safety of the bank when they caught sight of Raq, or the lazy flight of a heron which had been disturbed by a fellow-angler. Then came the moment I had been waiting for, when we would bathe in the ice-cold stream and laze on the bank in the sunshine. What gloriously happy days those were!

The Farm

Photo: Ilona Longbotham

Then back we would go to the farm for a meal. As we were privileged guests, instead of being banished to the dining-room, we were allowed to join the family in the friendly kitchen, with its huge centre table for the farm lads, and our small family table by the fireside. This settle on which I am now sitting was always Bram's favourite corner, with its old black-leather-covered sofa, and, as I write, Sallie is kneading her twenty large loaves of bread for her big family with as little concern as I would bake a teacake. For the evening meal, of course, the dining-room is used, for then the farm kitchen is given over to the lads.

When our meal was over and the lamp was lit, we always looked forward to a chat by the fireside. Bram would then lead Joe on to talk of his sheep and cattle, or they would talk apprehensively of that peculiar phenomenon, the Helm Wind, which betrays its coming by a heavy white line of cloud lying along the summit of the fells.[5] Joe would explain that if it does not cease blowing at the end of three days, it continues for either six or nine days, and after that indefinitely. No wonder the farmers dread it in the spring, for it destroys all the young grass, and sometimes it blows so fiercely that work in the fields has to be abandoned. The only time they welcome it is in a late harvest, for it then dries the stooks.

Stories would then be told of the old haunted house now replaced by Old Parks. Joe would recall that as he and his brother and sisters grew up, a bigger house became necessary, and that, while it was being built, they lived in the barn. Queer things happened in that old house. One morning, when the family arrived downstairs, they found the corner of the parlour carpet turned back in a double fold; and as Joe demonstrated it by turning back the corner of the hearthrug, I felt a cold shiver down my spine. The carpet was put straight, but to their concern the next morning they found it turned back again. This went on for some time, until one night they placed the foot of the piano on it; even this had no effect. Mr Potter then decided to stay up and investigate the matter. As he sat reading, for no apparent reason the lamp suddenly went out, and upstairs he ran at top speed, much to Mrs Potter's amusement. What surprised me most was that Joe said that his parents became so used to it that they took no notice of it. The children were too young at the time to realise its significance.

Finally, it was decided that the stone flag beneath the carpet should be lifted, and the children were told to call at the stonemason's on their way from school. Alan remembers standing in the lamplit parlour as the stone was lifted, disclosing human bones, together with a small piece of red cloth with buttons on it. From the day when these remains were reburied the carpet never moved.

As Alan was a small boy at the time, and one likes to get first-hand evidence of such stories, I have just been in to see old Mr Potter's sister, who lived with them for a time, and who lies here bedridden at the age of eighty-eight. "Aye," she said, "I saw the carpet turned back myself many a time. We thought nothing of it."

Sometimes Alan and his wife would walk across the fields and join our fireside circle. Margaret and Sallie would discuss the price their butter was fetching at the Penrith market, and we would laugh as Margaret, who had not long been married, would tell of a practical joke played on Alan and herself after their wedding.[6] When they had left the reception, their journey lost a good deal of its romance because of a vile smell in the car. Time after time they got out to investigate, but could find nothing to account for it. Finally, on the far end of the exhaust pipe under their seat, they found a pair of well-cooked kippers. They had been so placed that they would cook when the car was in motion, and lose their pungent smell when the engine was turned off.

Then, sure enough, the chat would veer round to the old haunted house again, and Alan would tell how one evening his mother had gone over the fields to see some friends at the Mains. Some hours later the farm lads and the maid were sitting as usual on the side settles by the kitchen fire, when those who were facing the door saw someone, whom they took to be Mrs Potter, come in, walk through the kitchen and into the hall. The maid, who was accustomed to help her off with her coat, followed her, but to her astonishment there was no one to be seen. Such was the effect on the girl that she ran screaming through the fields and met Mrs Potter half-way home.

No one could be less superstitious or more dubious of ghost stories than Bram, but what could we say to this? All I know is that I was in such a shivery state when bedtime came that, instead of taking my candle and going up ahead of him as I usually did, I refused to move until he was ready.

In old Mr Potter's time some very interesting Roman relics were found by archaeologists near the house in the Low Field, and Sallie has just been showing me some of the urns, necklaces and vases in her cupboard, all of which date from about 600 B.C.

How they all laughed when Bram went into the dairy and tried his hand at butter-making. The two sisters were living at Old Parks at the time, and it had looked so easy when Charlotte was doing it. "I'll do it for you," he said cheerily, and Charlotte, taking him at his word, went off to do another job. He started turning the handle of the old wooden churn with vigour, but his enthusiasm soon waned. First he used one hand, then the other, then both, while the family came in from time to time to laugh at his discomfiture. Charlotte eventually returned to find him thoroughly exhausted, and when she opened the churn he was disappointed not to see pounds of butter. When she said, "I've known it take almost half a day in winter-time," he vanished.

In pre-war[7] days farmers had a bad name for being conservative, and those in Cumberland were, I believe, the last to introduce new methods on their farms. "Before the war I could have counted all the tractors in this district on one hand," Bob said, as he took me across the fields to show me a curlew's nest he had found. It was when we visited the farm in 1934. that Joe showed us his new tractor; then followed motor-lorries, the milking machine and the rest.

Though Bram knew that these things must eventually come to his farm (as he always called it), if it was to prosper, he was secretly pleased that Joe was in no hurry about it. He hated to see machinery replacing so many of the things that were dear to him and spoiling the appearance of the countryside. He liked to watch a team of horses plodding slowly along in front of the plough, followed by white-winged gulls, but he never watched the noisy, smelly tractor, for to him it was an offence to the quiet of the countryside. He liked to sit on the haycart as it swayed down the hill from the High Barn and listen to the clip-clop of the horses on the cobbled stone yard, but he never wanted to sit on the motor-lorry. He missed the rumble of the wooden cartwheels in the farmyard, now replaced by pneumatic tyres. He rode about the farm on Beauty on his earlier visits, and it grieved him to see the number of horses slowly but inevitably growing smaller and smaller.

When he was younger, he remembered seeing the grass cut by hand, and he often recalled the skill shown by the reapers as they kept in line together, and with rhythmic, graceful movement wielded their scythes, laying low the drooping swathes. It fascinated him to watch them as they paused from time to time to sharpen them. As they began at the heel, he listened to the clear metallic ring of the blade, which faded away to an echoless grind as, with steadying hand, they neared the point. This interval afforded the men a chance to straighten their backs, and to talk of the weather or the crops. To him there was music in the swish of the scythes and the song of the soaring lark above. No wonder he resented the harsh, noisy jangle of the mowing-machine.

When staying here alone he once wrote to me, "You'll be sorry to hear that the paraffin lamps and candles are no more, for they now have electricity even in the buildings." I knew what he meant. What became to Joe and Sallie a saving of labour, to him meant the loss of something intangible which he would never be able to recapture. The soft, shadowy yellow light of the paraffin lamp as we sat round the fire at night seemed more friendly than the hard glare of electricity; and the flickering beams of the candle-light, as we lay in bed, had always been associated with the music of the stream below, the bleating of sheep, and the call of the plovers in the Low Field, all of which filled him with happiness.

But electric light in the farm buildings was worse, for he loved the time of night when he followed Joe into the back-kitchen, and they lit their storm-lamps. "Rats, Judy," Joe would call, and the keen little Yorkshire terrier would bound ahead of them across the yard. Then I would see their storm-lamps swinging in and out of the various buildings and hear Judy's excited barks as she disposed of one rat after another, while Joe took a last look at his stock to see if they were all right for the night.

Harvesting, in his early days at the farm, was more leisurely and more friendly, too, for the help of the women-folk was always needed to get it all in, and from early morning till late night they would work in the sun-baked field. Charlotte would laugh at his incompetence as he clumsily tried to tie the straw round his sheaves of oats, and would show him the knack needed for this seemingly simple operation, or the men would chuckle to themselves when his stooks collapsed like a pack of cards, for they never would stand erect the first time as theirs did. Hot and tired with his efforts, he would glance from time to time towards the farm until, to his joy, Hannah appeared in the doorway carrying a basket covered with a white cloth. His toil was over at last, and he could sit with them all on the hedge-bank as they relaxed and chatted over their 'ten o'clocks.'

But all these changes were merely an offence to the aesthetic side of his nature. His real grudge against the mechanisation of farmlands was that it destroyed thousands of nesting birds. To quote Bob again, for it is he who drives Joe's tractor: "Aye. I've known me drive over twenty plovers' nests in a day." In the more leisurely days of the past, as Joe swayed from side to side to balance the iron plough which Bonny and Darling were pulling, he could see the nests ahead of him and avoid some of them. In any case, the birds had a chance of escaping from the cruel blade which sliced the brown earth even if their eggs were destroyed. An intelligent farmer would leave a corncrake's nest in an island of grass, knowing how rare these birds were becoming in this country.[8]

Bram never imposed these ideas of his on any farmer. He knew that the Ministry of Agriculture had at last become enlightened on the value of certain birds in the destruction of insect pests that ruin crops, and he looked forward to the day when all farmers would learn that these birds were their allies and not their enemies.

He loved to feel that there was one thing that could never be mechanised, and I would climb the hills with him and listen to him as he chatted with the old shepherd, as his collie dog, lanky and panting, sat obediently awaiting his master's command. One wave of his arm, and off the dog would run to round up the sheep grazing in the distance. To me, they were mere dots on the horizon, but the keen eyes of the shepherd could detect if any were missing. Two staccato whistles, and off the dog would race into the far gully and soon reappear with the wanderers. As we walked together down to the valley with the sound of the bleating sheep in our ears, he would say, "While these mighty hills remain, they'll never be able to mechanise that."

It is a comfort to me now to feel that he was born before the end of the last century, for otherwise he would not have been able to recall and pass on to others these simple country ways of life which are all too quickly becoming a thing of the past.

He was no prophet, but we have often talked of something he said to Joe in the very early days. Curiously enough, though slow to mechanise his farm, Joe was one of the first people in Cumberland to own a wireless set. More curious still, considering that we lived in a town, it was at the farm in September 1923 that we first 'listened in.' What a set it was, with its three naked valves and its endless ramification of wires. After screwing ourselves into the most uncomfortable positions imaginable, so that four of us could share two pairs of headphones, and enduring innumerable catcalls and groans, we finally heard "2LO[9] calling," and what was alleged to be the band of HM Irish Guards. How excited we were at this miracle!

Bram then went out with Joe as usual, to have a look at his sheep. Gazing up at the complexity of wires that stretched from tree to tree, he stood a few moments listening to the music of the stream and the soft cooing of the woodpigeons in the spinney below. Then it was that he said, "Perhaps in the years to come we shall not only be able to listen to the sounds of the town, but town-dwellers may be able to listen to these beautiful sounds too."

Little did he know then that he himself would some day fulfil his own prophecy, for perhaps he did more than anyone else to bring the real atmosphere of the country to tired city workers by broadcasting to them the plaintive pipes of the curlew and the rustle of the corn in the evening breeze. It was at Old Parks, perhaps more than anywhere else, that he absorbed so much of the atmosphere that made his broadcasts in later years so true to life. Not one of our relatives ever saw the farm during those twenty-two years. Though we took our children once or twice when they were small, it seemed to be an understood thing that this part of his life was reserved for me alone.

And I shall have some peace there, for peace comes dropping slow,
Dropping from the veils of the morning to where the cricket sings;
There midnight's all a-glimmer, and noon a purple glow,
And evening full of the linnet's wings.

William Butler Yeats

Chapter 9 Notes

1   Turning off the main road in the direction of Old Parks Romany would see the Pennines to the East, notably Cross Fell.

2   These 'mere upstarts' include Scafell Pike, the highest peak in England.

3   The distinctive shape of this Lakeland mountain makes clear why it is referred to as Saddleback, but its Celtic name, Blencathra, is preferred today.

4   The reference to Cross Fell here is confusing. Eunice seems to be implying that Saddleback, Skiddaw and other Lakeland hills to the West make one vista, whereas Cross Fell is in the opposite direction (East) viewed from Old Parks.

5   This distinctive line of cloud, which precedes the ferocious Helm Wind, is known as the Helm Bar. It sits snugly across the top of the North Pennine fells, notably Cross Fell, to the East of Old Parks.

6   Romany came to Glassonby to officiate at that wedding. Margaret later recalled that, after his address, Romany said to the couple, "Never let the sun go down on your wrath," then to Alan, "And I hope the price of sheep improves."

7   Pre WW1.

8   Interesting that the corncrake was already becoming rare. They suffered a further serious decline in the 1950s and are now just about extinct in Cumbria, and indeed England.

9   In 1922 2LO became the second radio station regularly to broadcast in the UK.

Joe and Sallie Potter with Son Des

Chapter 10

The Caravan

The year 1921 was a memorable one, for it was then that he bought the caravan which was afterwards to play such an important part in his broadcasts. In those days caravanning had not become the popular pastime that it is today; trailer caravans were unheard-of, and in any case he would have scorned anything but a horse-waggon, or *vardo*, as it is called in Romani.

We were exploring the Eden near Appleby one day when some caravans drew up at the roadside. On enquiry we found that they were going to Brough Hill Fair,[1] so we changed our plans and went there too. Knowing that he would not find any genuine Gypsies amongst the crowd of *gorgio*[2] van-dwellers, he searched around until, in one corner of the ground apart from the rest, he spied some waggons and real Gypsy tents[3] made of blankets stretched tightly over bent hazel sticks. Their scorn for the sham Gypsies is always shown by this aloofness.

I kept in the background for a few minutes, but it was not long before they had recognised him as one of themselves. Then a conversation took place which was quite unintelligible to me – a mixture of English and Romani. I was impatient to know if they knew of a caravan for sale, but he, being wiser, talked of the Smiths, the Lovells and the Grays. Oh yes, they had met a family of the Smiths only a few weeks previously. I knew that he had gained their confidence because they invited us into their *vardos*. Gypsy women are like all other women – some are house-proud, others slovenly. Some of the waggons were spick-and-span with spotless curtains, shining brass fittings and most ornately carved woodwork; others were dirty and untidy.[4]

Eventually he broached the subject of the *vardo*. Yes. One of the Lovells had died, and his daughter had married a *gorgio*, one of the women said scornfully, for they look askance at marriage outside their own race. We were then taken to see it, and my heart fell as we climbed the steps of a dirty, gaudily painted van. "Just the size we want," whispered my husband. He knew that this was all that mattered at the moment, and saw possibilities in it that I did not. The owner talked of everything but the price, and so did he, for he knew their methods of bargaining. It seemed an eternity to me before we had accepted their figure of £75 and the *vardo* was ours.

Losing no time, we hired a horse and drove our shabby, gaily coloured caravan to Carlisle. Bram was wildly excited. For the first time in his life he owned a home of his own, and we talked of all that we would do to improve it. Finally, we reached our manse in Fisher Street, behind which was an open yard, and there the *vardo* was placed.

So eager were listeners to his broadcasts in later years to know exactly what it looked like, that I must give a few details. In appearance and size it was much like the pantechnicon-shaped caravans used by road repairers in country districts. It was twelve feet long by six feet wide, and most important of all, seven feet high. So many modern trailer-caravans are attractive and better fitted than ours ever was, but they are an agony to the taller members of the family. It had two casement windows, as well as the one in the top half of the door which opened separately, as those in all Gypsy vans do. Inside it was completely bare, and outside at the back it had a large cupboard – another sign that it had been used by Gypsies, for into this could be pushed the poached rabbit or the pilfered sticks.

Our first visit was to the Sanitary Inspector, for we knew little of the previous occupant, and the following day a couple of men arrived to squirt their disinfectant into every crack and cranny.

Having paid £75 I was worried as to what the alterations and decorations would cost, but I had reckoned without my versatile husband, and it was not long before I discovered that, like his father, he was a good joiner. Words fail me to describe the joy of those next few weeks. We could hardly sleep for planning and scheming, and we filled reams of paper with drawings of what we wanted. After purchasing the necessary tools, we put in a fourth casement window, a roof ventilator, a partition to divide the living-room from the kitchen, locker-seats, and Bram's clever fingers produced a folding table, cupboards and shelves galore.

There were moments of exasperation too, for he was not very accurate in his measurements, and his shelves were often either an inch too long or too short. Being over-thorough too, he never used a two-inch nail if he could use an eight-inch, and he seemed always to be pulling nails out instead of knocking them in.

Unfortunately, the weather was extremely hot, and by the time we were ready to start on the paintwork, it had developed into a heat wave. But, so eager were we to finish it that even this did not daunt us, and so, in broiling heat, we went on scraping off the old paint, both inside and out, and then repainting it. What fun we had – what splashings from head to foot, for we were both novices. No job that we ever did together gave us so much pleasure. The climax came when, clad only in our swimming suits, overalls and sand-shoes, we climbed up to felt and tar the roof. It was so hot that it was impossible even to kneel down. Had we been more sane we would have left it until cooler weather; but no, we must finish it at all costs. The tar ran everywhere except where it was meant to go, and we spent half our time unsticking ourselves and our shoes from the roof.

When the *vardo* was ready it did not take us long to decide where it was to stand. There was only one place, Penton; but alas! so inaccessible was the Mitchells' house, that we chose a spot farther down the river on the Canonbie side, near Harelow Mill.

The rivers Liddel and Esk divide England from Scotland, and to reach the. chosen spot we had to cross the border and negotiate some very steep hills. In our enthusiasm, however, we had forgotten one thing – a good brake. It had only one loose shoe-brake, which was quite inadequate to hold back the increased weight. Comma, the horse, was incapable of drawing it except on the level, so we were obliged to call at a farm and hire a second horse. Each time we reached the brow of a steep hill we had to tie a couple of ropes to the back axle and enlist the help of every farmhand in the neighbourhood to hold it back.

Whether my assistance proved of any use I don't know, but I can see the *vardo* now as it rocked and swayed like a ship in a gale, whilst I almost lay on my back and tugged at the rope as I skidded down the hills. When we reached Harelow Mill Farm, the lane leading down to the river was extremely narrow, and we stuck half-way down. Not until the farmer had cut away a part of his hedge were we able to move. We both heaved a sigh of relief when the *vardo* came to rest on a grassy knoll by the river, surrounded by fields, woods and glens. What more could we want?

Getting Under Weigh

The Caravan at Rest

Photo: *Ilona Longbotham*

Our first job was to put up our bedroom. This we had purchased from John Rubb – a large army-sized tent with floor-boards. This was no easy matter, especially in windy weather. Having hoisted the tarpaulin, mine was usually the difficult task of standing inside it and holding the pole upright while Bram pulled out the skirts and knocked the tent-pegs into the ground. It was at this point that he would suddenly remember that he had forgotten his mallet, and I would stand there, swaying backwards and forwards, smothered by the heavy tarpaulin. Then, to my delight, 1 would hear him knocking in a few pegs with his usual thoroughness, but just when I was beginning to breathe again he would say, "Oh, I must have the opening facing the river," and so, with great effort, out would come his pegs again and down would flop the earwig-covered tarpaulin, as I perspired and groaned under the weight of it. Not until we had camped for years did the tent spread its skirts evenly the first time the pegs were knocked in. There was no operation that tried our tempers so sorely, but there was always the joy of lighting the camp fire and a soothing cup of tea when the job was finished.

Being a townswoman, it took me some time to get accustomed to sleeping in a tent. Even when we went to bed at the same time, I used to lie and wonder which of the moths and daddy-long-legs that fluttered round the storm-lamp would decide to land on my face, or I would shiver with fright if I heard weird sounds that I could not account for. But when I was left alone it was just terrifying.

The river Liddel, with its boulder-strewn bed and deep pools, is much beloved of anglers, for salmon and sea-trout lie in its depths. The biggest of these fish seemed to have the unfortunate habit of feeding[5] after dark, and so most of my husband's angling was done at night. My evenings were usually spent following at some distance behind him along the river bank, as he waded from one pool to another. Until it became really dark, I was happy – then I had to make a choice. Should I stay and allay my fears by talking to him and thus spoil his fishing, or should I grope my way back to bed? I usually chose the latter and soon regretted it, for then it was that the owls would reserve their most ghoulish shrieks until they passed over the tent, or a bat would fly through the opening.

He had, too, an unpleasant way of getting up in the early hours of the morning, and I would wake to find myself alone. His quick ears had heard the sound of the river in flood, and he knew that there were fish waiting to be caught. Or he would be examining the veneer of mud left on the river bank when a flood subsides to see which night-prowling birds and animals had left their footprints, and when he came back he would tell me excitedly that a heron or otter had been about. I do not think that he had any conception of what I went through during that first year, and it never seemed to occur to him that I might be nervous When Glyn was with us, he could not understand why I would not put him to bed in the tent and go night-fishing with him. With an air of odd surprise, he would ask, "Whatever is there to be afraid of?"

When he had to return to his work in Carlisle, Glyn and I were left alone. When bedtime came, I called Raq into the tent, tied up the flap securely, got into bed, hid my head under the bedclothes and hoped for the best. Then it was that the tent would become temperamental. Heavy rain would fall, and the canvas would contract, soaking our bedclothes as it flapped in the wind. I knew well what was coming, but I postponed the evil moment. I lay there watching the pole. Yes, it was anything but perpendicular. Up I got and fumblingly unlaced the flap, and groped my way out into the darkness to tighten the ropes, stubbing my bare feet against the pegs as I stumbled about. Then I hurried back to bed again.

One stormy night Bram and I were awakened by a terrific hurricane which swept down the glen. As the pole swayed perilously above us and the tent bellied in the wind, I gasped, "Which way is it going to fall?" "Over our bed," came the consoling reply. As luck would have it, the tent managed to right itself, and we settled down once more. Half an hour later we were wakened by an ominous sound. There was no mistaking it. The river, swollen by the heavy rain, was in flood, and we were but ten yards from the top of the bank. We got up, half dressed, and debated whether we should move the tent, but decided to wait.

Meanwhile, he was testing the rise of the river with a twig which he had stuck in the bank, while I was bundling some of our possessions through the pouring rain to the safety of the *vardo*. Then I sat down on the bed, shivering and waiting, as through the darkness I could see the muddy brown torrent rushing by. Higher and higher up the bank it came, and it was not until we had begun to take out the tent-pegs that it receded a small fraction, and we knew that we were safe. Anyone but my husband would have been thankful to get under the bed-clothes again after such a chilling experience, but instead, he proceeded to put on the rest of his clothes, fetched his rod, and went off fishing.

Though I fished a great deal, I did not become an experienced angler and was never proficient enough to use any but his inferior rods. What made it rather difficult for both Glyn and me was that we were never allowed to fish in any water where there were any fish, so we usually contented ourselves with sitting on the bank with hazel sticks and string, trying to catch eels. In a letter which Glyn wrote to me recently, he says, "My recollections of those early holidays are of long hours as we sat on the bank fishing, but I always suffered from incipient guilt-feelings, because the fish never attached themselves to my hook, as they did to Dad's – as though they knew that I wasn't really trying very hard."

The galling thing, too, for both of us was that once we had managed to land an eel, we always had to call for his assistance to prevent it squirming back into the water, and to kill and clean it. In time, however, he taught me not only how to do this, but also how to skin and clean rabbits.

Looking through the caravan window one afternoon I saw him gazing intently at what looked like a thick black line of tar which stretched from the bottom of the tent to the top. I found that it was a huge colony of ants, trekking over the tent, as I thought, because they had not the sense to go round it. It was an amazing sight. That night we had just settled comfortably in bed, and were about to put out the lamp when, to our horror, the whole tent collapsed on us like an umbrella. He grabbed Raq and with difficulty managed to put out the lamp. We then crawled out under the tarpaulin on to the wet grass, and spent the rest of the night in the caravan. The next morning we discovered that the ants had not only spent their evening eating through the top cap of the tent, but had spent the rest of their night in our bed. When I became agitated, he just laughed and said, "They're quite harmless." Though I spent the rest of the day waging war on them, for weeks afterwards, as I lay in bed, I would see them swarming out of the seams of the tent where they had been in hiding.

There was never a time of year when he could not find interest at the caravan. When fine, he was out all day bird-watching; when wet, he was fishing. But when it rained ceaselessly, housekeeping became a problem. I would perhaps discover that the water-tank needed re-filling when he was miles down the river, and up to the pump at the farm I would trudge with my buckets. When we ran short of bread, he'd say, "I'll go for you," and at that moment he had every intention of being helpful; but in the interval, he would have seen a kingfisher flying towards the far bank, and he would be off to search for its nesting-hole. I could never rely on him, and looked forward to Glyn's school holidays, when he did most of my shopping for me. Though we camped in Scotland our nearest shop was in England, two and a half miles away, and the only means of reaching it was across a dangerous swinging bridge which spanned the river. In rough weather I dreaded this bridge with my armfuls of provisions, because both hands were needed to hold the wire rail and many of the wooden foot-planks were missing. When I was half-way across, the bridge would sway so violently that a loaf would go toppling down into the turbulent waters below.

Friends who came from Carlisle to visit us had to cross this bridge. "Don't forget to help them across," I would call as my husband went off to meet them. But, likely as not, he would shoulder their cases and stride ahead, and then become so absorbed in watching the rings made by a rising trout in the water below that he would forget to tell them that only one person should cross at a time, and they arrived at the caravan in such a nervous state that they almost contemplated fording the river when the time came for their return.

But in spite of all these drawbacks, during the whole of the next twelve years it never occurred to either of us that we might spend a holiday elsewhere. A Carlisle friend once commiserated with me over the fact that I never had a holiday free from cleaning, cooking and washing-up. It was certainly only "a change of sink" for me, as another friend amusingly put it. But she was incapable of appreciating the compensations that were mine. How could I explain to her the hundred and one things of interest that Bram found each day and the joy we found in the solitude of camp life. I was never bored, for the days flashed by all too quickly. We made our own fun and our minds were so attuned to each other's that we would laugh from the pure joy of being together. To see his shining eyes as he came up the *vardo* steps with a creel of freshly caught trout, or a handkerchief of mushrooms to fry with the bacon for breakfast, was more than enough reward.

It was always a sad day for us both when our stay at the caravan came to an end, and we took down the tent and hung it in the barn, for we had a great affection for it. It had withstood the storms and gales of many years with never a leak, and as we lay in bed and read the name of the maker – Budd of Bermondsey – on the canvas, he would often say, "I'd like to thank that man for all the pleasure he has given us." Locking up the *vardo*, too, gave us a pang, and as we crossed the field, burdened with luggage, I can see him now, glancing back wistfully at it for the last time.

Lest I should have given too much of the lighter side of our camping life, and not enough of the deep satisfaction and peace that it gave him, I should like to end this chapter with a favourite extract of mine from an article he wrote to the *Cumberland News*, to which he was contributing a weekly nature column.

"I am writing this on my caravan steps. The scene before me makes me feel that for too long I have been a pedlar in small things. I do not know what it is about it that makes me feel that my life has been too circumscribed, but I do know that what I now see before me both sweetens and uplifts me. The turquoise sky, the soft babbling of the curling water, the lily-white gulls sailing like thistledown above me, all bring me something mysterious and satisfying, something that rebukes the darker side of my nature, and makes me feel that the best that is in me is one with the intangible beauty lying behind it all."

But we sleep by the ropes of the camp,
and we rise with a shout, and we tramp
With the sun or the moon for a lamp,
and the spray of the wind in our hair

J E Flecker

Chapter 10 Notes

1   At that time Brough Hill Fair was the biggest of all Gypsy fairs, whereas today it is a much smaller affair and Appleby Horse Fair is the largest.

2   *Gorgio, gauje* or *gadga* is the Romani word for non-Gypsies.

3   These tents are known as bender tents.

4   This is a surprising statement as the Romani people are generally much more fastidious than the average housewife.

5   When salmon and sea trout return to the rivers of their birth to breed they do not, in fact, feed. It is, therefore, a perplexing question as to why they will rise to an artificial fly. One theory is that they are being territorial.

The beautifully restored Vardo Today
(at the Bradford Industrial Museum)

Chapter 11

Nature Expeditions

One of my husband's most precious possessions was his camera, and many were the hours he spent studying the various catalogues before he bought the special one which he always used for bird-photography. When I encouraged him to buy it, I had no idea how it was going to upset our domestic arrangements, for, at times, taps dripped incessantly, and it was quite impossible to have a bath because his valuable plates were being washed. When, however, he secreted himself in the box-room in order to develop them, it was Lizzie, whose twelve years' devotion to him while she was in our service should be recorded, who stood guard at the door to see that no one opened it and ruined his plates. I like to think that I was responsible for buying him an equally precious possession. On one occasion when in London I took a great risk and bought him an expensive pair of field-glasses. Knowing nothing about them, this was rash. However, they proved to be an exceptionally good pair and gave him untold pleasure, and he rarely went bird-observing without them slung on his back.

In spite of the time he spent on his hobbies and church work, he was never too busy to take an interest in medical matters, for he had far more than the ordinary layman's knowledge of the subject. This was probably hereditary, for his mother used her own herbal remedies for most complaints, and they were usually effective, if unorthodox. If either of our children was not well, it was always to their father they went, not me, for he had a natural gift for healing, and would have made a good doctor. He had an uncanny instinct, too, for diagnosing the ailments of the members of his congregation whom he visited, many of whom were only too ready to talk of them. His convincing manner alone was sufficient to reassure them that they would get better. When, therefore, his father was found to be suffering from diabetes, he was doubly grieved that he had not realised that his enormous appetite in earlier days was due to some deeper cause. As it was, the disease had taken a firm hold before the symptoms were recognised. Owing to his failing eyesight he was obliged to retire from the Mission, upon which a public presentation was made to them both for their twenty-six years' devoted service. He had been greatly loved by the children in the slums where he worked, and as he and his wife entered the meeting, a shabby-looking boy pushed a dirty, crumpled piece of paper into her hand, which read, "From twelve boys in this street whose very sorry for him, who likes him, and what for does he leave us when we like him."

As well as this, Bram was concerned over Polly, who for years had been suffering from heart trouble. He knew that the only way for her to prolong her life was to leave his parents and get a complete rest, for she was only in her early forties. But unfortunately, her devoted nursing of his father, who eventually became blind, hastened her end, and she died a year or so later. This was followed soon afterwards by the death of his father at the age of fifty-eight. His funeral was the last to be conducted under the shadow of the Liverpool cathedral, and as we were putting him to rest, it was a curious sight to see the men working on the huge scaffoldings far above us, and to hear the echoes of their tools reverberating through the vast building.

The position of his mother was now a sad one, for her public work became impossible without the help of her husband. When she offered to come to our Church and, with his help, hold a ten-day Mission, how could he refuse? But to accede to her request to assist her with similar Missions in other places would have been an embarrassment to him. And so, with the companionship of Nellie, who succeeded Polly, she settled down to a quiet life in Liverpool.

Meanwhile, our life in Carlisle seemed to be full of innumerable exciting happenings, which appear so trivial when written down, that I feel it must have been his vivid personality that made them interesting. There was the morning when, with shining eyes, he dashed into the house and made me drop everything and go with him to Sebergham to see some corncrakes that were nesting in the garden of the village policeman – a most unusual thing, for these birds are not only particularly shy, but are becoming more and more rare. There was the day, too, spent at Baron Wood near Penrith when he gave me a fright. He left me as usual to wander off alone looking for nests, but when he did not turn up for our picnic lunch, I went in search of him. To my consternation he was standing waist-deep in the middle of the lake with what looked to me like a bandage tied across his face. In front of him there floated the rotting carcase of a dead sheep, and on it was the nest of some bird which he was photographing. He had found the odour so overpowering that he had tied his handkerchief over his nose! How I wished that I, too, had a camera!

Then there was the time when he rushed off to Raine's shop in Botchergate because someone had told him there were four live bitterns on view. But unfortunately, these unhappy birds, having been blown out of their course when crossing the North Sea, had been found on the marshes in an emaciated condition, and had been brought to the taxidermist to be stuffed. It angered him to see rare or small birds of any kind on sale, for there was hardly a mouthful to be got from many of them. As we walked along the shopping streets together, I would entice him across the road if I saw larks, snipe, dunlin or golden plover exhibited in the poulterers' windows.

To tell of our many expeditions together to the galleries at Ravensglass, Crofton Hall, Gayle, and Moorthwaite Loch, and of days watching the wildfowl on Rockcliff Marshes, would take too long, but one incident at Monkhill is perhaps worth recalling. He was wandering round the lake where gulls, coots and widgeon abounded, when he noticed that Raq was chasing a wild duck. Seeing that she did the usual broken-wing trick in order to lure the dog to follow her, he knew at once that her nest would be in the vicinity. It was not long before he had discovered it with fourteen eggs in it. Though he was never guilty of taking birds' eggs, he had a broody hen amongst his poultry at home and, being anxious to watch the young ducklings as they grew up, he put four of the pale green eggs in his pocket. That evening he was due to preach in the little village chapel at Monkhill, and just as he came out of the vestry, he remembered the eggs, and with awkward gait mounted the pulpit steps. So restricted was he in his movements that he was obliged to cut his sermon short that evening.

Eventually he arrived home with the eggs intact, and, to add to the usual menagerie we always kept, the four young ducklings were hatched out. At first, just watching their antics as they sported in the bathtub in the garden gave him pleasure, but one day he dug up some worms for them, and after that they refused to eat anything else. Though he loved a garden, he was never fond of digging, and in time he became exasperated, for every inch of the soil had been turned over and still they wanted more. When they grew older, we were in the garden together one evening when he heard a familiar "Honk, honk" overhead, and pointed upwards to a flock of wild ducks which were flying high above us. To our amazement, three of our ducklings suddenly rose into the air and joined their kith and kin in the sky. I can recall now the look on my husband's face as he stood watching them until they were mere dots on the horizon. How thrilled he was that these youngsters, who had never before heard the call of the wild, knew by instinct that they were meant for the freedom of the skies, and not to be cooped up in a town garden. The fourth timid duckling he gave to a farmer living near Carlisle, after making him promise not to pinion it. It mated with one of his farmyard ducks, and the breed was afterwards known as 'Evens's strain.'

There was the time, too, when he and Arthur Chant, who is now County Architect of Shropshire, went on a walking tour in Wharfedale. I have before me an article which Arthur contributed to the *Cumberland News* telling what kind of a walking companion he found my husband to be. He described how, in contrast to what he calls his own "cart-horse-on-cobbles gait," my husband slipped along so quietly that "the curlews just nodded to each other and said, 'He's one of us, lads, carry on.'" He also comments on what he calls "the curious fact that all the plovers, larks and curlews have laid their nests in the very line he is going to walk over," whereas he himself cannot even find "a mare's nest." He tells of the interminable hours my husband spent talking to gamekeepers, stone-breakers, poachers and others, "while I had to stand for hours first on my right leg, and then nervously change to my left, fearing to break the spell."

He then continues, "Weary after the day, we give our leaden packs one last tired hitch over our shoulders, and take the long road that leads down from the hills to some enchanted village. After peering where the light shines most invitingly from mullioned windows, we find ourselves in the house of someone who, unwittingly caught at her doorway, found herself entertaining angels unawares. My companion, with pack off, and stockinged feet toasting before a roaring fire, invests the hearth with a strange and kindly friendliness. Whilst an inspired Daleswoman finds his happiness infectious, and hides her surprise by bustling about as she hews large rashers from a mighty ham and smashes a wealth of eggs into the frying-pan, she sends her man out for more logs, and the family gathers round.

"He soon wins the confidence of the youngsters who, with their own experiences lit up by his childlike enthusiasm, find themselves talking with a new wonder and surprise. It was as if he set the everyday affairs of life to a strange and lovely music. Here was a guest indeed. Laugh? I should think we did. We haven't laughed like this for years."

It was with Arthur, too, that he once tramped the country north of the border. For the first few days they fared well, for Bram's persuasive powers soon induced farmers to allow them to sleep in their Dutch barns or granaries. When, however, they reached the more lonely districts, they were surprised to receive rebuffs when they called at farms. It was not until they reached Dumfries and noticed how everyone stared at them that the reason for it all suddenly dawned on them. There had been an implied contract between them that neither of them would shave, and they had no idea of their fearsome brigand-like appearance. Even the barber, when they burst in on him, thought it was a hold-up, and his customers were quite alarmed. No one would have taken my husband for anything but a tramp on many of his outings, but after this he was always careful to shave.

Arthur and his wife often came to the caravan and fitted in well with our free-and-easy life. It is not many months since they visited our home, and the way we picked up the threads of friendship just where we had left them in Carlisle was delightful.

The more remote the country the happier my husband was, and many were the times we stayed together at the lonely inn near Sedbergh and climbed the heights together to find the peregrines and buzzards which nested in the ravines of Cautley Spout.

My activities, however, were soon to be curtailed by the joyous arrival, in 1924, of our daughter, whom we christened Romany June. Though I was able to take her with us a few months later when we went to stay near the Farne Islands off the Northumbrian coast, it was Glyn who had the privilege of going with his father to visit the late Viscount Grey of Falloden. It had always been an ambition of my husband's to visit his bird-sanctuary, and permission was granted for him to do so.

To his surprise, instead of being conducted round by some member of the staff, they were received by Sir Edward, as he was then called, and his wife, and it was not long before they found that they had a great deal in common. Sir Edward was a keen angler and, like himself, had done a great deal of his bird-observing when patiently fishing some river or stream, and so they chatted away happily. Bram had pictured him as the austere, distinguished-looking Foreign Secretary; instead he found a simple, friendly, rough-suited country gentleman.

Talking of the necessity of wearing drab-looking clothes when bird-observing, he then told my husband an amusing story against himself. One very wet afternoon Lord Montague and a friend were motoring near Falloden when they passed a bedraggled-looking tramp. "Let's give the poor devil a lift," said one of them. When they pulled up, they found that it was Sir Edward.

While they sat chatting, Glyn was being entertained by the squirrels who popped into the study, helped themselves unconcernedly to the tray of nuts on the desk, and then scampered out again. As they made their way down to the sanctuary, Sir Edward kept stopping and tapping a box of mealworms which he was carrying, and birds of all kinds flew down from the trees and alighted on his shoulder to be fed. When they examined a long-tailed tit's nest, he told how he had given the job of counting the feathers used by these birds in the building of one nest to one of his gardeners, who had a big family of children. They counted sixteen hundred and fifty, each of which the bird had searched for in the nearby fields.

When they reached the ponds, Bram was astonished to find that all the foreign birds were unpinioned and free to come and go as they liked. They returned to the Arctic regions each spring, but in the Autumn they came back to Falloden. "But how do you know they are the same birds?" he asked. "Oh! they come and feed out of my hand the day they come back," was the reply.

As Glyn and he were about to leave, and they stood on the terrace looking down the long avenue of fir trees through which gleamed the waters of Beadnall Bay, he was very touched to hear Sir Edward say, "It is six years since I have been able to see that lovely view," for his eyesight had been failing for years. Even then, his gracious hospitality was not ended, for he walked with them all the way to the entrance gates to see them off.

On their way home, Bram asked Glyn what he had thought about it all. He was chiefly disappointed that, when they had been asked to stay for tea, his father had refused the invitation. He also seemed surprised that when Sir Edward needed more bread for his ducks, he had run back to the house for it himself, instead of getting a footman to bring it on a silver salver. What pleased him most was that Lady Grey had stuffed his pockets with red currants. This all showed that, unlike his father, his leanings were not towards Natural History.

During the remainder of our stay my husband spent a good deal of his time observing the sea birds on the Farne Islands, and it was whilst there that he performed an operation on a gull, which he often described in his later lectures. Amongst the thousands of kittiwakes, puffins and gulls that surrounded him, he happened to notice that this bird was in distress, and discovered that it had swallowed a fishing hook and line. Using his penknife, he slit its crop, and after extracting the hook and line, he used it to sew it up again. He then carried the gull to a flat rock which overhung the sea, and many who heard him tell the story will remember the look of joy on his face as he described how it lifted its beautiful wings a few times, and then soared up into the air and disappeared from view.

In the meantime he had purchased an English setter, and she and Raq became great pals; but unfortunately one morning, when chasing each other round the garden, Meg inadvertently kicked Raq down the cellar steps and his injuries were such that he died. Not only was my husband inconsolable, but Meg was too, and so he then bought a pointer, whom he called Pete. When he took the dogs for walks, Pete in particular attracted attention. Sometimes, when he was out, curious-looking men would call and ask to see the dog, and when I had grudgingly taken them round to the kennels, they would spend endless time examining his points. One day a man called and offered £100 for him. We were dumbfounded. We had no intention of being rushed, and so during the next few days we mentally spent the £100 over and over again. Within a week Pete was dead. He developed St Vitus' dance,[1] and we lost him and our £100. My husband's real love, though, was for cocker-spaniels, and Pete was soon replaced by a second Raq.

What he called the "stupid formalities of introduction" were of little concern to him at any time, and in one of his articles to the *Cumberland News* about this time he wrote, "If you will only go for a walk with the conviction that each person you meet is an open book of enjoyment, and will take the trouble to turn over the first page, your dog will do the rest. A wag of his tail, a cool muzzle thrust into an unresisting hand, and you have made another friend."

Two months before we left Carlisle, having been prepared by one of his restless moods, I guessed that he was planning another expedition. Out it came at last. We were both to go to the lighthouse on Ailsa Craig, an island off the West coast of Scotland. This was impossible for me, because I was in the throes of packing and cleaning the Manse in preparation for our departure. In any case, I could not have left my two-year-old daughter. After days of preparation, he reached Girvan on the Ayrshire coast one evening in June 1926. He garaged the car, but the weather was so rough that he had great difficulty in persuading anyone to take him across the Firth of Clyde.

Before leaving home he had experienced some digestive trouble, and as he stood on the beach and saw the lonely rock in the distance, he enquired of an old fisherman what would happen if he needed a doctor. "If you're sick, they'll send up yin licht," he replied, referring to the rockets used by the lighthouse keepers. "If you're awfu' bad, they'll send up twa, but if you're deid, they'll send up three." This he found none too comforting a reply. Finally, he managed to persuade one of the fishermen to take him, but the boat was small, and the farther they went the more the gale increased. Until then, he had been full of the joy of his adventure, but as the boat plunged through the heavy seas, he felt so ill that he was hardly conscious that they had arrived at the huge rock island. When he saw the lighthouse keepers waiting to receive him, he thought his troubles were at an end, but there was no beach except at low tide, and after being rocked about uneasily for what seemed hours, waiting for the seventh wave, he and his belongings were tossed on to the base of the rock.

On the huge rock above him stood his hosts. He looked around for the way up, but all he could see was a crane and a pulley, and by this means he and his belongings were eventually hoisted aloft.

Arriving at the Lighthouse on Ailsa Craig

With the usual Scottish reserve, he was received courteously but not effusively, for the men did not know what type of man they had to entertain, and in their cramped quarters this mattered a great deal. Finally, they reached the ivory-white lighthouse, and I imagine that Bram's friendly smile soon thawed the ice, for it was not long before they were on the best of terms.

I suffered agonies of mind those next two weeks, for it was impossible to get letters from him. The rock was a very dangerous one, and the only means of reaching the nests of the thousands of gannets, guillemots, kittiwakes and black-headed gulls[2] which nested on its heights was up a narrow goat-track only eighteen inches wide. Shouldering his two cameras and hiding-tents, he would make his way up to the summit and fix his hiding-tents to photograph the shyer birds. But to reach the more inaccessible nests he had.to lower himself from ledge to ledge with a rope whilst fragments of loose rock which he dislodged fell around him. One false step, and he would have crashed on the rocky boulders eleven hundred feet below.

One day he was in one of his tents on the summit when a terrific thunderstorm broke, and, before he knew it, the tent rose like a balloon into the air and disappeared. He scrambled beneath the shelter of a big boulder, but so violent was the storm that he was thoroughly scared. The lightning streaked in and out of the rocks, and the noise of the thunder was almost drowned by the reverberation of the waves as they raced one another into the huge caverns beneath the island. Then he happened to notice thousands of birds sheltering unconcernedly under the ledges of rocks around him, and the sight of them both amused and reassured him. If they were not afraid, why should he be? Later, at low tide, he went to search for his tent and discovered it on the beach below.

His admiration for the lighthouse men was unbounded. Nothing was a trouble to them as far as he was concerned; they quite embarrassed him by fetching and carrying his things. In spite of many wasted plates, he secured some excellent photos, and spent most of his spare time in an outhouse at the base of the lighthouse which he had fitted up as a dark-room. One evening he was sitting there quietly when, to his horror, one of the men opened the door. He had come to fetch a shovel. Twenty of his best plates were ruined!

At last, to my intense relief, he arrived home safely. That evening some friends happened to call, but my pleasure in their company was spoilt by a curious smell that pervaded the room. I mentioned it after they had gone, but he laughed and said that it was pure imagination on my part. He could smell nothing unusual. The next morning he went off to Tullie House Museum to tell his friend, the Curator, about his adventures, for it was with him that he had climbed Garrick Fell to find a peregrine's nest. While he was gone, I sniffed around amongst his belongings, but could detect nothing to account for it. When he came back, he said, "I've found out what the smell is. Before I could tell Mr McIntyre where I'd been, he said, 'You've been somewhere where there were gannets.'" The peculiar odour of these birds had so impregnated his clothes that the Curator recognised it at once, and it took weeks of airing to get rid of it.

After all I have written of my husband's tireless energy, it is strange to have to tell that he visited an Edinburgh specialist just before leaving Carlisle in 1926. The verdict, unfortunately, was that the indigestion he had been experiencing was due to duodenal trouble, and he was put on a diet. A trouble of this kind is an enigma to some people, for it often lies dormant for years and then reasserts itself. Thus it was with him, and so energetic was he during the next years that few people knew that he was not in perfect health.

When staying with his friend, Jonathan Gray, at the North British Hotel in Edinburgh, a little man whose face seemed familiar walked into the lounge where he was playing the piano, and before long he found himself accompanying Harry Lauder as he sang, "I love a lassie" in his own inimitable way. His friendliness impressed them both.

The time had now come to say good-bye to our numberless Carlisle friends, for Bram's wide interests and his long stay had brought him in touch with people far outside his church work. His weekly nature articles, his angling, his music, his photography, his love of sport and dogs, and the fact that he was a freemason, had all made a walk with him up English Street one continuous greeting. When, therefore, a cheque was presented to him, he was touched to find that the subscription list not only included his own church friends but some of the most important and the most humble citizens of Carlisle.

I have dealt longer than I intended recounting in some detail these twelve years, but as the remainder of his ministry was spent in the industrial towns of Yorkshire, I feel that he had more chance of self-expression in Carlisle than at any other period of his career.

He felt his departure keenly. Not only had he been supremely content in his church work and friendships, but he was leaving behind a part of himself in the quiet hills and valleys of Cumberland.

There's a waterfall I'm leaving
Running down the rocks in foam,
There's a pool for which I'm grieving
Near the water-ousel's home.
And it's there that I'd be lying
With the heather close at hand
And the curlews faintly crying
'Mid the wastes of Cumberland.*

Nowell Oxland

---

*From a poem composed by Lt Nowell Oxland, on board ship on his way to Gallipoli, where he was killed in August 1915.

Chapter 11 Notes

1   Sydenham's chorea, also known as St Vitus' dance – a disease involving severe involuntary shaking.

2   This should be black-backed gulls. Both great and lesser black-backed gulls nest on Ailsa Craig, but not black-headed gulls which are ground nesting – on marshes near still water.

Dinner with the Lighthouse Keepers

Chapter 12

Huddersfield

Our journey by car from Manchester to our new home in Huddersfield was not an auspicious one, for the moors, with their murky heather and tired-looking grass, looked gloomy and menacing. Each time we rounded a bend, we looked in vain for the pine woods and spinneys we had left. Unfortunately, we approached the town from its more sordid side; countless mill chimneys were belching forth huge columns of smoke, and the working-class districts with their back-to-back houses were drab and ugly.

For some time after our arrival, Bram was homesick for the beautiful Eden valley. Sadly, he put away his fishing-rods, and if when travelling farther afield we passed a clear, sparkling stream, he would get out of the car for the sheer pleasure of looking at it.

With his friendly disregard of formalities, he soon came to know and love the Yorkshire people, and as he was born in the North and had lived there the greater part of his life, it is not to be wondered at that he singled out Northerners for his special affection. The hospitality we were soon receiving was prodigal, and that shown to us by F L Moorhouse and his wife stands out above the rest. It was with 'FL,' as he was affectionately called, that Bram went one day to New Mills to see a water-diviner at work. As he stood and watched the man grip the hazel-rod firmly between his hands and then walk to and fro across the field, he was fascinated. Suddenly the rod, which pointed downwards, came miraculously to life and jerked upwards, and the water-diviner said calmly, "There's water under here." "Are you sure?" asked FL. "Yes," he replied, "and it's sulphur." Bram then asked if he might try his hand at it, and they all laughed as he walked up and down the field with no result. The water-diviner then placed his badly scarred hands on Bram's wrists as they walked along together, and the violence with which the twig suddenly twisted upwards when passing over water, made him wince with pain.

Despite the friendliness shown to us, for a time I wondered if he would be able to exist in industrialism, but it was his car that eventually enabled him to discover the beauties of the dales and wind-swept moorlands.   What there was of interest around Huddersfield, too, he soon found, and one of his favourite hunting-grounds was Bretton Park.   On his first visit he had difficulty in convincing the gamekeeper that he was a bird-lover, and not the usual type of passing motorist who disturbs game-birds and scatters his picnic litter on the grass.   One morning, the gamekeeper rowed him across the lake to photograph the grey Canada geese which were nesting on one of the islands.   After promising to fetch him at four o'clock he then left.   Hour after hour Bram patiently sat in his hiding-tent waiting for the mother-bird to return, and it was nearly three o'clock when his first chance came.   Just as he was preparing to release the shutter, to his dismay he heard the gamekeeper's voice, "I thought you'd be getting bored."   Bored?   He could almost have laughed aloud.   But even this was not as disappointing as the time when he laboriously erected a platform near a heronry in the Hellifield district and, after waiting for days, failed to get a single photograph.   What risks he took to get a good picture!   It was not until long afterwards that I knew that when photographing the rooks' nests from the top of the church tower in Manchester Road, he had nearly been blown off the parapet by the fierce March gales.   As it was, when he returned home, he was covered with soot and grime.

On one occasion our Sunday School teachers, returning from a country ramble, saw a disreputable-looking tramp coming towards them, and were about to put their hands into their pockets when they recognised their own Minister.   It caused a good deal of merriment, especially when he explained that he had spent most of the afternoon in and out of some furze bushes watching the antics of a stoat.

I think it was in 1929, when preaching at the Lancashire town of Nelson, that he first met Rennie Woods.   Rennie and his wife were weavers in a cotton mill, but he was meant for a wider life, for he was an artist in photography and had a fair knowledge of bird life.   How sad that he should still be spending his life listening only to the rattle of looms. When Bram suggested that they should spend a holiday together photographing birds on the rocky coast of West Scotland, Rennie's face was a picture. It was an unheard thing that Fair Week, their one week's holiday in the year, should be spent anywhere but at Blackpool. What would his family think?

He arrived at our house on the Sunday afternoon, and as he sat demurely by my side in the pew that evening, the congregation little knew with what eagerness he and Bram were awaiting the final words of the benediction. The abrupt way we took leave of our friends after the service must have caused surprise, but every minute was precious, for they had planned to leave at daybreak the following morning. For the next hour the house was in a state of confusion as cameras, stands, hiding-tents, sleeping-bags, billycans and hundreds of photographic plates were bundled into the car.

It was hardly light the next morning when I stood in my dressing-gown and waved them good-bye, and watched Raq circling round as he tried to find a niche in the crowded corner of the back seat.

Rennie, who for years had dreamed of such an adventure, simply could not believe that it was really true, and when they had crossed the Border, and he saw the Galloway hills for the first time, he said, "Happen some-un'll gimme a clout on t'head an ah'll wakken up." Bram, who rarely made his plans beforehand, had not the least idea exactly where they were making for; all he knew was that there were sea birds galore on that wild, rocky coast, and lodgings did not matter when they could sleep out under the June sky.

Eventually they reached a quiet fishing village and, after making a few enquiries, they garaged the car and raided the one and only shop for provisions. Their next job was to find a fisherman who would row them out to the distant, uninhabited promontory known as Almorness Point. The piles of luggage which filled the herring-boat perplexed the fisherman, but his expression was rather one of pity when he asked them what time he should fetch them, and was told "In a week's time."

They explored the island[1] and found an old hut in which the fishermen occasionally slept at night when visiting their nets. Apart from hard planks, there was no bed of any kind, so filling their sacks with sea-wrack, they took it in turns to sleep with the rats on the floor. A candle stuck in a bottle served as a light, two jam-jars as mugs, and their only knife was used both for cleaning the fish they caught and buttering their bread.

On the 'Island'

What a marvellous week they had! The island was rich in bird-life – ringed plovers, oystercatchers, dunlin, mallards, sheldrakes. What more could they want? Bird photography is by no means the easy pastime that some people imagine it to be. It is hard work, for in addition to the weight of cameras, heavy plates and hiding-tents have to be carried from place to place. No sooner was Bram settled in a tent than Rennie would arrive to say that he had discovered a rarer bird half a mile away. Down the tent would come, and they would tramp over rock and shingle to put it up again. A hiding-tent can rarely be used until a couple of days after it is put up, because the birds must be given time to get accustomed to it; hence the need for so many tents.

My husband was particularly susceptible to the comfort of his large easy-chair at home, and yet he would sit without complaint day after day on the hard ground in his small, cramped tent, two feet square. He was fond, too, of his pipe, but even this pleasure he denied himself, lest the smoke should scare a bird away. So shy were many of them, that he would sometimes stay there a whole day without getting a single photograph. But he was never bored.

Though they both revelled in it all, they suffered many disappointments. A dark-room was fixed up in the corner of the hut, and when they developed their plates each evening many turned out to be unsatisfactory.

By the end of the week they had lost all count of time, but by careful calculation they decided that the fisherman would be fetching them on the following day. Though they had not taken half the photographs they wanted, regretfully they had to pack up. When he arrived home, he said proudly, "I've got a whole series of the common gull." This seemed to me a very ordinary bird, but when he told me that it only nested in about three places in the British Isles,[2] I was able to appreciate his good luck.

His knowledge of wildlife, by this time, was becoming more generally recognied, which induced his friend, Ernest Woodhead, to ask him to contribute a weekly nature column to the *Huddersfield Examiner*. Their friendship began at one of FL's famous parties, when this amazing man of over seventy joined in the charades and games with as much zest as we did. We never met a more interesting man. Not only had he become editor at the age of twenty-eight, but he had been a Rugby International and one of the best amateur runners in his youth. But what astonished us most was his erudition. At the age of seventy, he added a knowledge of Spanish to his other languages by attending classes at the local Technical College. At the age of eighty he began studying Russian, and, incidentally, joined in the dancing at some local function, and in between all these activities, he travelled abroad to further his knowledge. With it all he was a deeply religious man, and Bram and he had many heart-to-heart talks.

I have not dwelt at length on my husband's church work because it varied very little in the different towns in which we lived. The Huddersfield church was a down-town one, and he found the work disheartening, for though he attracted a large number of outsiders to his services, it was beyond his powers to restore it to the prosperity of former years. But a letter I have received from Fred Lee shows that he accomplished more than he knew. "I have attended Buxton Road chapel for over sixty years, and, during the whole of that period, I can recall no minister more beloved than your husband."

To describe his public prayers would be unfitting, but they were so often commented on that they must have been helpful. "Each service he conducted was one act of worship, and many felt it was worth-while attending if only to hear him pray," writes a member of one of his congregations. He put so much of himself into them that I can hardly imagine the effect of them in print, but I am told that two of them are included in the Rev R Walter Hull's book of modern prayers – *In this Manner, Pray Ye.*

He was no scholar; he did not delve deeply into theology, nor attempt to explain many of the more intricate mysteries of the Christian Faith, some of which he frankly owned he did not understand himself. In simple language he would state what he himself believed, and was inclined rather to try to rid religion of the man-made ritualistic incrustations of the centuries, and present the life of Christ in its simplicity and beauty.

He had no voice specially reserved for pulpit utterances, as so many preachers have; whether he was reading the Scriptures or praying, it was the same unaffected voice that afterwards became so loved. "I have never heard the Bible read so naturally," writes another. He loved the poetry of the Psalms, and he made the dramatic stories of the Old Testament live. Religion to him was a very practical thing, for he had little mysticism about him. He would tell us that holiness was not some vague, nebulous virtue, but wholeness, and that being holy meant that one served God and one's fellow-men not only with one's emotions, but with one's mind and with one's bodily energy.

His pulpit attitude towards life was usually one of optimism and thankfulness, and his sermons and prayers were veined with gratitude for being alive, for the quiet, simple things of life, the treasures of the world of nature, the wealth of friendships, the joy experienced in helping others, all of which, he would tell his congregation, were to be had "without money and without price."

He rarely used the word 'sin,' but would talk of missing one's aim in life, and not living up to the highest that one knew, rather than the committing of a dastardly act. This at once took away the very comfortable[3] feeling some of us had always had when sin was mentioned. Though a great deal of what he said may have been considered unorthodox, he put what he believed into such simple everyday language that the most illiterate person could not fail to grasp his meaning.

On one occasion, when preaching at Cardiff, a Gypsy was seated in his congregation. This man afterwards wrote to the Secretary of the Gypsy Lore Society, of which both he and my husband were members, "I was pleased to shake hands with Romany after the service. I spoke to him in broken Romani and he replied, but we only had a few words owing to the crush." He then went on to say that in his sermon my husband had helped him by translating the word 'love' in relation to loving God as 'goodwill,' rather than as the word is used today. He continues, "Romany said he used to be bothered because he could not make himself love God, but when he learnt Hebrew and found that the different cases of the word had different meanings, and that it did not mean loving God as a man loved a maid, it no longer worried him." I mention this because my husband dwelt a good deal on the misuse of this word, and felt that it was one of the biggest stumbling-blocks to the Christian religion.

To put into words the effect of his preaching on other people is beyond my power, so perhaps if I end this chapter with a few quotations from letters, it will help to convey it.

"He gave me a vision of the true beauty and meaning of life. His was no conventional religion, but real and living."

"I always forgot I was listening to a sermon, for I felt that he was having a personal chat with me."

"I seemed to find him at his greatest in the pulpit. I was thrilled by the nobility of his thought, shot through with a rich human passion and sympathy that endeared him to us all."

"Life has become richer to my family through his ministry."

"I am not a member of any church, but he struck me as being more akin to the real thing than anyone I had previously heard."

"His sermons were eloquent in their simplicity."

*I will make mention now of the works of the Lord, and will declare the things that I have seen.**

Chapter 12 Notes

1   Almorness Point is, as Eunice has said earlier, a promontory, not an island. Even today the peninsular remains remote and isolated. Eunice is no doubt influenced by this being the location called 'Shingle Island' in *Out with Romany by the Sea.*

2   This is an interesting piece of information as it illustrates a reversal of the all-too-common trend of decline. The breeding areas of the Common Gull, since the eighteenth century, have been extending in Britain, albeit still predominantly in Scotland

3   Comfortable in the sense of 'smug;' a feeling that one is without *real* sin – completely missing the point that considering oneself thus commits one of the greatest sins, that of pride.

Buxton Road Methodist Chapel, Huddersfield

Chapter 13

Halifax

My husband's caravan was now resting in an orchard on the bank of the river Esk in East Yorkshire. This was not an ideal position from his point of view, for it was not sufficiently secluded, but he had placed it there rather as a compromise to the family, who wanted to be within easy access of the sea. One morning he opened his daily paper and read with much concern that terrific floods had swollen the river and that Sleights' bridge had been washed away. He was quite convinced that his beloved *vardo* was now far out on the North Sea, and was only consoled when he learnt that, though the farmhouse had been flooded out, only the wheels of the caravan had been submerged. He was also secretly pleased, for he now had a genuine excuse for moving it.

After a long search on the Eskdaleside moorland road, he found what he wanted, a lonely, grassy slope over-looking wooded glens and deep gullies, and the *vardo* was driven to its new resting-place. In one of his weekly articles he wrote, "On one side my caravan catches the tang of the sea as the breeze blows up the valley; on the other, the fragrance of wild thyme wafted down from the moors." As we stood on its steps we could see the old quarry, the haunt of a family of foxes, for whom he always seemed to be making excuses when the farmer accused them of raiding his poultry; beyond this stretched limitless miles of heather-covered moorland. Below, we could hear the music of the river which ran between high, rocky gorges, the home of otters and kingfishers. We soon became familiar with woodpeckers which were at work in the trees, and heard their harsh, derisive calls, and he would sometimes show us the signs of a badger that frequented the wood nearby.

Whilst standing by the *vardo* one day, he drew my attention to some woodcock which were flying overhead, "One of them is carrying something," I said. Greatly excited, he fetched his binoculars. It appears that naturalists have differed for years as to whether woodcocks carry their youngsters or not, but as he had not seen it himself, he was never sure about it. That I, of all people, should have pointed out to him a woodcock carrying its young filled me with pride, for it was the only occasion on which I remember showing him anything of real interest.

We made our own path across the fields to fetch our milk, and it gave us an almost childlike pleasure to see it becoming more and more defined as the weeks passed. We liked to feel that it was our path and that no one else ever trod on it.

No plans were ever made for the day, and when he disappeared I never knew when he would turn up again. I loved the place when he and I were there alone, but the children were now of an age when they needed other interests, and one half of me always seemed to be wanting to follow him through the woods, whilst the other half was drawn towards the children and reassuring them that there was plenty of interest for them in the country if they would only look for it. I was in a dilemma. My husband would rather stay at home than spend a conventional holiday elsewhere, and yet they were too old to be told what kind of a holiday they should enjoy. Year after year this family conflict arose, making me most unhappy. No amount of persuasion would convince him that the country was not completely satisfying for everyone; they were not content to be buried in the wilds, two miles from the nearest bus, for unfortunately, at that time he was the only one of us who could drive the car. So tiresomely obstinate was he at times over matters that interfered with his usual mode of life that I saw no way out of the difficulty. Finally, however, he compromised by driving us over occasionally for the day to the seaside and returning for us at night. Not until we had bought a beach hut at Sandsend on the sandhills far beyond everyone else's was he happy away from the caravan.

Though beach huts on the East coast were removed by the military authorities at the beginning of the war, for some reason or other ours was not touched. Today it stands there alone,[1] a reminder of glorious summer days, and a memorial to his tireless energy, for though he did not actually build the hut, he made many improvements to it. The encroaching sea would wash away its foundations, and he would spend days staggering up the sandhills with every available huge boulder he saw lying on the beach.

Romany at Sandsend

To me those were happy days, for, alas, by this time swimming was the only pastime that we as a family shared together, and even Raq would join in the fun. How we laughed when Bram ran down the beach wearing his swimming suit both inside out and back to front! He never could get it right unless I was there to help him. And what appetites we had for our picnic lunch afterwards.

It was on one of our later war-time visits to Sandsend that we were perturbed to find that the beach hut, having survived some terrifically high seas, was almost toppling down the bank.

Civilians at that time were forbidden on the beach, and it took us some time to get permission from the military authorities to attend to it. Pocketing the permit, we made our way towards the sandhills, and it was not long before my husband, who was always remarkably agile, had squeezed his way through the barbed wire and made a passage for me. We were filled with importance at being the only people allowed on the beach, and gloried in the pleasure of it. From time to time I noticed that June was waving to us from the cliffs, but the busier we became strengthening the foundations of the hut, the more I pretended not to see her. We then noticed a man walking towards us along the beach. "Another lucky man," we thought, and laboriously hauled up another heavy plank of wood washed up by the tide. As he came nearer, we saw that it was a soldier. He questioned us, asked to see our permits, and then told us that we should have used the entrance to the beach where he was on guard. We apologised, and he allowed us to finish the job. When we left the beach, June came running towards us excitedly. She had been told that parts of the beach were mined. No wonder she was excited.

During our third year in Huddersfield my husband was far from well, and so we toyed with the idea of his retiring from the ministry. But forgoing a salary of £320 needed some thought, especially as we had recently parted with £500, the whole of our savings, to a friend who was on the verge of bankruptcy. Before we could make up our minds, however, he received an invitation to a church in the neighbouring town of Halifax, where the work was easier.

So, the September of 1929 found us in a well-furnished manse which stood on the bleak, exposed ridge of one of Halifax's many hills, and was towered over by Wainhouse's Folly. This mighty tower, which served no useful purpose, had been built by a crank out of spite to one of his neighbours; it cost him forty thousand pounds and was eventually sold to the Halifax Corporation for four hundred. As it was close to our house, and anything but per-pendicular, it was a constant menace to me and my small daughter, and when fierce gales swept across the valley, we often thought our last moment had come. But to my husband it was a constant source of interest, and I can see him now, as he hurried to fetch his binoculars to examine some sparrowhawk or peregrine that had found refuge on its summit. Added to this, our outlook was often depressing, for the house stood in a cemetery, and a constant procession of funeral carriages drew up in front of our windows. He was more than friendly with our sexton, who was one of our most regular callers. Not only had they funerals to arrange, but when unusual birds frequented the cemetery or a robin built its nest under a half-open glass wreath-cover, it was Johnnie who came to tell Bram about it.

A letter from Inspector Allingham of Halifax reminds me of an incident which, though it ended tamely, brings out a trait in my husband's character. When a very young constable, he was on duty one wild night when he happened to notice that our study window was open. He listened intently, thought he could hear someone inside, then took a chance and rang the bell, expecting the intruder to dash out of the window. Meanwhile, Bram had opened the door. His letter continues: "I shall always remember that moment, for when I told him my suspicions, he said, 'We'll soon settle him,' and before I could get inside, he had walked straight into the room and switched on the light. There was no one there, but I did admire his courage and coolness. He certainly was a 'well-plucked un,' and a man I always admired."

The discomforts of our house detracted little from our happiness, for the people among whom we worked were grand Yorkshire folk, mostly of the artisan class, with whom my husband always got on well. The friendly atmosphere in the church vestry on his first Sunday morning also appealed to him, for whether they were employers or employees, they addressed each other by their Christian names, and it was not long before he, too, was saying, "Good morning, Edgar," or "Charlie."[2]

If enthusiasm was needed to launch a scheme, it was always his personality that carried it through, but he never liked to discuss or plan business matters before-hand. When I reminded him of a committee meeting ahead, he'd say, "Jot down what you think we ought to discuss. Don't bother me with it now, dear." This was all right, but even when the day arrived he didn't want to talk about it, and it usually ended with, "Tell me in the car as we go up." Then, as likely as not, when he came to an item which I had added to the agenda, he would glance at me helplessly, as if asking, "What was this all about?" But once he had grasped it, no one could deal with it better than he, and though he disliked committee meetings, his fondness for his officials put him in such good humour that we just rollicked through the business. One of them writes, "He had a wonderful way of dealing with awkward members. There was rarely any fear of a scene when he was in the chair, for he had a way of soothing a cantankerous member as though he were smoothing the feathers of a ruffled bird."

Having been a scoutmaster when in Carlisle, he took a special pride in the troop connected with our Church. Owing mainly to good leadership, they had an excellent record, and fifty of them today are serving with the forces; unfortunately, eight of those whom my husband knew have already lost their lives. The scoutmaster writes most appreciatively of the impression he made on his boys. Especially grateful was he for the way he would get up an hour earlier on Sunday mornings during the summer months and motor up to their week-end camp at Luddenden Dean. I can well imagine that he would be at his best as he sat and talked to them in the open-air, with Raq at his feet, and the scouts squatted in a circle round the smouldering camp fire.

Romany with Scouts

During our ten years in Halifax I hardly remember a Sunday when we had our car to ourselves to and from church. No wonder it was called the King Cross bus, for Bram would go miles out of his way to fetch the sick and aged, and there were very few other members of the congregation who were not given a lift at some time or other. I am reminded of this by C O Mackley, a master at the local Grammar School, who, when writing to me, said, "I shall never forget the thousand and one ways in which he was always making work for himself to make life less of a burden to others."

Amongst his many activities he both wrote and produced several plays for the young people, which gave him scope for his love of colour. He would spare no pains to get artistic backgrounds and lighting effects, and would go to endless trouble arranging the folds of the Eastern robes worn in a Nativity Play so that the lights enhanced their beauty. As I watched him, I often felt that he derived a deeper satisfaction from it than the audience did.

Meanwhile, the graveyard manse had become uninhabitable, and a very pleasant house was bought for us in Rothwell Road. After waiting for twenty years, he had the joy of a good garden, and what pleased him just as much, commodious outhouses which he used as kennels, workshops, poultry houses and sheds in which to house the various injured birds and animals he often brought home, and the stray dogs for whom he always had a tender solicitude. But when he walked across the little rough croft nearby, and said, "This would be an ideal place to keep a goat," I protested, for he forgot that he was often away from home, and that it would fall to my lot to plod through rain and snow to milk Nanny.

It was his love both of animals and flowers that got him up at four-thirty one morning when passing through London. After visiting Covent Garden Market just for the pleasure of revelling in the scented avenues of carnations, sweet peas and daffodils, he went to the Zoo only to find that it was not open until nine o'clock. However, he walked round until he found a gate through which stores were being carried and went in. While engrossed in watching the birds, an official spotted him, and he found himself outside again. Nothing daunted, he walked round again and asked a workman who was entering another gate where he was going. "To find Mr Johnson," was the reply. He followed the man in, inspected the various animals and, each time he was asked his business, replied "I'm trying to find Mr Johnson," and then made determined efforts not to do so. By this time, he was arousing suspicion, so he decided that he had better find Mr Johnson, but unfortunately, when he reached him, a burly policeman stood at his side, and he once more found himself outside the railings. Even then, he did not give up hope. Learning that the Superintendent was about, he asked permission of the gate-keeper to speak to him, with the result that he was finally allowed to remain in the grounds.

Once Whipsnade had been opened, and he could see the animals in their natural surroundings, he rarely went to the Zoo, for, having watched the lordly peregrine falcons enjoying their freedom on the craggy gorges of the Cumberland hills, it worried him to see them imprisoned.

His opportunities of studying wildlife in Halifax were so limited that it was touching to see his pleasure when he came across wild creatures. One night when we were taking Raq for a late walk, he suddenly stood still. He had heard far above us the calls of a flock of curlews who were migrating to the moors. I cannot describe the thrill it gave him. Those lonesome cries were

141

to him the pipes of Pan, calling him back to the Cumberland estuaries from which they had probably come, and it moved him strangely that these wild moorland birds were passing over the mill chimneys of an industrial town.

Our second year in Halifax, in a sense, ended for me twenty years of blissful married life, when our home was indeed our castle, and none but our friends intruded on our privacy. It has been said that once a man is in the public eye, he is no longer his own master. How true this was of my husband, for it was his very ability to portray the countryside to others which debarred him from enjoying it to the full. Though the next years of his life brought him fame, it deprived us of much that was precious. I soon found that his increasing popularity was becoming a threat to the seclusion of our home life, and realised that I should have to share him with the public. Proud as I am of all that the name 'Romany' meant to so many people, the happiest years of my life were those when he was known only as Bramwell Evens.

I also love a quiet place
That's green, away from all mankind.

W H Davies

Chapter 13 Notes

1   This old photograph shows
    an isolated Sandsend' beach
    hut of that era. Probably
    not Romany's, but similar
    and also looking precarious,
    perched on the edge of sand
    dunes. It is, of course, not
    there anymore.

2   One should not underestimate how unusual such informality was
    at that time. In the editor's early ministry (1960s-70s) there were
    still older parishioners who wished to be referred to as Mr, Mrs or
    Miss Xxx.

Kings Cross Methodist Chapel and Wainhouse Tower, Halifax

PART 2

Chapter 14

He becomes a Broadcaster

One afternoon my husband was walking down Market Street, Manchester, when someone who recognised him spoke to him. "You're just the person they could do with on the Children's Hour," he said in the course of conversation. "You've done some broadcasting, haven't you?" My husband replied that he had given several talks to schools both from Leeds and Newcastle, but had never taken part with others in a mixed programme. Before they parted, this friend promised to mention his name to Olive Schill, the organiser.

He often wished afterwards that he had met this man again so that he could have thanked him for what proved to be the opening of a door into a much wider and more interesting life. I hoped, too, that his name might have been forthcoming when my publishers advertised in the press for any information about my husband that might prove of interest, but I have heard nothing.

A few weeks later a letter arrived from the BBC suggesting the usual audition, and asking him to bring with him a few nature incidents suitable for inclusion in the programme. This passed off satisfactorily, and he was engaged to take part in the Children's Hour the following month.

Even today letters received by the BBC show that there are still many listeners who imagine that the Romany walks took place out-of-doors. This being the case, it may be wondered why I should wish to dispel this illusion, but, as the BBC eventually disclosed the fact that they took place in the studio, it may be of interest if I tell how the broadcasts were presented.

When the day of my husband's first engagement arrived, he was received by the organiser and asked, "How do you wish to be announced?" for, at that time, all those who took part were either

Uncles or Aunties. This came as a shock. Certainly not 'Uncle Bramwell' nor 'The Rev Bramwell Evens.' On the spur of the moment he replied, "Romany," and Romany he became.

What a fortunate choice it was! It not only helped his broadcasts by making him anonymous, but an inartistic name might have spoilt their whole effect. From that day he was not only called Romany by everyone at the BBC, but it was not long before it took precedence over Bramwell Evens everywhere he went. The only person who disapproved of it was our small nine-year-old daughter, who had been christened Romany June, for she felt that she had a prior claim to it.

He was then ushered into the studio and introduced to Muriel Levy, Doris Gambell, Eric Fogg and Harry Hopewell. He had no idea what part each of these artistes was to play in the programme; all that he knew was that he had to tell two nature stories from his own experience and that each must not exceed five minutes in length. The red light then went on, and they all gathered round the microphone, and it was not long before Uncle Eric's hilarity and the charming naturalness of Auntie Muriel and Auntie Doris had drawn him into the impromptu fun and banter which was always such a popular part of the Northern programme.

Though, naturally, a little nervous when he arrived, their friendliness and the jolly atmosphere that prevailed soon restored his confidence. These people, so quick to respond to each other's fun, were just the audience he needed to tell his stories well. He was sure that they would react in the same way to the pathos of the story of Phan[1] the otter, or the beauty of Brune[1] the mallard. Meanwhile, Muriel, who always compered these programmes, was signalling to him that his turn had come. But as he began to speak his heart fell. His friendly audience had melted away one by one, and he was left alone to tell his story to the soulless microphone. Out of the corner of his eye he could see Harry turning over his songs on the piano, Doris and Eric on the chesterfield studying their scripts, and Muriel at the other end of the room carrying on a conversation by means of signs with the effects man. So this was what 'behind the scenes in the Children's Hour Studio' meant. It was so different from what he had imagined. He had always depended so much on his lecture audiences with their eager, expectant faces for his inspiration, and these people were not even listening. He did not, of course, understand that as it was a variety programme, each artiste was concerned only with his own performance. However, in spite of this set-back, he told his story and entered with zest into the remainder of the programme, little knowing that this was the strange beginning of the 'Out with Romany' walks, and many years of happy partnership with Muriel and Doris.

This was followed by similar programmes, but it was not until he had been broadcasting for several months that it occurred to anyone that he had the ability to hold the interest of the public for more than five minutes on his own subject. It happened on one occasion that Harold Dean – who, incidentally, Romany and I always considered to be the best story-teller to the smaller children that we had ever heard – was unable to fulfil his engagement. How were they to fill up the time? Could Romany enlarge on his subject? Of course he could, for he was far more at home without a script than with one. "Ask me anything you can think of," he told Muriel and Doris, and so when his talk ended, they fired at him impromptu questions at random. So quickly did the time pass in their interest that he was surprised when Muriel nudged him and pointed to the clock – a hint to bring their chat to an end.

By this time, listeners were expressing their appreciation of this part of the programme, and so he was asked to prepare a script which would include Muriel, Doris and whichever Uncle happened to be booked for the Children's Hour on that particular day. These scripts were a jumble of scribbled notes which Muriel had to sort out and fit in between songs and other items, all of which were interspersed with her own original patter. This was often concerned with the behaviour of Eric's famous deaf earwig, Montgomery, which always escaped from its matchbox and turned up in the most unexpected places just when the programme was in danger of becoming dull. But Romany was none too happy; jolly as the atmosphere in the studio always was, it was an unnatural background for his descriptions of peaceful country life, and the time allotted to him was too short to get the artistic effect he wanted. Just when his talk was becoming so realistic that listeners were imagining themselves walking across a field with him, someone would break the illusion by saying, "What about a song from Auntie Doris?" and the sound of the piano would bring listeners back with a jolt into the studio. The *Radio Times* announcements of the programmes in those early days, too, were odd, 'Romany takes us along and hears Uncle Harry sing, Green grow the rushes, O,' or 'Eric, having returned from his holiday, pays a visit to Romany.'

Then, too, just as in real life, he was sensitive as to the people who accompanied him on his walks, and preferred those who had some appreciation of the beauty around them, so in his broadcasts he was ill-at-ease if anyone took part who had no real interest in the subject. This happened often, for, as I have said, any Uncle who happened to be booked for that day took part.

Eric was an exception, of course, for until Romany became firmly established in the hearts of his listeners, Eric, with his keen sense of humour and his aptitude for getting into trouble of every kind, was a distinct asset to the programme. Whilst Muriel and Doris followed Romany quietly along a lane, questioning him in their musical, childish voices, Eric would be enlivening the proceedings by falling into a ditch, getting stuck half-way up a tree, or sitting on an ants' nest. All this may sound very tame to those who never heard these early programmes, but I feel it will give pleasure to some to recall the many laughs they had over his absurd antics.

For some years before this, Frank Nicholls had been an established favourite in the Children's Hour, and as he had adopted the character-part of Adam, the gamekeeper, and read nature stories to the children, my husband's engagements for a year or two were few. But as soon as the organiser saw that he had a peculiar knowledge of his subject, and that his programme would not conform with others under her control, she gave him more scope for developing it on his own lines, and it was not long before he was writing a forty-five minutes' script and choosing the artistes who should take part. This suited him well, for the extra time, previously taken by other items, enabled him to imbue even the most unimaginative listener with the spirit of the country before the exciting incidents happened for which the children were waiting. He was now free, too, to depict a complete and harmonious picture of a walk, as he knew it to be, and, together, we schemed and planned to make it a true and vivid impression of English rural life.

By the time that the organiser left the Children's Hour at the end of 1933 the programme was established, and neither its form nor its presentation altered during the next ten years. Romany felt that she had contributed more towards its success than any other organiser who followed her, for she had allowed him to develop it in his own way.

Her successor was Janet Beith, a niece of Ian Hay, the novelist, and herself the author of several best-sellers. She showed a sympathetic appreciation of the broadcasts, and it was with a sense of relief that she looked forward to them, for, as each region functioned separately in those days, her work entailed a good deal of organising and rehearsing. But once Romany's script had been typed, and the necessary sound-effects chosen, it needed little supervision, and better still, no rehearsal beforehand. This lack of rehearsing was all a part of his design to make the walk sound realistic. Once he had discovered how gifted his helpers were, he found that their laughter and exclamations of delight were never quite so spontaneous if the freshness of what he described had been toned down by repetition.

By the time that Olive Shapley had taken Janet Beith's place at the end of 1934, the programme was being chosen by the children as the most popular of all, and each time a Request Week poll was taken, Romany's name headed the list. Olive Shapley was not only a lover of nature, but had great personality, and in her Romany found an organiser after his own heart. When, occasionally, she took Muriel or Doris's part she would become so interested in what he was saying that she too would break away from her script and ask questions of her own in the most natural way. To her, as to Janet Beith, the Romany Friday was a welcome day, and such confidence had she in those taking part that she usually left them in control. I do not want to underestimate the responsibility of the work of the various organisers, for if anything had gone wrong they would have been held responsible, but I do know that they always referred to Friday as their easy day, and if they had to be away from the BBC for any reason, they would choose Friday, knowing that, with the help of competent effects men, the Romany programme would run itself. The broadcast, therefore, was unique in that it did not need a producer in the same sense that other plays did.

In those days signature tunes preceded most of the programmes, and when Romany was asked to choose one he had no difficulty, for he had often asked Eric to play 'The Lullaby of the Leaves' for the sheer pleasure of hearing it. Listeners little knew what effect this had on him. For a man of his temperament the bustle of studio preparations was the wrong atmosphere; he should have been able to come straight to the microphone from an outdoor walk. But when the red light went on and Eric began playing the opening bars, he would sit down, relax, close his eyes, and I knew that he was being soothed into a tranquil mood.

When Eric left Manchester to conduct the Empire Orchestra in London, the North Region suffered a great loss. His contribution to the popularity of the North had been outstanding, for he had provided the lightness and fun which some of the other Regions lacked. The tragic news of his death some time later came as a great shock to my husband, especially as only a week previously he had been with us all in the studio. Having an engagement in Manchester, he had chosen the day of the Romany programme to visit his three old friends. As we stood round the piano, and he played the signature tune once again, his eyes filled with tears as he recalled their happy broadcasts together, and wistfully he wished himself back with them again, for he had never been as happy in London as in the North. My husband regretted that he had not kept in touch with him, for a friend in whom he could confide might have averted his sad end at such an early age. We thought it strange that no public appreciation of him was given by the BBC, for he had served both the North Regional Music Department and the Children's Hour for many years. Surely a man who gave so much pleasure was not less worthy of praise because his end happened to be a tragic one. All that Romany could do was to plant a tree near the caravan in his memory.

Perhaps I should have explained how it was that I came to be in the studio, though restrictions as to visitors were few before the war. My husband, *unfortunately*, had to send his script to the BBC to be typed ten days or more in advance. I, emphasise the word 'unfortunately,' for naturalists will appreciate the absurdity of his having to portray a true picture of what could be seen and heard in the English countryside ten days ahead. He would perhaps have written that the migrant willow warblers had not arrived in this country, whereas, in the interval, he might have seen one; or there may have been snow when he wrote the script, and he would then find that it was brilliantly fine on the day of the broadcast, thus altering the whole character of the walk. Consequently, when we received the typed script by post, it usually needed corrections and additions, necessitating further clerical work when we reached the studio.

The first time I went to the BBC I was very much impressed, for even to have been inside in those days gave one a sense of superiority. As we went up in the lift and along the corridors, I imagined that everyone we encountered was some famous radio personality, and as I was carrying my husband's foolscap script, I hoped that they imagined the same of me. Later, I found that most of them were either engineers, clerks or messengers, and that the most important officials rarely emerged from the seclusion of their offices. After introducing me to Muriel and Doris, Romany went down to the canteen for tea. Spreading out our scripts on top of the piano, I then dictated to them the necessary alterations to their copies. Though I did this for many years, I never ceased to marvel at their ease of manner. As they pencilled them in, they would chat perhaps about their future programmes or private affairs, but what astonished me more was that they only asked for their own cues. A whole new paragraph might have been inserted for Romany, but all they wanted was his last word. How often we laughed over his 'last word.' "But he won't stop on his last word," Doris would exclaim; "he's sure to think of something more to say."

In those early days, too, I would arrive at the studio expecting to see them feverishly studying their scripts, which they sometimes did not receive until the morning of the broadcast, but instead, I would find Muriel at the piano and Doris trying over a song for some other programme. On one occasion, I found Muriel in the canteen gossiping with a friend over a cup of tea. When she saw me, she said, "Oh, by the way, my script didn't arrive by post this morning." It was then less than an hour before the broadcast was due to begin, and she had not the least idea what it was all about. I expected her to get up at once and rush upstairs for a copy, but not a bit of it. She calmly finished the conversation, and her cup of tea. Sometimes one of them would arrive late and say to me, with a sweet smile, "Correct mine for me while I go and have some tea, there's a dear." And then she would start the broadcast without having looked at either my additions or deletions.

It was the same with Romany. Sometimes he would be returning from a lecture tour on that day, and I would meet him at the studio with his script. If his train happened to be late I worried needlessly, for as long as he had time to glance through it, he was never concerned. Just as he disliked using notes of any kind when lecturing, for his brain worked more quickly when stimulated by his audience, so he found it more difficult to inspire Muriel and Doris when reading a script. All this was not carelessness on their part, but due to confidence born of years of team work.

While we were at the piano busily correcting our scripts, all kinds of noises were going on behind us, for Terry Cox, the effects man, was experimenting with his various gadgets. Then an engineer would come in to test the microphone, and Doris would be called away to try over a few sentences; or perhaps all of them might be needed if a difficult sound-effect was required, such as scaling a cliff or hiding with Raq in a corn-stook. Otherwise, when we had finished, Muriel and Doris would go off to the canteen, and Romany would reappear. His eyes would light up when he saw Terry, for he could always be relied on to subdue the sounds to fit the quiet atmosphere of the walk. "As long as Terry is there, it will be all right," he would say. But capable as he was, and the same can be said of Jack Hollinshead,[2] there were things that he was not above learning from Romany – the difference between the sound of Raq's feet as he paddled into a stream and that of Muriel's, the sound made by the wings of a plover as it swooped down on an intruder, or the irregularity of Comma's hoof-beats; the hours that Romany had spent listening to country sounds had not been in vain. Then he would disappear into the listening-room to hear the bird records the organiser had chosen, for he alone knew which fitted in best with his walk, and also whether Terry's imitation of the yep-yep of a distant fox was true to life.

When the broadcast was due to begin, I made my way to the listening-room, through the glass window of which I could see them at the microphone. Then it was that my real pleasure began, for though I knew the script by heart, I had only to shut my eyes and I was away with them up the lane, into the caravan and across the fields. Meanwhile Terry is putting on a record here, and manipulating a gadget there, with such skill and unobtrusiveness that his presence is giving them confidence. But what is Romany saying? That isn't in the script. Muriel and Doris seem interested, and are asking him all kinds of questions. How cleverly they are playing up to him. Now Terry is exchanging glances with the organiser, and looking helplessly at his script, hoping that one of them will soon give him his cue. But Muriel and Doris are chatting on, and Romany has certainly forgotten his 'last word.' Now they're back again. But why is he moving away from the microphone like that to show them the nest? Oh, Doris has noticed, and is pulling him back just in time. How they are all enjoying it. Now Muriel is bending down to pat Raq, and as he wags his stumpy tail, he looks up at his master adoringly, as if saying, "This is a queer kind of walk. Why not let's go on a real one?" There goes Romany again, wandering off on another bypath, and as he describes the fox they are watching, he is waving his script about so excitedly that I'm sure the listeners will hear the crackle of the paper.

Now they're back to the incident on the top of the last page. No wonder they are all glancing at the clock, for it's only five minutes to six, and they're nearly at the end. How will he fill up the time? What will he talk about? Why has he stopped in the middle of a sentence to search his pockets? Oh, yes. He's looking for the pheasant's feather he picked up this morning.

"You put it in your inside pocket." He's found it at last. They've now more to talk about than the time will allow, and they're being faded out. There's the red light for the six o'clock news.

To describe what they saw on these walks to those who did not hear them is not easy, for though on paper the dialogue looked absurdly simple, it was their personalities which brought the scenes to life. My husband had been able to use his knowledge of bird and animal life when lecturing, but it was the broadcasts that gave him his first opportunity of using his varied and unusual knowledge of rural life. The children are most likely to remember the exciting adventures as they waded the river to rescue the otters, climbed the belfry tower to watch the rooks, or followed the tracks of the trapped badger, but others will recall with pleasure the natural way in which Romany would comment on the most commonplace things as they sauntered along. He would show them the beauty of the golden crops swaying in the breeze, the charm of a passing red admiral butterfly, the dew sparkling on the delicate tracery of a spider's web, the bronze and gold leaves of a shapely beech tree, the gossamer wings of a green dragon-fly, and the vividness of the red berries on the mountain ash. All this was interspersed with useful information given in such a delightful and often amusing way that the child listener was not conscious that he was learning anything.

A great deal of the fun, of course, was provided by Raq[4], as he chased the rabbits, scented out the stoats or fell into the stream in his anxiety to track a moorhen. Romany would rarely mention anything which he himself had not seen, and if, during the winter months when there appeared to me to be little of interest, I suggested that he should include information of foreign birds or animals he had seen in the Zoo, he would laugh and say, "There's plenty to see in the English countryside in December." Often, too, I would show my ignorance by hinting that the script would be enlivened by the inclusion of a certain thrilling story of some animal, and was quietly told, "It's hibernating now, dear."

One afternoon we listened to an imitation of his programme given by one of the other Regions. When it was over, I asked him what he thought of it. He praised it, but what struck me was that he criticised things which I had not noticed, such as, "A woodcock would have risen into the air sooner," or "You never find that bird amongst the turnips." It was this accuracy of detail and wide knowledge of every aspect of country life, gained by years of patient observation, that enabled him to put his information into the form of a walk, whereas his imitators, who were usually limited to one line of nature study, would trip up on some detail, showing that they were not conversant with the countryside as a whole.

During this time, letters were being received by the BBC showing that as they went on their walks, calling to see Mrs Fletcher at the farm, or meeting the gamekeeper on his rounds, listeners imagined that the broadcast was taking place out-of-doors. This was a surprise to Romany. The BBC had never stated that it took place outside, but if he was presenting it so realistically that they were following him into the woods and fields, he would emphasise the illusion still further. Thus it was that, instead of the customary Children's Hour introduction, the announcer merely said, "And now, children, we are going out with Romany," and a deliberate pause was then made before voices were heard fading in from the country lane. When the broadcast was over, instead of the usual illusion-dispelling announcement that "Those taking part included Mary Smith as the fairy godmother, etc.," their conversation faded out in the middle of a sentence, and the listener naturally imagined that they were continuing their walk. So cleverly was it done that even some of the BBC officials told Romany that when listening to other programmes they visualised the studio in which they were taking place, but the moment that Muriel and Doris's voices faded in, they immediately found themselves walking along the lane to meet him.

This reaction of the public, together with the liberty allowed him by the BBC, all combined to give him the atmosphere he wanted, for the listeners had inadvertently done for him what he could not do for himself. Had our English climate been kinder, and the BBC prepared to use the microphone out-of-doors, it would have been just as easy, and more satisfying for him, to have taken them for a real walk, but it would not have been so instructive, nor as effectively done in the short time at their disposal.

The time had now come for Olive Shapley to leave the Children's Hour, and none regretted her departure more than my husband. Thus, one organiser followed another, and still the Romany walks went on. Nan Macdonald, who arrived in 1937, proved not only most capable and punctilious over details, but appreciative of the artistry of the programme.

It was not until the following year that Romany gave his first broadcast to 'All Regions.' How strange it sounded to Northern listeners to hear Nan explaining who Romany was, and the meaning of the word '*vardo*.' To our amusement, some of his new listeners wrote him encouraging letters on his first effort, but it was not long before the programme gripped the imagination of his wider public, and he became a national favourite.

When war broke out, his troubles began. Trying to get into the BBC was like getting into a fortress. A soldier with fixed bayonet guarded the entrance, policemen scrutinised our passes, the stairs up which we had so often run when late were barricaded, and keen-eyed commissionaires met us as we stepped out of the lift. They knew Romany well, of course, but those on guard below did not, and often when he arrived alone, he would have forgotten his pass,[3] and they would have to telephone up to make sure that this unusual-looking man, accompanied by a dog, had no evil intentions.

It was during some of these waits that he made friends with a fine-looking young policeman, and their mutual interest in cricket and outdoor life made the time pass quickly. On his arrival at the BBC on the Tuesday after the severest of the Manchester blitzes, he was distressed to hear that this man had been killed by a landmine whilst on duty.

Then came the war-censorship of his script, and what was worse, not a word must be added after it had been typed. To be cramped in this manner was heart-breaking; it took away so much of the naturalness of the walk if he could not extemporise as he stood before the microphone. Apart from a reference to the weather, what could he tell the enemy about birds and animals that would help them, he wondered. Despite these restrictions, in his enthusiasm, he would often forget and deviate from his script. He just couldn't help it. But even Nan would smile and overlook it when his script was found to be too short, and they went on chatting until the fade-out, for the Romany programme had never suffered the indignity of having its time filled up with musical records.

Nan's work, too, was not as easy as that of her predecessors. Owing to the war call-up, the competent effects men had been replaced by inexperienced ones. As I stood with her sometimes in the listening-room, she would turn and look at me despairingly, all her gesticulations having been in vain, as a record of a running stream was put on so loudly as almost to drown what Romany was saying. Then, too, the more frequent introductions of country characters added to her work, for they were all novices at broadcasting.

Despite Romany's difficulties, so content was he when talking of the wild creatures he loved that, as I watched him before the microphone, I often thought that he was entirely content with his audience of two. He was certainly too absorbed in the walk to give a thought to his wider audience. Was it chance, I wonder, that Muriel and Doris happened to be in the studio on his first visit? Had he searched the British Isles he could not have found two more understanding helpers, for year in, year out, they showed the same fresh interest and laughed with the same pure enjoyment.

Wherever beauty dwells
In gulf or aerie, mountains, or deep dells,
In light or gloom, in star or blazing sun,
Thou pointest out the way, and straight 'tis won.

Keats

Chapter 14 Notes

1   These are, presumably, names that Romany used in the broadcasts. In the *Out with Romany* books they are Sleek the otter and Quill the mallard

2   Eunice calls him Jack Hollingsworth. Jack Hollinshead (1915-2019) was a sound engineer at the BBC. He started at Manchester BBC as a sound effects boy in 1930 and continued in sound engineering all his working life. He was much valued and remained, long after his contemporaries had passed on, a source of information about the Romany broadcasts.

3

```
          B.B.C. PROGRAMME PASS
    To be  surrendered on leaving B.B.C. Premises,
    after final performance.
                                    No.  4145

    Name      G. B. Evens       lls

                            NORTH REGIONAL
    Admit to B.B.C. studios in     OFFICES; M/or.

    Issued by           d.R.A.M.Hl

    Period of Validity       7 . 12. 43 .

    Signature of Bearer
          STUDY INSTRUCTIONS OVERLEAF
```

This would have been Romany's last BBC Pass as it covers a period beyond his death.

4   Apparently, Raq was not always quite so well behaved as we are led to believe. In the end, unless he was actually needed in script he was banished from the studio.

Doris Gambell

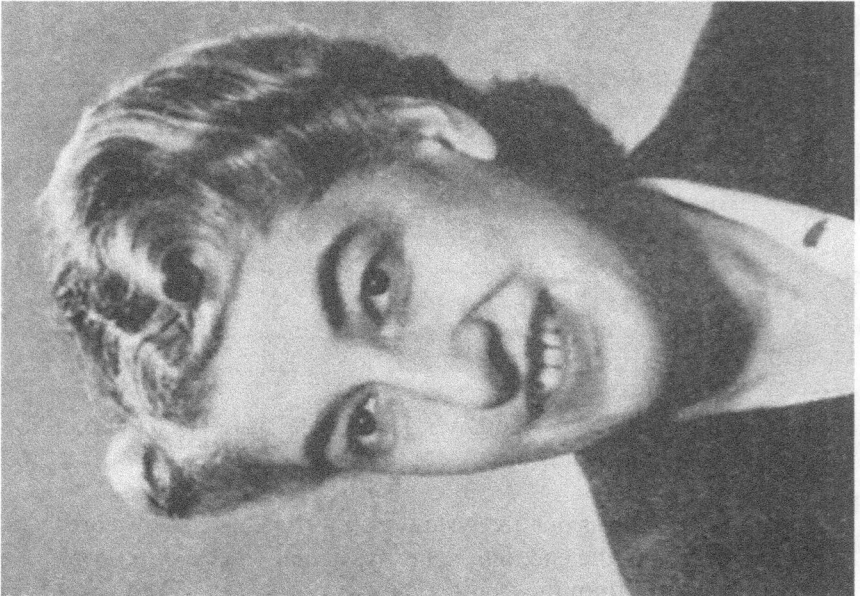

(1948)

Muriel Levy

Chapter 15

What his Listeners Thought

In one of his books, T S Lambert, a former Editor of *The Listener*, sums up the ideal broadcaster as one who has sympathy, simplicity and freshness. These words recur in many of the letters received from listeners.

"Often, when I have felt depressed, the sympathy in his voice has cheered me." "The broadcast was so real and moving and his voice so full of tender feeling." "My invalid sister seemed to forget every ache and pain the moment she heard him speak."

The simplicity and freshness of the walks is best expressed in a letter which appeared in *The Listener*. "Many years ago, I vetoed the suggestion that we should purchase a receiving set with the excuse that it would be certain to need a new valve when one of the children needed a pair of new shoes. Shortly afterwards . . . I heard Romany in the Children's Hour, and that settled it. We really believed that the Romany programme was the real thing. We walked with them every step of the way; we stepped into puddles, we saw the owls up in the rafters of the barn, we saw Jim the gamekeeper coming to meet us. We had no trouble visualising the tea-table at the farm, and a look of glee went round our own table on the occasion when Uncle Eric put an egg into his pocket. I cannot say when we made up our minds that it was all astonishingly clever acting; it is enough to say that it made no difference. Those children are grown-up now; one in East Africa, one in Canada, but I can safely say they would all jump at the chance to listen again."

The talks inspired a very personal intimacy. If my favourite announcer were to visit my home, I should feel flattered, but I should receive him conventionally, and probably find myself trying to speak more precisely, but no one ever felt ill at ease in my husband's company, and in many homes he was received with an affection which almost embarrassed him. Letters from people who had never seen him just say, "We loved him dearly." "He had become as one of our family." And a Scottish listener wrote, "He was known as 'dear Romany' round here."

He was always touched to receive letters from country people penned up in towns, telling of the poignant recollections conjured up by his walks. One of them wrote, "I am a native of the heath, and now that I am exiled, the out-on-the-heath atmosphere of your walks is so real as to be almost painful." Another wrote, "Your broadcasts make me home-sick for the village I lived in when a boy."

Townsfolk wrote saying that his talks made them feel that they were missing a great deal, and that they longed to live in the country so that they might share his pleasures. These letters he found difficult to answer, and though I have not the ability to express exactly what he said, he told them that if they were to be content in the country, they must have not only a love for it, but an understanding spirit; they must be able to give something from within to their outward surroundings, and have the capacity to attune their minds to nature.

In later years, it thrilled him to receive letters from men and women in the Forces, especially those abroad, and to feel that they had not only listened to him as children, but that he had been privileged to open their eyes to a new world of beauty and interest. As they wrote of the wildlife they had seen in the hot, sandy wastes of North Africa, it touched him to read of their longing for the freshness of the cool, green fields of their homeland. Men, in lonely outposts on remote islands, told him that his broadcasts had saved them hours of boredom, for they had occupied their time watching the sea birds around them.

Taking into consideration the popularity of the walks, and the fact that it was the only original programme that had run consecutively for so many years, it was strange that, apart from publishing a few complimentary letters, they received less than a dozen lines of appreciation in the BBC press during my husband's lifetime. Though he never complained of this, I knew that it was a disappointment to him.

Consequently, when in June 1942 I showed him a copy of *The Listener*, he was both surprised and delighted to find a charming appreciation by Herbert Farjeon, the well-known dramatic critic, and author of many clever and witty revues on the London stage. After having devoted a week to listening to the Children's Hour, and commenting on the high level of the programmes in general, he wrote, "But Tuesday! I have omitted Tuesday only because 'Out with Romany,' being supreme, must be separately praised. I can't, to be plain, praise it enough......Here, I would hazard, is the BBC's best creation." My husband was delighted. To get such appreciation from a critic of his standing was worth the years of waiting.

An official of the BBC, quoted by various newspapers, said recently of Romany, "He was outstanding not merely because of his wide and curious knowledge of country life and his knack of conveying it vividly over the air, but because of a microphone technique which seemed to be natural to him. The microphone never cramped him; indeed, when broadcasting, he seemed to be almost ignoring it."

It was this technique which made his programme different from others, and I like to feel that he was the first to introduce it into broadcasting. Just as he had no special voice reserved for pulpit utterances, so before the microphone he talked and laughed as naturally as he did at home. This helped more than anything else to give the illusion that they were actually out-of-doors.

'Northerner,' of *The Yorkshire Post*, wrote, "Romany's great achievement was that he took his listeners away from the loudspeaker into real lanes, fields and woods, which never relied on word-painting for their existence." After referring to his retirement from the ministry of the Church, he went on, "It is probably true to say that his most effective ministry then began. With the microphone as his pulpit, his congregation was numbered in increasing millions. Children in city slums began to go out with Romany, and to discover the hedgehog in the dead leaves, peep into the hedge-sparrow's nest with its blue eggs, or listen to the plop of the vole under the river bank. They were entranced by the reality of a ramble which never went beyond the four walls of the studio."

The educative value of the broadcasts was shown by an appreciation received by the BBC from the late Minister of Education, H A L Fisher, and by the large numbers of school teachers who based their nature lessons on the Romany walks. Many of them not only encouraged their scholars to listen, and to read his books, but sent him batches of essays written by the children on his last broadcast in order that he should select the best of them.

In a sense it was unfortunate that the programme was limited to the afternoon, for it was of equal interest to older people. Although a calculation during that period showed that nine million adults were finding the Children's Hour as entrancing as the four million children who listened to it, the majority of business people were debarred from hearing my husband's programme. Nevertheless, the number of his adult listeners from all spheres of life increased year by year; many of them tuned in by chance, and here they were, so held by their natural longing for these simple pleasures, that they found themselves compelled to listen to the very end.

Elsie Sprott, who is head of the lecture section of the BBC, tells me that when lecturing on broadcasting in different parts of the country, appreciations of my husband's broadcasts were amongst the most frequent she received from her audiences, and that when lecturing to troops, many of the Education Officers told her that they used his talks for observation lessons when training the men.

It would be monotonous to give further appreciations, but it may be of special interest if I tell what his fellow-artistes at the BBC thought of the programme, for their listening, naturally, was in a different category from that of the ordinary listener. I must digress here to explain that though I had always been keenly interested in the theatre and in radio plays, my husband was entirely ignorant of even the names of famous stage and radio personalities, owing to his absorption in his own world to the exclusion of almost every other. People of importance in spheres outside his own were of no special interest to him, and I never remember his going out of his way to meet any of them.

When, however, he began to broadcast, I sometimes found this attitude of his most irritating, for many of the well-known stage personalities who frequented the Manchester Studio, recognising him, came up and chatted to him, and he neither bothered to remember their names nor thought it of sufficient interest to mention it to me afterwards. On one occasion while I was busy in the studio, I found that he had been having tea with Cecil Trouncer, of whom I had always thought highly. I was naturally green with envy. "Oh, was that his name?" he replied casually afterwards. "He is a charming man, whoever he is."

When Doris came to see me some months ago, she was astonished to hear that I had not at any time met any of these people, neither was I aware that he had. She laughed and said, "How like him," and then went on to tell me of some of the compliments that had been paid him. Muriel, too, in a letter wrote, "Many of them regarded ours as the finest programme with the most far-reaching effects on the air. They frequently asked, with open mouths, how it was done." Since then, however, some of these artistes have expressed their appreciations to me.

Ronald Simpson was one of these, and Laidman Browne had not only met him frequently, but had been into the Children's Hour Studio "to see how it was done." The tribute he has paid my husband is so charming that I feel I must quote it at length.

"I have never seen the Indian rope trick done, but I have been on a country ramble when sitting by my own fireside. I have explored fields and hedgerows, watched an old dog-otter teaching his youngsters diving tricks, torn my trousers on bramble bushes, had tea in a caravan – and all this on a cold, dark November evening.

"I first became acutely aware of the genius of Romany about the year 1937. I had enjoyed his programmes ever since, and, like all good listeners, I had come to accept the realism of his rambles without bothering my head as to how it was done. Then came the day of the 'Otter Family.' I found myself holding my breath as we scrambled through the brushwood to the edge of the stream. Then Muriel tore her stocking and Doris sat in a bed of nettles. I was afraid their whispered exclamations would warn the object of our stalk. Then came Romany's low caution, 'Don't make a noise. Look! Can you see him? Just by that brown stone under the bank.' I saw it all myself. For five minutes I watched that father otter pushing his youngsters in and out of the water, nudging the timid one, cuffing the quarrelsome one, darting after the adventuresome one who had headed out midstream. It was Raq that broke the spell. His bark, as he came bounding over the fields towards us, had alarmed the happy family. There was a sudden flurry of water, and when the ripples stilled against the muddy bank, there was no sign of the otters. I sat back in my chair feeling most annoyed with Raq. Why had they brought him? At this point I realised that I had been listening to a 'studio' broadcast, and yet, so completely had I been under the spell of Romany that I almost believed he was out-of-doors. But – was it a 'studio' broadcast? I listened again. The explorers were now having tea in Romany's caravan. It couldn't be from a studio. This was too real. I listened intently. Yes, perhaps it might be from the studio, and yet – no. It was out of the question. The microphone must be hung in the caravan and......In this manner I wavered for several minutes in indecision until a glance at the clock – 5.35 p.m. in wintry November – cleared all doubts as to its being an outside broadcast.

"What was there about this man that he could so mesmerise his listeners, that I, after many years of microphone experience, could be in such doubt about it? I could not think that it was entirely studio technique, merely superior work by the 'Effects' department; it was something far removed from mechanical miracles. When I met him a year or so afterwards, and watched him at work, I realised that he was one of those extremely rare people who are completely unconscious of the microphone. He never 'gave a performance,' and I am certain that he would not have liked anyone to have said that he was acting a part, for these walks were very real to him.

"All experienced broadcasters know that the microphone possesses the power of transmitting a sense which, for want of a better word, we call 'sincerity.' I find it difficult to describe how this sense can be developed and exploited, if, indeed, it can be developed at all. But there is no doubt that a few, very few, are gifted in this peculiar way. The late A J Alan was one. Romany was another. I have talked to many friends in the radio world about Romany's broadcasts and, without exception, when I have waxed enthusiastic about some particular adventure of his, they have capped me by saying, 'Oh yes, but did you hear him when they found the litter of baby foxes?' I shall never forget the delight of listening to him, and it has been a great shock to me to learn that there is only one recording of the 'Out with Romany' programme in existence."

One of the things which struck me very forcibly in the reading of these letters was that many of these busy radio stars were regular listeners to the programme. Derek Oldham wrote, "Though I never knew who your husband was, I loved him very much, and used to mark my *Radio Times* whenever there was to be another ramble." And Leslie French, after describing him as a "friendly, lovable personality," says, "The programme was one of the few that I really looked forward to with delight."

What lies behind a good deal of what I have said about my husband's lack of interest in the BBC world is expressed in a few lines from Dennis Noble; "He was in truth one of God's own creatures, so close to Nature that he was of the real fresh air, and the first breath of Spring." Though outwardly, he might be in the canteen chatting happily to these people while waiting for his programme to begin, in spirit he was already sauntering along the shadowed aisles of some wood, to be joined, presently, by thousands of others who would not experience such pleasure had his mind been on mundane things.

Nevertheless, it seems a pity, for his own sake, that he did not realise what high compliments these artistes paid him. He was vaguely aware, of course, that some of them were taking part in important programmes, but had he known that they were experienced actors, who knew everything there was to know about stage and radio technique, their commendations would have been of so much more worth to him.

I could fill reams of paper telling how much of this praise was due to the help given by Muriel and Doris, especially of their sensitive understanding of his every mood; like most artistes, he was temperamental. Herbert Farjeon has expressed it best in the article I have already quoted from *The Listener* – "Romany alone would be enough; but the two little girls! Who are these vocal geniuses? Have the voices of two children with their spontaneous wonderments, their broken exclamations, unfinished sentences, half laughs, interrupted interruptions, ever been, and will they ever be, more perfectly presented?"

They were not children, of course, but Mr Farjeon was but one of thousands who naturally thought they were. To a great many Northern listeners their identity was well known, for they had listened to Auntie Muriel and Auntie Doris in the Children's Hour before Romany began to broadcast.

It may be of interest to others to know that Muriel is married to R Fayer Taylor and has a charming small daughter called Angela. To tell of her versatility would take too long. In addition to her gifts as a broadcaster, she is a writer of children's books, plays, revues, press articles and countless BBC scripts. Doris Gambell is well known as an accomplished singer, and her services are in great demand all over the country. Her broadcasting talent had been recognised long before she began to help Romany, and Northern listeners will recall with pleasure, amongst other programmes, her clever characterisation of the small child Rosemary.

The identities of those who took the minor parts in the broadcast may also be of interest, though they would be the first to own that they were not worthy to be mentioned in the same breath as Muriel and Doris. Romany's method of choosing these people caused comment at the BBC where there were so many talented artistes available, for the majority of them were ordinary working-class people, who had never stood in front of a microphone. But his object was to preserve the illusionary character of the walks by not introducing those whose voices were well known to listeners, and to use simple, unsophisticated people as much like his own village friends as possible. As long as they did not try to improve their speech when they found themselves before the microphone he was satisfied.

Searching for likely people afforded us much interest and amusement and, after trying out several village children when on our journeys, we found the farmer's boy we wanted in our own kitchen. Jimmie, the chubby-faced, small son of my dear domestic help, Janie Widdop, was sharp-witted and, with his smeary face, unruly hair and shabby clothes, he looked exactly the part when he came down after school to fetch his mother. But we hardly recognised him on the day of his first broadcast with his shining, clean face, plastered hair and smart new suit, bought for the occasion. Nevertheless, he took his part well. Today, he is proud to be known as Sub-Lieut. James Widdop of the Fleet Air Arm.

The gamekeeper's wife we also found nearby. Clara Growther was taking part in a play in one of our church concerts and, as we sat and laughed at her broad Yorkshire dialect, we knew that our search for Betty Woods was over. Not only did her personality make her the centre of the stage, but she talked as unaffectedly in public as she did when we visited her in her unpretentious home in Farrars Court. When before the microphone she was self-possessed and restful, which to Romany mattered a good deal. Of her first impressions of the studio she says, "Ah allus tried, when ah were theear, to mind mi own business, an' not speeak till ah were spokken to. Soa, ah tuk all in, and said nowt." Good old Betty. How well she understood Romany. I could never under-stand why she would not come with me to the canteen and have a cup of tea beforehand, but she now tells me that she was so utterly bewildered by the ramifications of the countless corridors that "Ah were that flayed a gettin' lost, ah felt if ah left it, ah sudn't get back ageean afoor red leet went on. Yer see, tha's that many places, yer could sooin looise yersen." So that was it.

How we found a husband for her in Jim, the gamekeeper, was more unusual. Among the commissionaires at the BBC, who for years had taken us up and down in the lift, was Pat McGlyn. I often wondered why Romany deliberately chatted with him at length each time he saw him, but Sergeant McGlyn was hearty, bluff of speech, and in build the big, burly type which suggests a gamekeeper. Surely, we thought, seeing that he had retained his natural mode of speech after years of contact with BBC personalities, he would not attempt to imitate them when before the microphone. Finally, we decided to try him out, and found that we were right. So accustomed was he to going in and out of the studios that the microphone presented no terrors for him. In fact, at times, he had to be restrained when, in his easy-going manner, he would add lines to his script which were not always appropriate. However, he made a good gamekeeper and remained in the programme for many years.

Finding the right boy to take the part of the evacuee took longer. We even tested some of the more intelligent boys at the local school. None proved suitable, but it was amusing how some of them hovered round our garden during the next few days in the hope that we had not yet made our choice. Then it was that Romany remembered Rennie's son, Gordon,[1] who was working with his parents in a mill at Nelson. He was alert and, like his father, had shared outdoor adventures with Romany. We wired, and the reply came back, "Gordon will be proud to help you."

I can see him now waiting for me outside the BBC on the day of his first engagement. Unfortunately, there was no empty studio available where I could rehearse his part with him beforehand, and we finally found ourselves in the gallery of the Concert Hall, where so many instruments were being tuned up that we could hardly hear each other speak. This worried me, but the broadcast soon showed me that Lancashire dialect was so much a part of his everyday speech that he needed far less rehearsing than most of the other dialect characters. Nick, for it was Nick, the evacuee, that he then became, was quite unperturbed when he reached the studio, and once he was perched on his box in front of the microphone, he stuck stolidly to his script, never turning a hair in spite of the curious things that were going on around him. Even when the others howled at some of his comical sayings, he never moved a muscle.

He took his part so well that, when the broadcast was over, Wilfred Pickles came into the studio and asked him to take a part in a play in which he was interested. Nick's eyes lit up with pleasure at the thought of becoming a future radio star, but Romany and I exchanged glances. We knew that if his voice was recognised by listeners as Romany's Nick, the whole validity of the broadcast would be imperilled. "Do as you like, but if you accept, I shan't be able to use you again," Romany said. As it happened, his father was in the studio on that day, and before Nick could reply, he said "Certainly not. It's an honour for you to be in Romany's programme." Poor Nick! We felt sorry for him, for it might have led to many BBC engagements, but the popularity he afterwards gained, and the importance of being besieged for autographs after being written up in his local paper, more than compensated for the disappointment.

The farmer and his wife we found in later years near our new home. While Romany worked in his garden, everyone who passed exchanged greetings with him. Amongst these was John Gore, the respected caretaker of the Council Offices. As Romany leaned on his spade, John would comment on the size of our turnips or bemoan the depredations of the caterpillars on our cabbages, and all in such a slow, drawling, lengthened voice that it was not long before we had decided on him for the part of Johnson, the farmer.

Then, too, we had often been treated to some good mimicry of Lancashire dialect by our near neighbour and friend, Winifred Ashworth, for having been brought up in Burnley, she found it easy to relapse into the broad vernacular she had been accustomed to hearing in her youth. Both these characters proved a great asset to the Romany programme, but unfortunately, they were brought in too late to gain the success that they deserved.

The only others I can recall who took the country character parts were Janet Beith, who made a most admirable farmer's wife as Mrs Fletcher, and Wilfred Platt, the son of Romany's friend at Northwich, as the farmer.

I had almost forgotten the most important, to me, of all the outside helpers, for, with the idea of introducing a younger child to ask the more simple questions, Romany brought our daughter June into the broadcast on several occasions. Though she was only fourteen at the time, she took her part well, but the curious thing was that, contrary to our expectations, her voice over the air sounded older than those of Muriel and Doris. However, not only had she experienced the thrill of broadcasting with her father, but as we had written to her school to get permission for her to return late on account of her first engagement, she spent her first few days surrounded by an admiring crowd, and climbed several rungs of the ladder of school importance.

The BBC received many requests that the programme should be broadcast either in the evenings or on Sunday afternoons, "so that Father can listen to it," for many a father arrived home just before six o'clock to find his wife and family in a state of tense excitement as they listened to some adventure. On one occasion a man wrote to say that on returning from work one evening, he banged the front door behind him, and was reprimanded by his small child whispering, "Hush, Daddy. Muvver's out wiv Romany."

An experiment was therefore made one evening in June 1939, but it was not repeated, because Romany neither wished to sever his connection with the Children's Hour nor to dispel the illusion of its being an outside walk by broadcasting on dark evenings. His loyalty to his own department was also one of the reasons why he refused to broadcast for Radio Luxembourg, another being that their advertising methods would have entirely spoilt the atmosphere of the walks. Why it was never included in the Sunday afternoon Children's programme to reach a wider public he never knew. I think those in authority considered it too non-religious for the Sabbath day. And yet, though he never mentioned religion, he seemed to convey the inner meaning behind everything good and beautiful, for he had both sight and insight.

Having already referred to my husband's BBC mail,[2] it may be of interest to tell what listeners wrote about. A great many told of the pleasure his broadcasts were giving, and recounted personal experiences on country walks. Some described unusual things seen, and asked him to identify them. It was incredible how vague many of these letters were; the colour of a bird was described but no mention made of its size or shape. The trustful letters from children were delightful, especially when they wrote, "I want to be a naturalist like you when I grow up. Can you tell me what I must do?" Though loth to disappoint them, he always advised them to treat nature study rather as a hobby, because he knew that unless they had the ability to impart their knowledge to others, a livelihood was impossible.

Sometimes as I carried the breakfast tray into the dining-room, I would see him chuckling over a quaint drawing sent by a tiny child of a four-legged creature, meant to be Raq, or almost in tears as he read of the joy his walks were bringing to some bedridden listener.

When breakfast was over, it was my duty to sort out and deal with his mail. Owing to the urgency of many of the letters which dealt with his lecture engagements, those from listeners usually had to be put on one side. There were, however, some which could not be ignored.

"My little boy and I are spending a week in Halifax. May we come and see you and Raq?"

"I have caught a baby hedgehog. What shall I feed it on?"

"I have bought one of your books for Mary's birthday. May I send it to you to be autographed?"

"The fish in my aquarium are dying. What shall I do ?"

"My wife and I have listened to your broadcasts for many years. We have a week's holiday from next Saturday. Do you think Mrs Fletcher would take us in at your farm?

"A yellow-hammer in our garden has deserted her nest of young ones. What shall I feed them with?"

"We are so pleased to hear you are lecturing here next Thursday. Will you come and have tea with my family and bring Raq?"

Children of all ages concocted letters merely to get his autograph in reply. Sometimes these would become a burden, for a small boy would write from a Prep School, and as soon as he received the autograph, letters would pour in from the rest of his class. Those from tiny children were enchanting. They usually began with simple phrases followed by more mature ones, showing exactly where mother had been called to the rescue to help with the letter, if not the spelling.

There were also a few not so easy to classify, some of which ran:

"Mary has a beautiful singing voice. Could you give her an introduction to the BBC?"

"I am sending you a nature poem that I have written and hope to hear you read it over the air next Tuesday."

"Pamela and Dennis would like to come with you on one of your broadcast walks. Can you arrange it?"

"I am sending you by registered post the manuscript of a book on country life which I have written, and shall eagerly await your opinion of it."

"Could you tell me where I could buy a dog like Raq?"

"If you are travelling with your *vardo* anywhere near our farm, will you call and see us?"

Added to these letters there were often those from narrow-minded people, and cranks of all kinds urging Romany to read the literature they enclosed and include the information in his broadcasts. Saddest of all were those from poor, demented people who, hearing the sympathy in his voice, would pour out their troubles to him in utterly unintelligible language.

Although we were generally unable to reply at once to letters from listeners, to my knowledge not one of the thousands he received during the years he broadcast remained unanswered. Though this part of my husband's mail was always of interest, I often dreaded the parcel post, for autograph books followed each other in constant procession, together with Romany books to be signed. Packing them up and re-posting them was a never-ending job. When they arrived, these parcels were easily recognised, being mostly the same shape, but it was the smaller parcels which caused me most concern. Listeners would send not only specimens of flowers, plants and butterflies for him to identify, but I would open a box and find a repulsive-looking beetle or a dead bird, and as my husband was often away from home, it would lie about for days, getting more and more noisome. Even the postman objected to these parcels, and as he came up the garden path, he would carry one at arm's length and say, "Here's one that needs opening." Or a neighbour would sometimes take in our parcels when we were away, and we would arrive back to hear that they were sorry, but they had been obliged to open one of them because of its offensiveness. Then, from the garden shed, they would produce a decomposed rook's head, or a verminous mole.

Occasionally the parcels were sent to the BBC, and had to be disposed of before Romany arrived there. June reminds me, too, that once I put a wedding-cake box aside in order that she might share the contents with me, and recalls her horror when she opened it and found a white cockroach. On the whole, however, we preferred these dead specimens, for my husband was often too busy to examine the live ones, and they would spend their time crawling around the house in the interval.

Though there were disadvantages dealing with my husband's mail I count it a great privilege to have been able to help him with it. Most of all do I value the friendships we made through these letters, for some of these listeners who still write to me today I number amongst my dearest friends.

I thank you for your voices, thank you, –
your most sweet voices.

Shakespeare

174

Chapter 15 Notes

1   Gordon Woods, like his father Rennie, was very interested in photography, and both, became projectionists in local cinemas. Rennie's photographic speciality was birds and Gordon's insects. Gordon was elected to the Royal Photographic Society, so no mean photographer. He was very secretive about his methods whereas Rennie was only too happy to dispense advice.

2   There were, of course, floods of sympathy letters to the *Radio Times* following Romany's untimely death, many people pointing out how regrettable it was that the 'exposé' of the studio setting of the walks, and Muriel and Doris being the 'children,' happened just before Romany died. (See note 4 on page 266)

The former Broadcasting House, Manchester

The ground floor became a bank so this photo-reconstruction may not be completely accurate.

Chapter 16

Writings and Idiosyncrasies

During our early years in Halifax when my husband's journeys were within easy reach of home, I was sometimes able to go with him. Best of all, I loved the days when he was booked to preach and lecture at some village chapel. It amused me to see how he accepted these invitations with alacrity at certain times of the year. If I told him that, owing to his numerous engagements, I was refusing a certain invitation from some tiny remote chapel in the Yorkshire dales, he would say, "Oh, try and fix it in either in May or June," for these were bird-nesting months.

When the day arrived, we would get up early, and while I prepared sandwiches for our picnic lunch, he packed his camera gadgets into the car. After searching for some quiet lane or stream bank near our destination, he would light a fire[1] in readiness for boiling a kettle, and then go off on his explorations.

Raq after a Swim at Burnsall

Photo:: Ilona Longbotham

I always thought that he preached and lectured with more zest after such outings; his sparkling eyes seemed to reflect the very freshness of the fields as he described to his audiences the beauties of their own countryside.

War-time rationing has now altered the character of these Methodist functions. In those days, when we arrived at the chapel, we would see women walking round to the back entrance carrying large market-baskets, covered with spotless white cloths, and our mouths would water at the thought of the tea-tables groaning under the weight of home-made, juicy, fruit tarts and rich currant cakes.

Standing in the pulpit of the little chapel, with its well-scrubbed floor-boards, highly polished pews, and its smell of paraffin lamps, he needed little inspiration, for through the open windows he could often catch the scent of newly mown hay, or hear the thrushes vying with the creaky harmonium as we sang the hymns.

On one occasion, during an afternoon service, I noticed that he glanced more frequently than usual through one of the windows. At first I was concerned, for we had left Raq in the car, and I thought that some of the village children might have opened the door and let him out. But no, my husband was smiling. In fact, at times, he seemed almost excited. His mind was certainly not entirely on his sermon, for every now and then his eyes would light up for no apparent reason. When the service was over, down he came from the pulpit and, instead of chatting to the people as he usually did, he hurried through the vestry door. Being curious, I followed him and found him making his way down to the stream that ran through the village. When I caught him up, he was chatting to an angler who was showing him the creel full of trout he had caught during the service. He offered to lend my husband a rod, and it was with difficulty that I persuaded him that there would be disappointment if he did not put in an appearance at the tea-table.

How friendly the atmosphere of the village teas always was. There were few formalities, and almost everyone addressed each other by their Christian names. Sometimes we would find ourselves seated at a long table next to the most uncommunicative-looking people, but before I had time to rack my brain for something to say, my husband was already talking and laughing over this and that, for he always felt at home with country folk.

In the interval between the tea and the lecture, it is the usual custom for some hospitable person to entertain the Minister, but when the time came, Romany was never to be found; he had gone to find the nearest gamekeeper or farmer, or to hobnob with the blacksmith. And so I spent my time making apologies for him and saying that I was sure he would be back soon, though I knew that he would not return until he was due to lecture. He felt that it was a waste of time not to use every precious minute; there was so much he could learn from these people, for most of them belonged to his own world. "They've not been students of any university, but they have graduated in the lore of the countryside," he would say to me.

The more well-known he became, the more difficult he found it to slip away on these occasions. Sometimes, as I followed a few paces behind him along a stream bank, I would hear voices behind us, warning me that some of his admirers were in pursuit. With an appealing glance at me, he would stride ahead, with Raq at his heels, and disappear from view, whilst I pretended to tie my shoelace and then engaged them in conversation. Not only had my close companionship taught me how much the solitude of such a walk refreshed him, but I had often seen him unhappy when in the company of those who were out of harmony with nature. I had also seen the result of this when he lectured afterwards with less enthusiasm.

Sometimes, he was asked to take the local girl guides for a walk, for to have been out with Romany was, to many of them, the height of their ambition. He rarely refused such requests, but if they expected to see many of the things which he saw, they were usually disappointed, because they talked and laughed happily as they went along.

When he was younger, he was inclined to be intolerant of those who knew little of his pet subject. If we met a party of hikers walking briskly along a main road, looking neither to the right nor left, talking loudly as they went, he was irritated. "Eyes have they, but they see not," he would say. Some years later a friend took us over his engineering works. The marvellous ramifications of cranks, gears and shafts meant nothing to either of us. Teasingly, I whispered, "Eyes have they, but they see not." He saw at once what I meant, and in later years, if he lectured at a school where the children seemed unresponsive and ignorant of even the names of the commonest birds, instead of being impatient, his attitude was more one of pity that they lived in surroundings far from green fields and running streams.

Arriving at a village in the North Yorkshire dales on one occasion with time to spare before his afternoon service, he borrowed a rod and waders from his host and went fishing. At three o'clock the small congregation assembled in the chapel, but there was no sign of the preacher. Five minutes passed, then ten, and the stewards began to show concern. Finally, one of them ran down to the river and found Romany fishing unconcernedly, quite oblivious of the commotion he was causing. Having left his clerical suit at the house some distance away, he had no alternative but to go up into the pulpit in what he was wearing.

He was very fond of staying at Gebdykes Farm near Masham, and a letter from Mrs Gill recalls the time when he lectured at Skeeby. The following morning he went down to fish in the beck for an hour before catching the train for his next appointment. So engrossed did he become in playing a big fish, that he entirely forgot the time and was only reminded of it when his host arrived by car with his suit-case. In his excitement when landing the fish, he had gone into the water up to his waist and, having no waders, he was dripping wet when he arrived at Piecebridge Station and was bundled into a carriage by the guard. Unfortunately, the compartment was full, so he had no opportunity to change his clothes. To his relief, one by one, the passengers eventually got out and he had the carriage to himself. But he had reckoned without the guard when he stepped out at Lancaster. This man had seen a bedraggled-looking fellow in a brown tweed suit get in at Piecebridge, and now, out came a man wearing a clerical suit and collar. This looked suspicious. Romany was in too much of a hurry to make explanations, but as he walked through the barrier, out of the corner of his eye he could see the guard pointing him out to a group of porters, and he was greatly relieved to get away from the station.

My delightful outings into the country with him stand out as red-letter days, for as soon as my young, inexperienced maids found themselves left alone in the house late at night, they came and went with unfailing regularity. This, combined with his increasing correspondence and the help I was able to give him with his literary work, made it more and more difficult for me to accompany him.

By this time the Epworth Press had published, *A Romany in the Fields*, *A Romany and Raq*, *A Romany in the Country*, and *A Romany on the Trail*. My husband was not entirely satisfied with them because not only did they contain too much dialect for the average reader, but having originally appeared as articles in the Methodist press, they had not been written with the idea of being printed in book form. Parts of them, however, are very readable, and the following extract from *A Romany on the Trail* has been included by his friend H L Gee, in his Anthology, entitled, *Good in Everything*.

There is a time in Autumn when Spring seems to return. It is the time when the pine wood puts forth vivid emerald shoots, which shiver like delicate tassels at the end of the dark branches. Such a day it was when the dog and I wandered through a wood. Oak and elm, birch and sycamore spoke of waning life, but the pine tree had kept Springtime hidden in her heart to gladden us when Autumn should touch everything else with sleepy fingers.

No wood is quite like a pine wood, with its carpet of pine needles, dark brown, save where a stray sunbeam fires its brown into copper. Overhead the dark green canopy of leaves sways with majestic rhythm, sensitive to the slightest breath of the South wind, yet too proud to stoop even before the onslaught of the savage North-Easter. I can see the young saplings, self-sown, standing beyond the edge of the wood, the ling and heather at their base claiming the territory which the young pines intended to make their own. In the wood itself, the heather has had its day, for the tall giants starved it of sunshine, and it simply is not.

Here and there, patches of bracken, straining up to catch the sun, look like graceful crinolines round the tree trunks, but other vegetation only gleams in small oases – the rest is brownness. In some woods I allow Raq to roam about as he will, but in a pine wood I feel it to be sacrilege, and keep him to heel; there is a hushed awesomeness and an aromatic breath pervading all things. The tall trees arch over the rides, and the golden glory of the sun at the end of each shadowed aisle glows and shimmers.

When he had completed five years of broadcasting it occurred to a far-seeing Northerner that there were greater literary possibilities in the success of the 'Out with Romany' programme. This was the late Harry Wharmby of the University of London Press, a subsidiary company of Hodder & Stoughton. To say that he came to see us at our home in Halifax is putting it mildly. It was more like a cyclone blowing in, for a man with such energy and persistence we had never met. He just took our breath away, and when we could get in a word edge-wise to ask a few questions, we gathered that he wanted Romany to write books especially for children, and that he was quite sure that he could get his firm to publish them. At that time the broadcast was the monopoly of the North Region, so this London publishing house was unaware of its popularity. But all the King's horses could not stop Harry Wharmby from doing what he meant to do, and his firm eventually published *Out with Romany* in 1937, which was an immediate success. I feel that my husband would like me to pay this tribute to this dear, pushful, indefatigable man. He was not only loved by Romany, but was a favourite with most Northern booksellers, despite the fact that they found to their cost that it was far easier to give him an order when he called than to refuse to do so.

And so, my husband set to work to tell in story form the lives of the birds and animals with which he was intimate, and his adventures with the boy, Tim[2], are told in a series of six books: *Out with Romany, Out with Romany Again, Out with Romany*

Once More, Out with Romany by the Sea, Out with Romany by Meadow and Stream and *Out with Romany by Moor and Dale.*

Glyn [our son] also wrote one from Raq's point of view entitled, *Romany, Muriel and Doris,* but as he used some of the material of the broadcasts, it is included among the Romany books[3].

I think it must have been my husband's natural dislike of a time-table that made the fact of having to write a book a burden to him. It was not that he did not enjoy the actual writing when he sat down to it. He would have been happy if, when the publisher called, he had said, "Any time will do, this year or next. Do it when you feel like it," but when he said, "We'd like it by the beginning of March," a harassed look always came over his face. How could he work to a time-limit? I knew exactly what would follow. The next morning he would get up early and start on it at once, just to get it out of the way, for it always hung over him like a cloud until he had finished it. The speed with which he wrote a book was incredible, for though with continuous proof-reading it was usually nine months before we had seen the last of it, by writing several hours each day he usually finished it in about three months. Radiant though his smile often was, it was nothing to the one he wore when he brought me the last chapter. He was free at last to get back to his hobbies.

One of his peculiarities was that once he had written a book or article, he lost all further interest in it, and it was an understood thing that he would not see it again in any form. He would hand his manuscript to me and say, "Make any corrections or alterations you like," knowing that I would not presume to improve on his knowledge of wildlife. But the curious thing was that he did not ask to see what I had done, nor do I ever remember his reading either a printer's proof, or a book or article when published. There was, however, one thing that never bored him. When a book was completed, and illustrations were needed, he would spend hours rummaging through his hundreds of photographs of birds and animals to find those worthy of inclusion, and for days they would be strewn all over the study floor whilst we decided first on this one and then on that.

We had always imagined that books for children were simple to write. Certain types may be, but to include every fact one knows about a bird in a life-story, and weave it in such a way that the child is not conscious that it is swallowing a complete natural history lesson, is anything but simple. It gives one little scope for descriptive or imaginative writing, for one cannot become lyrical over the snout of a mole or the castings of an owl. Though we were both quite aware that neither of us had any great literary ability, we were hampered by the fact that whatever else was left out, everything he knew concerning the bird must be pushed in somehow, making the story sound very forced and unnatural at times. He would come in to me and say, "I've forgotten to mention how the woodpecker uses its tail," and in order to include it, I would have to introduce more dialogue.

Another difficulty of teaching nature in story form is that almost everything takes place within a limited area and against the same background. Where an ordinary writer can vary his scenes from one town to another, and even one country to another, Romany was limited to the English countryside and, though he saw so much beauty in the hills and streams, he found it difficult not to repeat his descriptions when writing successive books. "See what you can do with it," he would say when he brought me his manuscript, and as I struggled to improve it I sometimes wished that he would take Tim to watch the humming-birds in South America or the lions in the wilds of Africa.

It is a significant fact that when beginning his last book, he said, "This is the last of this series that I shall write," for he felt that he had exhausted the number of British birds and animals whose lives were of sufficient interest to make a story of any length. I have a stranger fact still to tell, but this I must leave till later.

My husband was on excellent terms with his publishers – W Stanley Murrell, the Manager, and Henry Brown, who were also responsible for bringing out the attractive Romany calendars, and he had a particular fondness for Ewart Wharmby, who eventually took his father's place in the North. He was fortunate, too, in the artist chosen to illustrate his books and, though he had never met Reg Gammon,[4] his knowledge of birds made him examine his drawings very critically, and he would say, "This man must be a bird-observer as well as an artist."

His publishers had great plans for further publications, and he had half-completed an Annual for smaller children and a Bird Pocket Guide to assist children on their walks. They were, too, in the middle of publishing some of his stories in the form of School Readers, in the same way that Arnold's,[5] the Leeds educational publishers, had been doing for some years. This reminds me that G H Holroyd, the chief editor of this firm, was telling me the other day that he believed that my husband had introduced reading to hundreds of people who had never read a book in their lives. The interest of his lectures and broadcasts had induced them to buy the Romany books, and Mr Holroyd hazarded that there were countless homes where these had been the first ever bought.

At the risk of boring readers who did not hear my husband lecture, in fairness to him I must explain something which he would often have liked to explain for himself. Owing to the scarcity of his books in the early days, especially in the smaller towns and villages where he lectured, children constantly wrote to him for copies. We could, of course, have passed these orders on to our local bookseller to deal with, but the children wanted them autographed and, invariably, enclosed letters which required answering. This added considerably to my work, and I nearly wore my shoes out walking to and from the post office with parcels.

When he lectured for some literary society it usually happened that a bookseller in the town set up his own stall on the premises. If it was a Methodist Church, books were ordered from the Epworth Press, either by my husband or the minister concerned, and, as with all Methodist publications, the latter always benefited from the sale of them. But if neither of these methods was available, Romany sometimes took with him to his lectures a supply from our own bookseller, who received the full selling profit on every book sold. The children did not merely want to buy a book at a shop; they wanted to hand it to him personally to autograph, and to see their rapturous faces as they spoke to him and patted Raq more than made up to him for the uncomfortable feeling he sometimes had that the public might think that he was hawking round his own wares, and also depriving booksellers of their profits.

He knew that it was not his literary ability that induced the various newspaper editors to ask him to contribute to their columns, even before he made a reputation as Romany; it was his unusual knowledge of the happenings in the countryside week by week, and the humour and pathos with which he interpreted them. Perhaps I should have given more prominence to the large amount of writing he did for the press. For seventeen years he wrote two thousand words weekly to the *Cumberland News*, and his column of the same length to the *Methodist Recorder* lasted for twenty-three years. His contributions to the *Yorkshire Post* and *Huddersfield Examiner* continued for six and fourteen years respectively, and over a period of twenty-five years he must have written several million words. It may be wondered how he managed this each week, together with all his outdoor interests and public work, but he had a facile pen and never lacked material. He would draw up his big armchair before his study window overlooking the garden and fields, and the moment his pen touched paper his thoughts crystallised so quickly that he could write two thousand words without a break. As with his books, it was always a task that must not interfere with his hobbies, and so he would rise early and get it done before breakfast, or it would occupy his free mornings when away from home on a lecture tour.

It is only when thinking about it now that I can see how different he was from most people in so many respects. Artistic people usually lack money-sense, but he had an almost absurd way of ignoring it. Unless it was to pay for a new camera or some plants for his garden, I doubt if he either wrote or signed a dozen cheques all the years we were married. Figures always bothered him, and if on some rare occasion he walked into the Bank, it caused no little comment amongst the clerks. Except when going away, he rarely carried any money, and often he would arrive at a shop to find that he could not pay for his purchases.

We shared a common purse, but although I usually left a few pounds in a certain drawer in case I should be out when he needed money, he never could remember where to look for it. Though in the early days he may have known what his fixed salary was, in later years he had no idea what he was earning, for he was always averse to talking about money matters and would say with a smile, "Don't bother me with it, dear. I know everything is all right in your hands." Had I been worried, he would have been only too ready to discuss it with me, but as long as things went smoothly he merely ignored its existence. His trust and confidence was something that I valued very much. I found it somewhat exasperating, however, when I needed his advice as to how to invest some money, that he should still have replied, "Oh, you know best." Once or twice I managed to entice him to sit down while I explained things to him, but before I was half-way through, he became engrossed in his own thoughts and, before I knew it, he was sidling out of the room, saying, "That sounds all right to me." In spite of these discouragements, I did think that he would show some interest in the making of his own will. When the air-raids started and most people thought it best to make their wills, I asked a solicitor to call and deal with ours. After lunch, though I had reminded him of the appointment, I took the precaution of keeping my eye on him as he wandered around the fields behind the house lest he should forget all about it. In due course an elderly, dignified gentleman arrived. I began explaining to him what we wanted, and at the same time I signalled meaningly to Romany to come in. He was postponing the disagreeable task as long as possible. Finally, I opened the French window leading into the garden and called him. When he came in, he did not sit down, but after a few pleasant remarks he said, with one of his most engaging smiles, "You will excuse me, but my wife deals with all my business," and out he went again. The solicitor's face was a study. When the will eventually arrived, he signed it as casually as he signed an autograph book, and never even glanced at the contents. He was a transparently truthful man, and I do not remember his deliberately telling a lie. On the other hand, he had an irritating way of leaving it to me to tell white lies when necessary. He avoided answering the telephone, for the calls often concerned his engagements, which he was unable to deal with without my help. If, however, he did answer it and found himself being asked to lecture at some place to which he did not want to go, it was laughable to hear him struggling to frame his words to make them sound like the truth. In desperation he would come and consult me. "Tell them you are already engaged," I would suggest glibly. "You go and do it," he would plead, and when I had dealt with the matter, he would look intensely relieved.　He was a poor hand at prevarication. Sometimes when he was busy writing, I would tell a caller with whom I could deal that he was not at home.　The next time we met the person concerned, he would look most embarrassed, and was so sure that he would say the wrong thing should the matter be mentioned that he would mutter, "I'm leaving this to you."

I have already hinted at his oddness with regard to clothes. Though I bought everything for him except what he was obliged to try on, I had to use every wile I knew to get him to buy these. On one occasion I persuaded him to come with me to buy a winter overcoat. "Don't say the first one you try on will do," I whispered as we went inside, for this was his usual method of shopping. Unfortunately for me, the assistant recognised him and at once began to tell him how much he and his family enjoyed the broadcasts, and as their conversation on birds proceeded, I opened one showcase after another and tried to interest them both in overcoats.　When we had chosen one, and the assistant had been given several autographs for his children, we left the shop.　The following week when he. was going away, I brought out the new overcoat. He put it on, went down the path, and then came back. "This isn't the coat I chose, is it?" he asked. "It's far too heavy for me." Off he went in his old one, and he never put on the new one again.

The ritual was always the same before he went off lecturing. He would come in from the garden in his old tweed suit, and say, "There's no need for me to change, is there?" He would look at me appealingly, and glancing down at the knee of his trousers, he would say, "What's wrong with a patch?" He never gave up hope that someday he might not need to change. Then very reluctantly he would go upstairs. On his way to the bathroom he would wind up the old musical box which stood on the landing, and as it laboriously tinkled out its somewhat discordant strains, he would try to finish shaving before the last notes of *The Bluebells of Scotland* or *The Campbells are Coming* faded away. Then would follow an interval of silence. I knew just what was happening. He would be sitting on the bed struggling to remove the laundry pins from his shirt. He never could find them all. He would start putting it on, then call me, and I would find him standing helplessly with it over his head, unable to free himself because of a pin in one of the cuffs.

Like a child, he would then ask me which suit he should wear and, more often than not, he would eventually come downstairs wearing a collar that did not match the shirt, or the trousers of one suit with the jacket of another. So attached did he become to a brown, polo-necked jersey which he wore on his walks that, in order to prolong its life when the neck became over-stretched, I sewed on a press stud. Little did I know what I was letting myself in for. Sometimes I found him wearing the jersey inside out, sometimes with the fastening at the back, sometimes at the front, but wherever it was, he would always come to me to have the press stud done up, and if I wasn't about, he would go all day with it undone. During the whole of his life, press studs and safety pins, like the pins in his shirt, completely baffled him.

Packing his suit-cases when he went away for long periods was no easy matter, especially if he went by train, for he never could repack them tidily. However large the cases, I knew full well that he would arrive home with half his things tied up in a separate parcel, or if he travelled by car, I would find the surplus on the back seat. I moaned as I unpacked his crumpled best suit, for, in spite of the fact that time and time again he had knelt beside me on the bedroom floor watching how I folded his trousers in their creases, he was quite incapable of doing it himself, though he had the best intentions in the world. All this seems the more incredible because he was so skilful with his hands in other ways.

As he wore his best dark lounge suit only on Sundays, I then devised a scheme of my own. If he left home early in the week, I would post the suit to his week-end hostess and ask her to superintend the repacking and forward it to his hostess of the following week-end.

He did not often wear a hat, but when he did take one away with him he invariably came home without it. So frequently did it follow him that I always recognised the familiar square shaped parcel when the postman handed it to me, and said to myself, "It's that hat again." It was indeed fortunate that his hostesses were mostly friends of his who knew his vagaries, for one of them tells me that she posted it after him at least three times.

He would rarely open a conversation on anything trivial, though he would listen with interest to my small-talk. And yet when entertaining friends his personality made him the centre of every conversation and he had such a fund of unusual information and such, a convincing way of telling anything, that what other people said seemed of little interest when he was in the room. Even the way he sat put people at their ease. He would almost lie back in his armchair, stretch his long legs half way across the hearth, take out his pipe and, before he had started talking, his smile had become contagious. But though he was always well-informed on the events of the day, and knew all that his newspapers could tell him, nothing, would induce him to be drawn into a debate or discussion. In fact, he seemed to lose interest the moment a subject was opened out at any length, and I would see a far-way look come into his eyes which meant, "Go on talking. I've much more interesting things to think about." As the discussion proceeded it amused me to see him glancing restlessly around as though planning some means of escape. Then it came, as if reluctantly – "Oh, I must take Raq for a walk." What hours of boredom his dogs have spared him!

When at home, with his more intimate friends, they would sometimes chaff him that he was not a good conversationalist. In one sense, this was true, for he was not a good listener, unless the subject was one which interested him. He would reply politely to some remark, and then as the conversation proceeded, his comments seemed to become tinged with vagueness, and he would finally retire into his own thoughts in spite of my efforts to recall him into the general conversation. More disconcerting still, he would often return from his dream-world and open a completely different topic before the other was concluded. This was particularly noticeable at meal-times, for our dining-table usually overlooked the garden. June and I would chat away for several minutes; then one of us would ask him a question and find him gazing intently out into the fields. We would exchange knowing glances, and carry on. But when relatives or near friends were having a meal with us, I sometimes found it embarrassing if, in the middle of a conversation, he suddenly got up and fetched his field-glasses to examine some distant bird. Nevertheless, it was a great relief to me to feel that I could always rely on him to be the perfect host on more formal occasions.

When living with a person, one rarely looks at his life in retrospect. One is inclined to isolate the incidents of daily life rather than view them against their proper background. Though June and I have laughed a good deal when recalling his idiosyncrasies, I am bound to confess that, lovable as my husband was, the busier I became, the more exasperating I found them. The fault was partly mine, for in our earlier days I had laughed at his oddities and encouraged his helplessness. No wonder he was hurt when, in the middle of writing a batch of letters to catch the post, I told him abruptly that he must find his own hammer or field-glasses. This, of course, was one of the penalties we had to pay for his increasing public work, which not only turned our home into an office, making it impossible for me to share many of the carefree pleasures of earlier days, but caused the first rift in our married life.

Looking back, I can see now that he was not meant to be tied down to the conventions which enslave most of us. His ancestry, his artistic temperament and his natural leanings were all towards a life of freedom. I can see, too, why he often appeared to be self-centred. Having been bound down by town-existence for so many years, the marvel was that he found time to absorb the knowledge which afterwards provided other people with an escape from the fetters of city life.

I knew the stars, the flowers, and the birds,
The grey and wintry sides of many glens,
And did but half remember human words
In converse with the mountains, moors and fens.

John Millington Synge

Chapter 16 Notes

1   To light a fire (*yog*) where one stops (an *atchin tan*), is a truly Romani trait.

2   The character Tim was substantially built on the boy George Swalwell. See note 3 on page 239.

3   Reg Gammon's illustrations are an important part of the *Out with Romany* books. They provide accurate portrayals of the birds and animals Romany talks about.

4   E J Arnold also produced a series of Broadcast Echoes – books related to established programmes. Romany provided *Walks with Romany* as No25 in the series. See page 292.

The Log Fire (yog)

Photo: R Nicholson

Chapter 17

His Gypsy Ancestry

One day I was walking with my husband and his mother along one of the Liverpool streets, when she referred to a clergyman who was coming towards us as a *rashai*.[1] Although they frequently interspersed their conversation with Gypsy words – *rokkering* in Romani, as they called it – this was the first time that he had heard her use this one, and knowing that it was derived from the Sanskrit word for priest, he began to take a new interest in the Romani language. It may not be generally known that there exists in this country a Gypsy Lore Society[2] whose work it has been to collect all available information regarding Gypsies, and many books have been written on the subject. Little has been found out about them before the early fourteenth century, when they were first heard of in Europe,[3] but a study of their language has proved that they originally came from some part of India.[4]

The first record the Society has of the arrival of Gypsies in England is early in the fifteenth century. Though in the seventeenth century Smith was a Gypsy name, owing to intermarriages, and the fact that a Gypsy often adopted his wife's surname, especially if he had been breaking the law, it is not possible to trace our Smith family farther back than to Romany's great-grandparents, Jim and Elizabeth Smith. But as Jasper Petulengro,[5] beloved of Borrow, was one of the chiefs of the East Anglian clan of Gypsies, and his real name was Ambrose Smith, it is not impossible that Cornelius, who roamed the lanes of Cambridgeshire, may have been one of his descendants.

In collecting information about my husband's ancestors, I was naturally anxious to find out if he had inherited his nature leanings from any of them, but I was not optimistic, for he himself had never met a Gypsy with whom he could converse on the subject. The idea that they have an instinctive love of birds and animals is a fallacy.[6] Brian Vesey Fitzgerald, the editor of

The Field, who has been intimately connected with them for years, tells me that he has found it extremely rare, except for a natural care of their horses.[7] Incidentally, the views which he expresses on their character and fortune-telling in his book, *Gypsies of Britain*, entirely coincide with those of Romany.

My husband's relatives assure me that he was the first and only member of the family to show any interest in the ways of wild creatures, and this is borne out by the fact that when Cornelius's children left their caravan life, they showed no desire to live in the country even when they had the means to retire. Many people naturally imagined that, being a truer Gypsy than he, his mother would share his outdoor interests, but she was chiefly interested in his public work, and during the twenty-two years he had his caravan she only saw it on one occasion. His sense of nature was acquired through his own personal experiences when trailing the fox as it loped its way through Cholmondeley Woods, following the tracks of the otter along the bank of the Eden or patiently watching the curlew as it nested in the marshy land beyond the farm.

Nevertheless, he did inherit from his mother his charm of manner and, above all, the most valuable of his gifts – the unusual quality of his voice; convincing, persuasive and full of sympathy. This convincing tone was not always to our advantage, for not only did it make the most commonplace remark sound profound, but not until our children were old enough to doubt their father's infallibility did I dream of questioning any of his statements, though they often ran counter to my ideas of logic and common sense.

What I have said about this quality of his voice applies also to his Uncle Rodney, and I would even hazard that had it not been for this gift, none would have heard of the Smith family. Even the fascination that Gypsies seem to have for most people was of little importance in comparison. What an advantage it gave my husband in his broadcasting and public speaking; he was well-informed on his subject but he had not the scientific knowledge of some of the great naturalists of his day. What an asset it was to his mother and uncle in the persuasion of their converts; they were not more spiritually minded than the clergy and ministers whose half-empty churches they filled. But their voices! Who could resist them? Although I knew the pathetic story of their mother's death by heart, the first time I heard one of them tell it in public I shed copious tears. I attended scores of their meetings, and despite the fact that I deliberately steeled myself against this story, the effect of the pro-longed sob in their voices always made me fumble for my handkerchief.

A Joke with Uncle Rodney (Gipsy Smith)

Photo: Walter Scott

These missions often caused disheartenment amongst the clergy and ministers concerned, and dissatisfaction amongst members of the congregation, who were inclined to compare the methods used to the disparagement of those to which they were accustomed. After one of these missions I remember a very conscientious, hard-working young minister coming to see my husband in a state of great mental distress. He was convinced that he was a failure, that he must change his methods or give up his work. My husband, to his surprise, laughed at him and assured him that though his relatives were eminently fitted for Mission work, they had neither the training nor intellectual ability to occupy his pulpit year after year.

But to return to my husband's interest in nature, he added a great deal to his knowledge when he began to photograph wildlife. His camouflaged hiding-tent enabled him to get close to a nest, and though patience was not one of his virtues, he would sit in it for hours on end. One afternoon I was sitting on a hedge-bank some distance away from him. From time to time I made a point of looking round to see if there was anything which might interest him, but saw nothing. I was very astonished when some hours later he emerged from his hide-out and handed me a press article of two thousand words entitled, 'Seen through the spyhole of my hiding-tent.'

Knowing when and where to look for a thing was one of his gifts. Walking through a wood on a bleak March day, I would see nothing but coarse, brown bracken, but he would search beneath the undergrowth and show me tender green fronds, or the first fresh spikes of a bluebell pushing through the carpet of moss. When the birds had mated, he would lift the very branch of a fir tree from which the fragile nest of a goldcrest was suspended, or walk straight to a furze bush and disclose the speckled pale blue eggs of a linnet. He had only to turn his head to see something of interest. It was almost uncanny the way he sensed things. Stirrings in a tuft of grass I naturally thought were caused by the breeze, but he knew better, and he would find a shrew mouse lurking beneath it. He would notice a branch swinging slightly out of rhythm with its neighbours, and, sure enough, a linnet would be swaying on it. Sometimes he called Raq to heel unnecessarily, I thought, but a few paces ahead he would show me the gamekeeper's deadly trap hidden from view in the brushwood. A sudden change in the direction of a bird's flight would convey nothing to me, but to him it meant danger, and he would run ahead just in time to see a fox slinking up a hedge-side. There never seemed a time of year when he could not find something. To him this was life, and what he had left behind in the town an existence.

Though he specialised in the study of birds and animals, he had only a smattering of knowledge of butterflies and insects. He knew more about river and pond life, for had he not sat many hours by the Cheshire meres and Border County lochs? There was little he did not know about the work of country people; he could discuss the rotation of crops with a farmer, pheasant-rearing with a gamekeeper; he knew something of country lore, of the portents of coming rain when he saw rabbits feeding earlier than usual, or a waterhen[8] strengthening her nest against the coming flood. Of botany he knew little; simple country flowers lost their charm if long botanical names were used, and he would talk of jack-by-the-hedge, travellers' joy, poor man's weather-glass and lords and ladies.

He had exceptional eyesight for long distances, and when up on the moors could recognise a buzzard long before I even saw it as a dot against the clouds. His unerring sense of direction, his instinctive perception of the contours of a twisting lane, never failed him, and his ability to see far ahead in the darkness, all enabled him to drive his car almost as quickly at night as in the day-time. Once he had made a journey, he rarely forgot the way: his landmarks were not the inns and churches, but some giant tree or distant hill. One of my weaknesses is a map, and when I was with him I liked to follow our route. Had it not been for the pleasure it gave me, I might as well have put it away, for he rarely looked at one himself and trusted his sense of direction and the lie of the country rather than any information of mine. It was sometimes exasperating when he turned off in a totally different direction from the one I suggested, but invariably in the end he was right, and we always got to our destination more quickly by his methods than by mine. I would study my map surreptitiously, because I knew he liked to point out things of interest on the way. "Oh, you've missed that kestrel. Put the map away," he would say teasingly.

His keen powers of observation also stood him in good stead in remembering faces, and he could usually recognise people with whom he had had any definite contact. He had, too, the peculiar gift of being able to recall both the sound of the voice and the mannerisms of any person he had known even in his youth. On one occasion, when in a railway carriage, he noticed that the man seated opposite to him twisted his hand in a peculiar way when lighting his cigarette. He looked at him. Yes. There was a resemblance. "Do you know so-and-so?" he asked, referring to one of his college friends. "He is my brother," came the reply.

We were often asked whether either of our children inherited my husband's interest in nature. Unfortunately, they did not, but they both knew much more about wildlife than the average child. He taught me, too, a great deal, despite the fact that I was town-bred and came from a family which had no interest in the subject. Though what I know today is but a very little of what he knew, whenever I go for a country walk I can say with thankfulness, "One thing I know, that, whereas I was blind, now I see."

He loved birds and green places and the wind on the heath,
and saw the brightness of the skirts of God.

Inscription on W H Hudson's Gravestone

Chapter 16 Notes

1   *Rashai*, or *rashi*, can also be used as a proper noun. One of the editor's Romany friends always addresses him thus.

2   The Gypsy Lore Society, founded in 1888, to which Eunice refers was taken over in 1989 and is now based in America. Today Romanies would turn to the Romany and Traveller Family History Society, founded in the 1990s, to research their roots.

3   The first written record of Romanies in Europe is AD1100, but they were probably present earlier than that.

4   The Punjab area of Northern India.

5   The name Petulengro is basically Smith in Romani, *petul* being horseshoe, or by extension horse's hoof, and *engro* a person or people, ie, someone who shoes horses, a smith (blacksmith).

6   Whilst Gypsies may not love wildlife, they are knowledgeable enough of their ways when it comes to poaching!

7   As well as great regard for horses, many Gypsies, albeit not all, are proud of and take good care of their dogs, bantams and pet song-birds.

8   Waterhen is a colloquial name for the moorhen.

Gypsy Encampment – Waggons

Gypsy Encampment – Trailers

(Lorries and trailer caravans began to take over from horses and waggons in the 1950s)

Paintings by Beshlie

Chapter 18

Lectures

In the many appreciations of my husband which appeared in the press, he was referred to as a broadcaster, naturalist, preacher, writer of books and contributor to various newspapers, but little mention was made of the large part that lecturing played in his life. In later years his journeyings took him all over the country, and there were few towns in the North and Midlands which he had not visited, many of them annually.

Although he had been arranging his own private lectures for many years, it was in 1932 that Gerald Christy, of the London Lecture Agency, asked if he might act as his agent. My husband consented, but refused many of their engagements, for, though the fees paid were much higher than he was accustomed to ask, he disliked travelling long distances for one engagement, especially as he had more work than he could cope with nearer home. It often perplexed Gerald Christy, too, that he would refuse an important Celebrity Lecture because of a promise made previously to a small church in the same town; to him Methodist causes always came first.

It was with regret that I heard a few months ago of the death of Mr Christy, for my husband was very fond of him, and found him most fair in his dealings. He was a fine type of man, and held in high esteem both by the lecturers on his list and the societies with whom he negotiated. I hear that the goodwill of his Agency has been sold to Christina Foyle who, incidentally, on one occasion invited my husband to lecture at her well-known Luncheon Club; unfortunately, he was unable to accept.

His agents, however, dealt with only a very small proportion of the avalanche of requests that poured in from Schools, Literary Societies, Churches, Luncheon Clubs, Celebrity Lectures, Rotary Clubs and a hundred and one Voluntary societies. Though it may seem a bold statement to make, I doubt if any lecturer influenced a wider public than he did during the last twelve years of his life.

His audiences were by no means limited to the type of cultured person one associates with the usual Literary Society. Many of his listeners, who would never have dreamt of attending a lecture in the ordinary way, saw his name placarded in the town, and, having enjoyed his broadcasts, went out of curiosity to see what he was like. Then, too, he often had an afternoon matinée comprising the combined schools of one town. There were, of course, times when the attendance was small; sometimes an exclusive society would limit admission to its own members, or perhaps some church, unaccustomed to spending money on advertising on a large scale, debarred his radio listeners from hearing him.

Lecturing to schools was one of his chief delights. To stand on the platform of a large hall filled with eager-faced girls or boys always brought the best out of him, and at the close of his talk they would pelt him with intelligent questions of all kinds. On the whole, he found them more alert and responsive than most adult audiences, some of whom appreciated his humour, but did not grasp the truth that lay behind so much of what he said. A great many of the letters I have received recently have been from members of the teaching profession, for they, perhaps, more than others, recognised his ability to keep children interested. Quoting from a letter from F U Woods, Headmaster of the Bury High School, "Hundreds of boys and girls who have passed through this school will for a long time keep the memory of a most enthralling and instructive lecturer, and a delightful visitor." The headmistress of the Queen's School, Chester, writes: "His lectures were a sheer delight, and all too short for my girls." My husband was booked to visit this school on 1st May, 1944, and I was very touched to receive a letter from Miss Nedham the following day, saying, "I thought that I would like you to know that we have remembered Romany today."

I well recall the day when he lectured to the girls at Cheltenham Ladies' College. June had always been so proud of her father when she accompanied him to other schools, and had seen him besieged afterwards by crowds of admiring girls and boys, but her own school was different. Parents, who seem attractive in home surroundings, often unwittingly become a source of embarrassment once they cross the threshold of one's school, and for her father to have to run the gauntlet of all her school-fellows filled her with apprehension. "Tell Daddy to talk about so-and-so and draw his best caricatures," she wrote to me beforehand, but even I never presumed to tell him what he should talk about, for it depended so much on the atmosphere he found when he arrived. Though I had attended hundreds of his lectures, I felt most uncomfortable as I sat beside her in the gallery of the large Princess Hall almost facing the crowd of girls, and sensed her tense, strained feelings. When he made them laugh for the first time, she relaxed and whispered to me, "It's going to be all right, Mummy," and though I knew that it always was all right, I, too, felt relieved. In spite of the ovation he received at the close, she left me hurriedly to find out what the reaction of her special friends had been. Not until the next morning, when we met her and she told us that everyone had enjoyed it, did I really feel happy, and only when she added, "And they thought you looked lovely in that new hat," did I remember that it was a matter of deep concern to her, too, what I looked like. I am reminded of all this by a letter from Miss Popham, the headmistress, who writes, "I think your husband was a magnificent person, who did the most wonderful work. The girls who heard him lecture when they were quite low down in the school are still speaking of it with tremendous enjoyment. He did indeed appeal to every one of us from the youngest to the oldest." Incidentally, it was Miss Popham who first introduced my husband to The People's Dispensary for Sick Animals. When ways and means of raising funds were being discussed at school, June suggested that her father might help. As a result of this, at the close of many of his lectures he made an appeal for the society, and in this way he collected about £600.

In one of her books, Vera Brittain, whose name often appeared on the same list of Celebrity Lecturers as my husband's, contrasts the highly organised, well-paid lectures arranged in America with our English methods. Referring to the latter, she writes: "As soon as anyone becomes known as a lecturer, constant pressure is put upon him by political and social organisations to make him feel a moral obligation to speak for them, usually for his expenses only, but sometimes without the offer even of these. When my English agent arranges commercial lectures for me in provincial towns, voluntary societies from the same cities besiege me with invitations to extend my visit to address them gratis. This is not because I am in any way a remarkable speaker, but because the prospect of getting something at the expense of another Organisation is irresistible to minority groups with limited resources."

Romany, too, found this a problem. "We have no funds," an elementary-school teacher would write, "but my children never miss your broadcasts. Could you bring Raq?" Or: "Could you spare an hour to talk to the blind boys and girls in this Home?" How could he resist such requests? I remember once sitting in the car waiting for him while he visited one of these Homes. When he came out, he described to me how the children at the close of the talk, had asked if they might feel him and Raq. Their pleasure as they touched his hair and face and fingered Raq had affected him deeply.

The number of such invitations which he accepted without thought of reward were countless, but perhaps his generosity in this respect was most clearly shown in the number of Methodist causes to which he gave his services. In a letter to the *Yorkshire Post*, G H Holroyd of Leeds wrote, "I could instance scores of cases of good done by stealth for which he was responsible, and there are dozens of struggling Bethels who are going to miss him sorely."

I, too, could tell of innumerable instances of good done by stealth. Cases of unexpected hardship amongst his fellow-ministers appealed to him especially, and to save embarrassment, he usually gave anonymously. Some time ago I wrote to a friend who disbursed certain gifts for him, asking him to inform the recipients why they would no longer be forthcoming and the replies include the following tribute: "So Romany was the anonymous kind friend who thought of others. I am not surprised. He little knew how his gifts helped us during those years of stringency." Another, whose Church he visited for many years without reward, writes, "I am particularly moved by this further expression of his generosity. You cannot realise what the loss of our Big Brother will mean to me and to my Church."

Ronald Howgate, whose two excellent photos of my husband appear in this book,[1] reminds me of an amusing incident. Before lecturing at a certain Nonconformist Church in Yorkshire, he went to tea with the minister and, in the course of conversation, was perturbed to hear that the latter was very badly paid, though the Church was by no means a poor one. My husband usually varied his fees to suit the financial position of each Church he visited, and so when asked by the officials what his fee was, to their consternation he doubled the amount he had intended to ask. When they fumbled around and grudgingly gave it to him, he turned to the minister and handed him the cheque, saying, "Will you accept this from me to buy yourself some books?" He had many a laugh over this afterwards, but I don't think he was ever asked to visit the Church again!

As no lecture was complete without Raq, I must digress here for a moment to describe him to those who have never seen him. He is a fairly large cocker-spaniel, in colour known as blue-roan, but actually black and silver. His good breeding shows itself in his domed forehead and low-set ears with their ridiculously long flaps. Though for show purposes I suppose his hair should not be wavy, its beautiful silky permanent wave is the envy of every woman he meets. It is no wonder that he has a noble, dignified mien, for his ancestors include Lucky Star and Wildflower of Ware, the same family from which our old Raq came. He was born on the sixteenth of July 1937, and to see the miles he runs as he chases the rabbits at the farm shows that he is as vigorous as ever he was.

Surely he must know that I am writing about his master, for he is a sensitive, intelligent creature, and almost the whole time he lies curled up at my feet. Sometimes as he rests his soft, cool muzzle on my knee, he looks up at me wonderingly with his lustrous brown eyes, as if saying, "If I could only speak, I could tell you such a lot about him." His reminiscences of their walks, and their journeys together all over the country, would, indeed, fill another book.

When his master changed from his old suit to the rough tweeds he usually wore when lecturing, it was amusing how Raq sensed exactly what was going on. He would wait at the foot of the stairs, and the moment my husband appeared, he would prance round and round the hall. Then off he would run to the garage, and the moment I opened the door of the car to put the luggage inside, he would jump up on to the back seat. Once installed, nothing would induce him to come out again. His disappointment was great if his master travelled by train and had to leave him behind, but, in time, he resigned himself to being left with me, and made the best of a bad job.

Even when I had packed his suit-cases and had everything ready for him, my husband took more getting off than anyone I know. At the last minute he would appear, grumbling as usual because he had to leave home. Down the garden path I would follow him, brushing his overcoat as I went, and then straightening his tie, for he was the most dear, helpless person imaginable. Then back he would go into the house, and walk aimlessly from one room to another. When I had piloted him out again and thought I had got him safely in the car, he would again disappear; then I would find him at the back of the house covering some favourite plant to protect it against the frost, or merely looking longingly at his garden. He was in the car at last, and the ritual almost over, except for a final check-up on odd things he so often left behind – his pen, Raq's lead, bird-whistles and, most important, the precious wallet which contained the list of his engagements. On this I had written full details of the times and places of his various lectures, where he was to stay each night, and special notes against certain places, such as, "Look out for Mary Jones after the lecture," referring to some child listener who was looking forward to meeting him, or "Enquire how Mr Smith is after his operation," or "Don't forget to call on Mrs Robinson," referring to some invalid listener with whom he had been corresponding. Yes. He understood everything, and was off at last. After waving him good-bye, and just as I was closing the garage doors, I would hear the car stop. "Where am I going first?" he would call, for his wallet was now safely tucked away. "Birmingham," I would reply, and off he would go.

During the war years, food rations bothered him a good deal. At first, I went to endless trouble wrapping up separate little parcels for his various hostesses, according to his length of stay, but this system soon broke down, for one person would refuse tea, another sugar, another had plenty of everything, and he would return home with the margarine wrapped in his best suit and a thick layer of sugar at the bottom of his suit-case. I then decided only to send rations if he was staying anywhere more than one night, but he never seemed able to sort out the parcels and invariably gave them to the wrong people. To the credit of his hostesses, be it said, he never lacked anything. So well treated was he that on his return home, he would say to me, "It's surprising how much better off other towns are for food than ours is," and I would smile to myself as I pictured the hostess concerned standing for hours in a queue to obtain some special delicacy for her guest, and possibly depriving her own family of rations.

During the latter years I was sometimes able to relieve him of fatigue by driving him to his engagements. Arriving at the last minute, as he always did, when the hall was usually packed, I would perhaps find myself squashed in some corner, from which I could see neither the platform nor the blackboard. But it was pleasure enough for me to watch the audience. Before he came in there was an air of excitement as eyes turned expectantly towards the door leading to the platform, and some of the children, in their eagerness to see him, hung perilously over the edge of the gallery. Combined with this was a sense, almost of fear, amongst the adults that he might not look like the Romany of their imagination, and there was a sigh of relief when he mounted the platform. When he began to speak, they seemed to relax still further, and here and there I would see heads turned one to another. I knew exactly what they were saying. "It's the same voice," or "Just what I thought he would look like," for no radio personality looked his part more than he did.

Sometimes when he walked on to a platform he was in such high spirits that he would look round on his audience and smile. The effect was electric. Before he had uttered a word that smile had not only captivated them, but reassured those who had listened to him over the air that he was the Romany they had already learnt to love. How often one hears of disappointments suffered when wireless favourites are seen in the flesh. Even their photographs, in some cases, are sufficient to break illusions: This mattered a great deal in my husband's case, for listeners had pictured him as tall, black-haired, full of fun and with a pleasing voice. If a stout, fair, solemn little man had stepped up on to the platform, it might have spoilt all further listening for them.

After one of his lectures a man wrote to him, "I have been a listener to your programme for. many years, but I dared not risk attending your lecture in case I should be disillusioned." His friends, however, had assured him that Romany on the platform was quite as attractive as over the air, and he wanted to know the date of his next visit to the town.

I wonder if his chairmen knew what power they possessed, for my husband was very easily influenced by his environment. As far as his audiences were concerned he was fortunate, for he had not the usual barriers of reserve to break down which most lecturers have. They were already his friends although most of them had never seen him before. But what was this chairman going to do? I wondered uneasily. Was he going to introduce him with a few words which would create the right atmosphere for his lecture, or was he going to take this opportunity of being in the limelight to air his own views on some extraneous subject? Until a chairman had finished his speech I could never relax. Sometimes a pompous, self-satisfied local magnate would get up and hold the floor for twenty minutes or more, and when he had exhausted himself he would turn round, as if thinking, "Oh yes, of course, there's a lecturer here. He'll want an innings too," and I alone knew how much it was affecting my husband. He had come on the platform so brimful of ardour, for he was never happier than when talking of the creatures he loved; then I had seen his spirits gradually drooping as the audience fidgeted restlessly in their seats, while the chairman went on and on. How hard he was going to find it to lift them again.

Then there was the opposite type of chairman who almost stood up and sat down in the same breath, having said, "You've come here to hear Romany, not me, so I will ask him to give his lecture," or "A chairman's duty is to stand up, speak up and shut up" – this always took Romany unawares, for he had various preparations to make, which he usually did surreptitiously during the chairman's address – unrolling his drawing-paper, searching his many pockets for his charcoal and whistles.

On the whole, however, he was fortunate, for most organisers chose chairmen who were in sympathy with his subject, and I could see him warming towards them as they told of their pleasure in his broadcasts, and related their own experiences of outdoor life. He cared not how illiterate or inexperienced they were if they had an understanding spirit, for he loved honest-to-goodness ordinary people.

I have now come to the most difficult part of this chapter – to describe to those who never heard him what his lectures were like. How absurd it was that they were ever called lectures, for anything more unlike the ordinary idea of one cannot be imagined. He just chatted away to his audience without a note of any kind. "What are you going to talk about to-night?" I would sometimes ask on our way there. He would laugh and always give the same reply, "It depends what they're like," for it really hurt him to talk of some of the things about which he felt most deeply to an insensitive, unimaginative audience, and he seemed to be able to sense whether the atmosphere was receptive even before he began to speak. He never varied his lecture titles. It was always, "Out with Romany," which gave him scope to choose whatever line of thought appealed to him at the moment, and though he jotted down a few notes afterwards of what he had said, he visited some societies for twelve years in succession and had not exhausted his subject.

Just as in his broadcasts he clothed his nature lessons in play and story form, so in his lectures, by his descriptive powers, the originality of the sketches he drew on the blackboard, his imitations of bird-songs and his ready wit, he provided his audience with over an hour's entertainment. I cannot explain what it was that enabled him to communicate something vital to them. I think it was his natural simplicity and unaffectedness, his human touch, his deep appreciation of everything beautiful and the fact that he had never lost his childlike sense of wonder.

With it all he was a born teacher, and he would sketch a wren as a garrulous old lady, complete with bonnet and gamp[2], and before their laughter had died away they would be marvelling at the skill and artistry with which this bird builds its perfect little domed palace, using no other tool but her bill to weave the moss into felting. Or he would depict a podgy baby owl reclining in an armchair, and the next moment they were learning that an owl has the incredible faculty of being able to swallow a bird whole and afterwards disgorge the bones and feathers all wrapped up neatly in a pellet. Artists, perhaps more than other people, will be able to appreciate his skill in being able to sketch and talk continuously at the same time, especially when he was sometimes perched up on a small box and unable to step back at intervals to see the effect of what he was doing.

Lightning Sketches Drawn by Romany whilst Lecturing

Meanwhile, Raq had been left in an ante-room guarding his master's belongings, and woe betide anyone who dared to touch them. After lying patiently all through the lecture, the moment that he was waiting for arrived at last. That loud applause from the adjoining hall meant that his master had asked the children if they would like to see him, and so great was the volume of it that sometimes I wondered if he were not the more popular. When my husband left the platform to fetch him the excitement rose, as the children in the gallery once more nearly pushed each other over the edge in their eagerness to see him first.

So accustomed was he to this ritual that when he came ahead of his master through the door, he never made the mistake of running straight towards the audience. Up the platform steps he scampered at such speed that he almost knocked over the important personages seated there. Despite the commotion, he received public adulation so often that he would sit up and unconcernedly survey the audience with solemn dignity and an almost haughty air. One could imagine his saying to himself, "I well deserve this applause. No dogs that I know have taken part in broadcasts, nor had their photographs frequently in the *Radio Times*, nor had hundreds of other dogs named after them. This is all very mystifying, but if my master wants me to sit up here, of course I must obey him, but I'm sure he'd rather be out on a quiet country walk with me."

If the crowd was a large one, I then usually made my way out to put him safely in the car until we were ready to leave. But experience had taught me that I must lock the doors and leave the windows open, for the children, after searching every corner of the building, would eventually discover him there.

Meanwhile, the lecture being over, Romany is immediately besieged for autographs. Sometimes, as the people thronged past him, he would sit bathed in perspiration while he signed his name over and over again, at the same time replying to the question of some child as to Raq's age, or patiently listening to some adult's experience on a country walk. He was such an approachable man that all types of people felt that they could talk to him.

I must digress here for a moment to explain that, as neither of us wished in any way to spoil the pleasure that my husband's illusionary bachelor existence in his caravan was giving to many listeners, we had mutually agreed that I should keep in the background as much as possible when travelling with him, except, of course, in places where his private life was known. I can fully appreciate the feelings of women married to celebrities, who only experience reflected glory, but I expect they would find it curious if, like me, they had to be completely non-existent. So realistic did some listeners find his broadcasts that more than one tender-hearted soul, when writing to him, gently hinted that he would be far less lonely in his caravan were he to marry either Muriel or Doris.

My position made him unhappy at times, for it deprived me of the pleasure of meeting many of his admirers, but to us both, the success of the broadcast came first. I could tell amusing stories of the predicaments in which this often placed me, of the times when I have had to stand at the back of the gallery, or been refused admission because the hall was "full-up." This did not worry me, for, having heard his lectures often, I preferred not to occupy a seat which might be appreciated by someone else, but the trouble was that he was accustomed to search the audience for me during the preliminaries, and to put him at ease, I had to squeeze myself in somehow. I could tell of entertaining comments made to me about him by those who sat next to me, of their superior airs when they told me that they had already shaken hands with him, or of those who became almost unpleasant if I did not reciprocate their flattering remarks, or refrained from applauding at the end of the lecture.

But I must return to Romany surrounded by his admirers, for the moment for which I have been waiting has come. I search around for some officials to control the crowd which is nearly smothering him, but being unaccustomed to dealing with emerg-encies of this kind, they have all disappeared. So I squirm my way through the throng and gently hint to those who are monopolising him that they should move on and make way for others. This is no enviable job, for some of them look at me with astonishment, wondering who this interfering woman may be. When I reach my husband, I perhaps find an elderly man, quite oblivious of others waiting, in the midst of a lengthy story of something unusual he has seen, or a charming little girl standing for several minutes gazing up at him with wide-open innocent eyes. Can this really be her Romany? It seems so heartless to move her on. But I am fully compensated for my discomfort by his look of gratitude when he sees me. Then I keep my eyes open for listeners who have written to him beforehand, and whisper to him, "This is John, who sent you the drawing of Raq," and the small boy's eyes shine with pleasure as Romany compliments him on it.

I can fully understand how it is that many lecturers find autographing too exhausting on such occasions, and refuse to do it. But my husband belonged to the Children's Hour, and he could not disappoint a child. Unless he was not well, he never refused, and I like to think that there must be thousands of children and adults all over the country today who have something personal to remind them of him.[3]

In addition to the strain of their engagements, popular lecturers are often expected by their publishers to visit booksellers in the towns they visit to autograph their stock of books. This was a sore trial to my husband, for, instead of being able to pull up his car in a quiet spot outside a town, he had to reach the shops before closing-time and then sit autographing while one assistant opened the books and another blotted them and took them away. No wonder he usually took two fountain pens with him wherever he went.

Meanwhile, Romany has signed his last book, except for the few stragglers who waylay him as he makes his way out of the building. When we reach the car, we find it surrounded with Raq's admirers. There he sits on the back seat, holding court and complacently submitting to the adoration of the children as they crane their heads through the open windows in their efforts to pat him. Though, of course, he is unconscious of his importance, the crowds around him suggest visiting Royalty.

We push our way through into the car. Then out comes Romany's pen once more as a couple of panting children, who had run home for their autograph books, thrust them through the open window. I start up the car. The moment my husband has been waiting for has now come, and as we drive off through the darkness, he revels in the cool night air after the stuffy atmosphere we have left, in being able to relax after his strenuous efforts and, most precious of all, in the silence after continuous talking.

Romany and Nick

Photo: Rennie Woods

In spite of all this, lecturing was as great a joy to him as his broadcasting. Not only was he happy in his subject, but the thrill of being able to sway the emotions and feelings of both seen and unseen crowds never left him. There were times, however, when he had to fulfil an engagement after having been in bed all day with one of his severe headaches. "It's like a skewer going through my brain," he would say miserably as he got out of the car. Sometimes the stimulating effect of a crowded audience and his increasing interest in his talk would make him forget it, but at other times, though he laughed and outwardly appeared to be on top of the world, I could see that he was in pain, and I would sit anxiously watching the hands of the clock creeping on as I waited for the lecture to end.

Only those who are engaged in public work of this kind can understand how exacting it is. A business man can usually put aside his work when he is unwell, but a public speaker not only cannot disappoint a waiting audience, but, however ill he feels, is expected to interest, uplift and often amuse them. Few public entertainers, I am told, can stand the strain of a turn lasting more than twenty minutes, but my husband must have had a very strong constitution, for by putting the whole of his nervous energy into his talk, he held his audiences for well over an hour.

Yet in spite of these discomforts he had many compensations, for no man was more blessed with kind and hospitable friends than he. Some of the many hundreds who entertained him were Methodists, some Catholics, some non-churchgoers; all that mattered was that they enjoyed his broadcasts or his preaching and appreciated his company. It would take a whole book to tell of them all, but there were certain homes where, over a period of many years, he knew that he could stay indefinitely as a welcome guest. At the risk of boring my readers I feel I must enumerate these people, for I want them to know what the quietude of their home life meant to him, and how grateful I was for their solicitous care, especially when he was not well. There were the Turners and Eva Hardy of Acomb, the Domleos of Derby, the Howgates of Dewsbury, the Garrs of Nottingham, the Taylors of Middleton, the Fairweathers of Clitheroe, the Dodshons of Spennymoor, the Holroyds and the Battys of Leeds and Birmingham, the Coopers of Walkeringham, the Bradleys of Cardiff and of Newark; the Hartleys and Leighs of Bolton, the Beatties and Leslies of North-ampton, and the Craggs of Riding Mill. May God bless them all, and the many others whose hospitality lightened his journeys, for his lectures and preaching engagements took him to well over nine hundred towns and villages. What a comfort it was to him, after moving from one hotel to another, to reach the sanctuary of one of these homes and feel that he could settle down for a few days and become one of the family.

On one occasion when on tour in the Newcastle-on-Tyne district, he had booked a room at a country inn and was on his way to explore the countryside when the occupants of a small cottage recognised him, though they had never seen him before.

"Isn't it Romany?" they asked. "We've always listened to your broadcasts." When they heard his plans, they insisted on his cancelling his room and staying with them. After entertaining him royally for a day or two, they were almost indignant when he asked how much he owed them, and made him promise to stay with them whenever he was in the district. This was the beginning of his friendship with the station-master of Riding Mill and his wife. Incidentally, it was five-year-old John Craggs who, after telling his parents how much he loved them, added, "And I love Jesus, Santa Claus and Romany next best."

I think that he must have given all these people a great deal of himself in return, judging from the letters which I have received. "It is no exaggeration to say that it was a sheer pleasure to have your husband. Of all the guests we have ever entertained, he was outstandingly the easiest and most delightful one, and his memory is one which will not easily fade."

"After each visit to our home, he left my little family radiant with his personality for some time after his departure."

"We always consider this house enriched because he stayed with us."

And perhaps the nicest compliment to a departed guest comes from a distinguished Methodist Minister: "It has been my happy lot to stay in homes all over the country that were radiant with memories of your husband."

Friendship is a sheltering tree.

Coleridge

Chapter 18 Notes

1   Being such 'well-known' photographs of Romany, it has been deemed prudent not to include them in this edition for copyright reasons – at least one of these images is in the National Portrait Gallery – but to identify them, here are partial images:

Ronald Howgate wrote an article about Romany (GBE) which is held in the Oxford Dictionary of National Biography.

2   Gamp is an old-fashioned word for a large umbrella.

3   One young lad (Romany was staying with the family) had an unusual autograph book which required a thumb print. Romany obliged and also gave the boy an illustrated autograph.

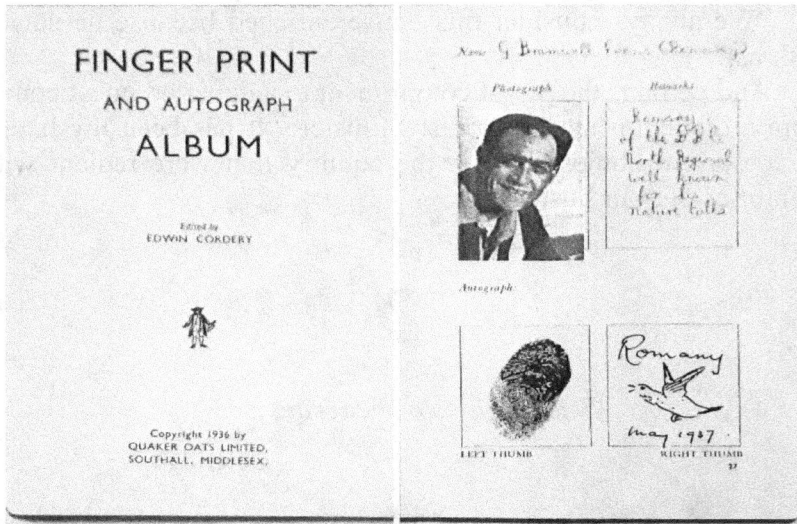

Source: Gosticks of Whaley Bridge

Raq's appearances at Lectures were eagerly awaited

Drawing by Leonard Hollands

Chapter 19

Hobbies

It was in the summer of 1931 that I was looking forward to a trip with my husband to the Bass Rock, off the East coast of Scotland. To my disappointment, a letter arrived saying that the lighthouse, where we hoped to stay, was a bachelor establishment and women visitors were not allowed. He then wrote to Rennie, who replied, "We're on strike at t'mill, and ah'm lakin.'" So, one summer evening in June found them rushing northwards, with the car once more packed with their photographic impedimenta and, of course, Raq.

"He wants" "Two pounds" !!!!
"You speak your mind". Rennie: "I dassn't."

Parking the car in North Berwick, they went down to the harbour to hire a boat. Their faces fell when they were asked to pay two pounds for a distance of four miles; they had only just recovered from this shock when Romany received another. In his exuberance of spirits, while waiting for the boat, he remarked on the weather to one of the occupants of a promenade shelter, for he was accustomed to talk freely to everyone he met. Her reply was to raise her lorgnette, look him up and down from head to foot, and then get up and walk away. He never looked very respectable on these expeditions in his old brown patched suit, but having lived with friendly Lancashire and Yorkshire folk for so long, this experience was new to him.

They feared lest the fisherman might add another pound to the fare when he saw their belongings practically filling the little boat. However, nothing was said, and after a fairly calm crossing, they saw the huge rock looming up two hundred feet above them, and the superintendent of the lighthouse with his assistants waiting to receive them. When they were ushered into the living-room, Romany, being undomesticated himself, was surprised to find how scrupulously clean the men kept it. He was impressed, too, by the considerate way they tiptoed about and lowered their voices so as not to disturb the man asleep in the adjoining bunk.

After the meal, they followed the men up the steep, winding staircase past the huge pulleys which turned the light, to the glass-prismed tower above, with its two hundred thousand candle-power incandescent mantles.

"Three hours on and six hours off," the superintendent explained when describing their duties.

"It must be very boring with nothing to do in this confined space," Romany remarked.

They laughed, and assured him that they had no time to be bored, for the huge weight, which works rather on the principle of a grandfather clock, had to be wound up by hand every half-hour. It was then that my husband realised the sacrifice and endurance of these fine men in their cramped, lonely existence. Whilst on duty a man is never allowed to leave the light, nor permitted to read or smoke, for the least dulling of the glass prisms may result in the wreck of a ship.

"But surely you have a fire of some sort in winter?" he asked. "Oh, no," was the reply. "Warmth would mean condensation on the glass, and where would the sailors be then?"

"What would happen if the machinery broke down?" was his next question. As though reciting a creed, they all replied, "The light must not go out. We would turn it ourselves." Mac then told how on one occasion he and his companions had no sleep for three days as they manipulated the huge pulleys by hand until the arrival of the breakdown engineers.

Early the next morning Romany and Rennie were off to the mighty bastions above the lighthouse where birds congregated in their thousands. This was Rennie's first experience of rock-climbing, and as he followed my husband down the cliff, he remarked, "If ah do slip, ah'll have summat soft to fall on."

It would be repetition to tell of all the birds they watched and photographed, but one morning they had, with difficulty, scrambled on to a projecting rock and were comfortably straddled across it when, suddenly, without any warning, a terrific blast of noise came from the huge mouth of the foghorn just above their heads. Like a snowstorm, thousands of birds swept from their ledges into the air, and only by gripping the rock tightly did they manage to keep their balance. Their nerves were so shattered that they abandoned the idea of taking any more photographs and quickly climbed back to the safety of the main rock, where they shared their one and only cigarette.

"Now Rennie! We have only one cigarette left,
So the fairest way is, for me to have
the cigarette, and you the cigarette card."

So the days passed happily, photographing the gannets and kittiwakes, and when the lighthouse-keepers were not busy, they would lower them in their boat to photograph the puffins on the base of the rock.

To my husband it was touching to see the excitement of the men when the supply ship was due to arrive with letters, newspapers, tobacco and provisions. Except on the first day, he had always seen them in their working clothes, but long before the ship was expected they donned their uniforms and stood looking through their binoculars towards the distant coast.

The time finally came for Romany and Rennie to leave the wind-swept heights of the Bass Rock for the dust and grime of industrial towns. For weeks afterwards, above the smoke of the mill chimneys and the noise of Rennie's looms, they could see the graceful flight of the white-winged gannets, and hear their monotonous chanting and the reverberations of the huge waves, as they dashed into the deep caverns beneath the rock.

When my husband was away from home for any length of time, it fell to my lot to feed any birds or animals there might happen to be in his outhouses. Before going off to the Bass Rock he had been busy doctoring two young crows which he had brought home with him from Greensit's farm at Tanfield. As they were newly hatched, he had to open their mouths forcibly and push the raw meat down their throats. They were so vicious that they often pecked him, and having watched the proceedings once or twice, I was not looking forward to the prospect of having to look after them. Great was my relief the day before he left, to find that they were beginning to feed themselves, for, as it was, I never relished the job of having to cut up worms for the smaller birds.

Delightful as our new house in Halifax was, it did not minimise our longing for a home of our own, and, in preparation for it, we began to collect pieces of antique furniture. When he went on a tour alone, he would often return with a disreputable-looking old oak bureau or table tied on the back of the car, which he had picked up for a mere song. He had a childlike delight in giving me a surprise, and would try to sneak his purchases into his workshop before I could see them, for he knew that, given time, he could make a good job of most of them.

All this encouraged him to take up joinery once more. He always seemed to be making things, but more for the pleasure it gave him than for the use they would be. He made a shoe-rack, but having made it, he was never known to put his shoes in it. After secreting himself in his workshop for days on end, he would proudly bring into the house a bedstead made out of the two sides of an old oak chest, or a stool hewn out of an oak beam. This afforded him so much joy that I had not the heart to tell him that he was making far more things than we should have room for; and when he brought in some unexpected bookshelves that he had laboriously made, I was faced with the dilemma of deciding which piece of furniture must be sold to make room for them. Though an artistic worker, as with his water-colours, he was inaccurate over details and was always in far too great a hurry to get a job finished. Because of the delight that it gave him to surprise me, I was not welcome in his workshop, but being impatient and a poor finder, to his annoyance he would be obliged to call me when he lost his screwdriver. This 1 would eventually unearth from beneath piled-up layers of wood-shavings, and the accumulated rubbish of weeks of work. He was completely happy when working in a muddle.

He had a special affection for grandfather clocks, and at one time we had half a dozen in the house, only one of which kept the correct time. He loved tinkering with them. "Who has been touching this clock?" he would ask as he went round the house winding and regulating them, and I would have to confess that in lightly removing a layer of dust, I had misplaced some pieces of wood which were correcting the balance of the pendulum.

He would handle a piece of old oak with reverence, smoothing the grain affectionately. In fact, wood seemed to convey to him something personal. The fallen trunk of a tree which we passed was just a piece of wood to me, but to him it was much more. He would see the old tree standing in the full pride of its foliage, and picture the many March gales it had withstood, and the birds that had found refuge in its branches. Had it not felt the scampering feet of the squirrels, and listened to

225

the soft cooing of the woodpigeon? No wonder he was always saddened when he saw a mighty tree ruthlessly cut down.

When at the *vardo*, he would sit by his camp fire for the sheer joy of smelling the scent of the pine logs, and watching the smoke as it curled upwards; on our picnics, he would scorn thermos flasks or "Teas served here" and make his own fire. To see his delight as he wandered about collecting wood, or sat gazing into the glowing embers, often made me forget that I was drinking smoky tea.

It gave him great satisfaction to discover anything, whether it was the first bird's nest of the season, the first violet on a hedge-bank, or a bolt on the roadside, which he was quite sure would fit the nut he had at home. The contents of his pockets vied with those of any schoolboy – nails, string, wire, dog biscuit, plant seeds, tobacco leavings and, of course, his favourite white ivory penknife. He had a mania for collecting and hoarding. Wood of any kind he could never resist, whether stacking up his workshop with valuable planks, or picking up a piece of firewood – a true Gypsy instinct. When he heard that the roof of an old church near Halifax was being pulled down, he bought several of the oak beams, though he had nowhere to store them, but like so many other things, he was quite sure they would come in useful some time.

One day a lorry drew up at our gate with the biggest old Spanish mahogany double-bedstead on it that I had ever seen. I protested to the man that it could not be meant for us. "Oh yes," Romany exclaimed on his return. "I can make a lot of things out of it," but after ruining his best saw, even he gave it up, and he presented it to our little West End Chapel to form their new pulpit. When his leisure was not spent in his workshops or out-of-doors studying bird-life, he was usually busy in the garden. This not only gave him endless pleasure but increased the number of his acquaintants. He was continually visiting someone's garden, or leading a procession of people around ours, and they would go away with cuttings, and then return later with something of theirs for him to plant.

One of his special gardening friends was Louis Sharp, and the competition between them as to what they could grow was keen.

They would teasingly disparage the size of each other's carnations and the height of each other's delphiniums, and try to baffle one another by using an unintelligible Latin name for some rare plant that one possessed and the other did not. One evening the Sharp family came to supper. I had been so busy preparing the meal that, until my attention was drawn to them, I had not noticed that the flowers I had put on the table had been replaced by others. When asked if they were from the garden, I replied, "Oh yes," for we were never short of flowers for the house. When their very unusual deep black petals, veined with pink and yellow, were commented upon, Romany remarked proudly, "You can't grow anything like that in your garden. They're called Inkiophalis." Mr Sharp, however, must have been suspicious, for he then examined the flowers more closely, and as he fingered them, his hands became stained with ink. There was no need to ask who had been responsible for this new horticultural variety!

During all these years our home had been open to bird-lovers and budding naturalists of all ages. In contrast to my husband's angling friends, I noticed that they were ever ready to tell each other of their discoveries. One of them would fix up a hide, photograph a certain bird, and then leave it for the others to use. Just when I had, with difficulty, persuaded him to get some writing done, George Edwards would arrive and, in a tone of solemn urgency, tell him of some unusual bird which he had found. For the next ten minutes, the house would be in a state of turmoil as he dashed up and down stairs looking for his various camera gadgets. Then, entirely forgetful of the hot meal which was ready, they would be out of the house before I knew it.[1]

In writing this book, I have regretted so much that he did not keep a diary of his bird-observations, but a friend of ours, Ilona Longbotham, reminds me of many of these expeditions. She proved one of his most useful scouts, for she would call and tell him when a certain nesting-bird which he had been watching was hatching out its eggs, thus saving him many fruitless journeys. It was she who first rigged up the hide near the kingfisher's nest on the Calder, and her diary reads, "I arrived about 10am to find that Romany had already been there for a couple of hours, and by fixing a stick near the nest on which the birds could alight, had managed to get eight photographs." It tells, too, of happy afternoons at Mildenhall Park stalking the deer and photographing the mallard's nest, and how, on our way home, Romany, noticing a yellow-hammer flying out of a bank, found a nest of newly hatched young ones. One of them was almost choked by the hairs which lined the nest, so he administered first-aid, and then replaced it. It would take too long to tell of the redpolls, sandpipers and kestrels they photographed when she came to the caravan, but as I am including the photograph which she took of him with two young tawny owls, I must mention the risk they took when handling them, for when doing the same thing a well-known bird-photographer[2] was attacked by the parent birds and lost an eye.

In spite of these pleasures, he often had a longing to escape from the grime-covered fields and woods of industrialism, and when the call of the Cumberland fells proved too strong for him, he would go off to the farm. It was strange how the very sight of those rounded hills gave contentment. I never fully understood their influence upon him, but however changing their moods, whether bathed in sunshine, as they stood silhouetted against the blue sky, or enveloped in sombre grey clouds, dark and menacing, they brought him a deep and abiding peace.

I will lift up mine eyes unto the hills,
from whence cometh help.

Psalm 121, 1

Chapter 19 Notes

1   Nowadays the obsessive rushing off to see a reported rare bird is known as 'twitching.'

2   The photographer was Eric J Hosking (1909-91), who, in 1937, was struck in the left eye by the claw of a tawny owl whilst returning to his hide.

Romany with young Tawny Owls

Photo: Ilona Longbotham

Chapter 20

Departure from Halifax

As Glyn and June grew up, it was interesting to watch how they were developing in some ways like their father. Glyn's aptitude for art, fondness for story-writing, and most of all, his utter absorption in his hobbies, made the presence of two absent-minded people in the house a trial. When visitors called to see us,[1] he would greet them, but when I encouraged him to make polite conversation he would wear an air of complete detachment as he looked up from the pad on which he was busy caricaturing our friends. He and his father shared a huge roll of paper which hung on the study wall, and when it was not covered with birds and animals, we would find amusing caricatures of ourselves. He did an extremely good one of Romany examining a wild flower, held in his hand, quite unaware that he had a large bird's nest with four open-mouthed youngsters on his head. What fun we had over it. He was full of original ideas, and, with his father's aid, produced a good 'Out with Romany' game which, unfortunately, could not be put on the market owing to the war. Perhaps it may materialise later.[2]

June, on the other hand, who today is a Petty Officer in the WRNS, showed signs of having inherited her father's dramatic ability, and was never happier than when taking part in amateur theatricals.

During these years, in spite of rigid dieting, his health was anything but satisfactory. After trying one expensive palliative treatment after another, he would temporarily recover; then would come the inevitable relapse. The August of 1937 found us at the caravan once more, but within a week of our arrival he was taken ill. Early one morning, I found him so much worse that I woke June, and though the nearest doctor[3] was nearly three miles away, she went off to fetch him. On hearing the symptoms, he came post-haste and within an hour an ambulance had arrived. So weak was poor Romany that the men had to carry the stretcher very slowly across the across bumpy, furrowed field to save him pain.[5] When half way across I suddenly noticed that Raq was following us and, much to his disappointment, I had to run back and lock him up in the caravan. This worried Romany, especially as Raq was ageing and none too well at this time. However, I reassured him by promising that I would return to him at the first possible moment. Several anxious days passed at the Whitby Hospital[4] before my husband was out of danger, and when he was well enough to talk things over, we came to the decision that he must either give up his broadcasting and lecturing, or retire from his Church. Knowing that his opportunities for preaching would be numerous if we decided on the latter plan, I eventually persuaded him to retire.

The following day, however, Edgar Isles, our Circuit Steward, came to see him, and as soon as he began to plead with him not to desert his congregation, I knew at once that I was defeated. They had been so tolerant of his absences when ill, and never by a look suggested that he should have done less outside work. In fact, as it turned out, they afterwards showed their appreciation by inviting him to stay a tenth year – an unusual term in Methodism. This, in itself, was answer enough to the outside critics who were, at this time, suggesting that he was neglecting his Church.

When he had gained sufficient strength, he was moved to a nearby cottage at Sandsend,[6] overlooked by brown bracken-covered hills and flanked by wooded valleys and streams. I can see him now convalescing, with the spray of the tide blowing on him through the open window. It was late September. The place was deserted and only an odd villager passed along the tiny promenade, nodding and smiling to Romany as he went by. How we both appreciated the quiet of those few weeks. Even the weather conspired to make him better, for it was so sunny and mild that he was soon able to sit on the wooden seat on the jetty, kept warm by the old salts and cronies of the village. They had tolerated the usurping of their cottages by the summer invasion of visitors, knowing that it would mean months of winter idleness when they could afford to chat and smoke, and through their telescopes watch the ships on the horizon as they plied their way from Hull to Newcastle. We revelled in the woods of the Normanby Estate, and felt a personal pride later when we heard that the Marquess of Normanby, whose familiar young figure we often saw bathing in pre-war days, had spent his time when a prisoner of war learning Braille, and then teaching it to his less fortunate companions. In one of his weekly articles, Romany wrote, "Many will bless him in future years for lightening their darkness."

What carefree days those were – no church meetings, no letters to write, no broadcasting, no everlasting telephone calls, nothing to do but sit and watch Billy Maclean following the tide out to his fishing nets, or the graceful flight of the gulls as they came almost to Romany's feet to be fed. To quote again from his article, "I have often felt that though the Marquess owns the rights of the beach, the real owner is Billy, the lean, bronzed, shabby fisherman who spends his days there, for what he does not know of beach lore is not worth knowing." If real possession means a deep appreciation of a thing, then my husband owned his woods and hills, for he found in them heart's content.

At this time *The Leeds Mercury* received so many enquiries asking for news of Romany that the editor, W L Andrews, whose recent contributions to the Brains Trust have been so much appreciated, said, "This Romany they're all concerned about must be a radio star. We'd better find out how he is." And so my husband was asked to send an account of himself to their columns. This so struck the editor's imagination that he at once offered him a contract to write a weekly article. The first of these appeared in December, under the title of "Out with Romany," and they continued when *The Leeds Mercury* and *The Yorkshire Post* became one paper under the editorship of Mr Andrews.

Before leaving Sandsend we heard that a nearby three-roomed cottage was for sale – an unusual occurrence on the Normanby Estate. We understood that some years previously, when the owner was living abroad, his neglectful agent failed to collect the rent over a considerable period of years and, by law, it then became the tenant's property. Whether at the back of his mind Romany had misgivings as to the future I do not know, but he said, "Let's buy it. It'll be a roof over our heads whatever happens."

Though distinctly better in general health on his return. the usual relapse soon followed. There was nothing for it but to face an operation, and so it was arranged that it should take place at the Private Nursing Home of Manchester Royal Infirmary at the end of February. He was also worried as to who would look after Raq while we were away, but this, unfortunately, was settled for him, for Raq died in his sleep a few days before we left home. Poor Romany.

The operation was completely successful but, by ill luck, pleurisy set in and for some days his condition was critical. So anxious were his many friends that I almost had to barricade the door to keep them out. On the second day, the Matron of the Infirmary came over to see him, bringing a friend. "He isn't fit to see anyone," I protested, forgetting that she of all people, being head of the Manchester Royal, had a right of entry. "How wise of you, Mrs Evens," she replied. "We'll come again when he is better." After an anxious week or two, he showed a distinct improvement, and from then on, never looked back. Most unbelievable of all, for the first time for years, he was able to eat anything without the slightest discomfort. This was indeed a new life for him.

But having too much confidence in his exceptional recuperative powers, within eight weeks he was back in his pulpit again, a very unwise step after a major operation.

On his return home, he felt the loss of Raq keenly, and the idea of transferring his affection to another dog was unthinkable. However, he visited the Greyclough kennels near Halifax, and fell in love with a nine-months-old Cocker-spaniel, so like the old Raq that he brought it home straightaway, and it was not long before it was following him about with the same devotion that the old dog had shown.

Each year he received so many invitations to join in the Christmas celebrations at local institutions, that when he was invited to visit one of the wards of the Halifax Infirmary, I was inclined to discourage him. "Perhaps I'd better go," he said at the last minute. How fortunate that he did, for when he reached the ward he found that its name had been changed to the 'Romany Ward.' As he walked in, he was confronted with a huge canvas depicting a gaily painted caravan, with a spaniel seated on the steps. In the centre of the room was a tripod and cauldron, and a very realistic Gypsy camp fire. Branches, complete with nests, swung from the ceiling, and birds of all kinds were perched on the trees dotted about the ward. He would not have missed it for the world, and when he enquired who had been responsible for it, he was told that Sister Winifred Robinson and her friend had painted the scenery and planned it all in their off-time.

During the following eighteen months at Halifax his new health made work a joy to him, and when, after his final Sunday evening service, our friends gathered to make a presentation and bid us good-bye, we felt it keenly. I cannot remember all the kind things that were said, but they are expressed in two letters which I have received lately. The Senior Circuit Steward writes, "We will ever remember with gratitude the ten years' service you both rendered, and will be more than fortunate if we are ever served again by a minister and his wife with such outstanding ability." And one of the Society Stewards says, "We just loved your husband." He loved them too.

Until that night I had been longing for the leisure that retirement would bring, for, though incapable of public speaking, I had done a great deal of my husband's church work when he was away from home. But as I sat with him on the platform surrounded by our friends, I realised for the first time that I was to be denied much happiness. Our twenty-eight years' close companionship, both in work and friendships, had come to an end. In future he would be away each Sunday, and I shrank from the thought of entering a strange church without him. Would no one come to me with their troubles, their gossip, their fun and their "Will you remind him of this or of that?" I was indeed retiring to a more private life than I wanted. No amount of leisure would compensate me for the loss of being able to share with him the joy of entering into the lives of ordinary people.

Perhaps I should have explained before this how it was that I was able to help my husband with his work, and it may not be out-of-place if I include here a little of my own background. My love of a pen was certainly inherited from my parents. My father, before entering the Congregational ministry, graduated at Cambridge and was a keen Hebrew scholar. As a child, whenever I ventured into his study I found him surrounded with books and papers, and if I made too much noise I can remember being told, "Don't disturb your father. He is writing Grandpa's life." My grandfather, Dr John Thomas, who was a well-known leader of political and religious life in Wales, was the editor and proprietor of a Welsh newspaper. He also wrote a novel on village life, which my mother translated into English, in addition to her other minor literary efforts.

When I left boarding-school I became private secretary to the Hon Emily Kinnaird, and the experience I gained when dealing with her correspondence, and wrestling with Bradshaw, stood me in good stead in later years. Until the day when I became my husband's secretary, he had been securely placed on a pedestal in my life, but I found him to be such a peculiar employer that he very soon tilted slightly from the perpendicular. One of my difficulties was that he objected to his public work and church work encroaching in any way on his home life, and that he had the capacity to close the compartment of his mind which dealt with them. For a man of his temperament, this was a natural desire, but as I spent five or six hours daily dealing with his work, it made my task extremely difficult. On arriving home from a lecture-tour, so eager was he to get back into his own world again that he would frequently sit down to tell me his experiences before he had taken off his overcoat. Then upstairs he would go to change into his old clothes, and the very tone in which he called Raq as he went outside had a finality in it, which meant, "That chapter is closed. I'm free again." But, unfortunately for me, it also meant that henceforth any reference I made to any writing I was doing for him would be distasteful to him.

A more exasperating man to work for cannot be imagined. It was only natural that he should have had no inclination for letter-writing, but the trouble was that he could neither be bothered to tell me what to say nor to discuss his future work. At first I would hopefully track him down in the fields or the garden each time I found myself in a quandary, but finding this fatiguing, I eventually made my own decisions and took the full responsibility of planning his public engagements. He might be vaguely aware that he was to visit Northumberland and Durham for ten days, but until I handed him his wallet containing his time-table the night before he left home, he had no idea what towns he was visiting. The same applied to his church meetings; he preferred not to know of them until a few hours before they took place.

In a letter which I received recently from June she recalls how we used to scheme together to get him indoors – "Do you remember how, when I had managed to coax Daddy in, he would listen to you for a minute, then would catch sight of a wagtail tripping across the lawn. With that disarming smile of his he was gone, and we knew that his literary efforts were over for that morning." Referring to an occasion when she managed to entice him in to write a personal letter which I thought should be in his own writing, she goes on, "How we laughed to see him sitting miserably waiting to do it, like a small boy kept in after school. Finally he asked you to dictate to him what he should say, which was more bother than writing yourself. Poor Daddy. He didn't like to see you doing everything, but he seemed quite incapable of doing anything about it."

In spite of these difficulties, I enjoyed my work and found it full of interest. My love of maps, too, made the puzzling out of his long journeys a pleasure, though fitting in lectures so as to give him the minimum amount of fatigue when travelling was like solving a jig-saw puzzle. It was only when his public work increased and my domestic help decreased that I found it a burden.

After breakfast I would hustle through my housework and shopping and optimistically settle down to write. I wrote everything by hand, because I feared that a typewriter would turn our home more into an office than it already was. Then the telephone would ring, the groceries would arrive; the telephone again, the man to read the meter; a small boy, "Please, is Romany in? I found this bird with its leg broken," and I would pilot him round the back of the house to my husband, and return to find the vegetables for lunch boiling over. Then it was that he would fall with a thud from his pedestal.

But all these minor troubles were as nothing compared with the deep hurt that was mine, for by undertaking his secretarial work, I had unwittingly separated myself from his real interests and associated myself with the side of his life which he found most unpleasant. With his natural instinct for shunning it, he would avoid coming into the room where I was writing in case it meant discussing something. When I went into the garden his eyes would light up on seeing me, and then it hurt me to see his face cloud over when he saw that I had a pen and paper in my hand. Although it usually ended in his pointing out to me the beauty of one of his choice plants or the dainty flight of a meadow pipit, as I walked back into the house I vowed that I would give it all up; he must employ his own secretary.

Sometimes as I sat pondering over these things he would walk past the window and smile, as if saying, "I'm quite happy, and, of course, you are, too." But I knew that complete happiness could only come to me if he could give up his public work, and we could roll back the years and idly saunter together along the banks of the Eden.

He is lifeless that is faultless.

Old Proverb

Chapter 20 Notes

1   Brenda Coxen, the daughter of Winifred Ashworth who played the part of Mrs Johnson, the Farmer's wife in the later broadcasts, tells us that Eunice used to answer the door wearing a hat. If it was a welcome caller she would explain that she was just back, but if an unwelcome caller, sorry, she was just going out!

2   The game never did materialise.

3   Dr English.

4   George Swalwell (Tim of the *Out with Romany* books), son of the farmer on whose farm the *vardo* was encamped, remembered this event. He and his brother Wilf helped carry Romany's stretcher. As Romany was transferred to the waiting ambulance he said, "Well, George, out of one caravan into another!" Despite the pain he had not lost his sense of humour.

This was 1937, but interestingly, when signing Wilf Swalwell's autograph book around that time, Romany signed as 'G Bramwell Evens' despite having for some years been broadcasting and being widely known as 'Romany.' Compare the 1937 autograph on page 219.

George, who was a lovely gentle man, was a great source of information about Romany. As a boy he used to locate birds' nests for Romany and help building hides. He spent time with Romany watching kestrels (Kek and Fan in *Out with Romany by Moor and Dale*), and foxes (Flash in *Out with Romany*).

It was from George that we learned that when staying at the *vardo* Romany often preached at the Brunswick Road Methodist church in Whitby.

5   Whilst in the hospital, Romany would sign autographs for sixpence, the money going to a patients' welfare fund.

6   That cottage has since been demolished to make way for a car park. It stood at the bottom of Lyle Bank.

Romany and June at the Sandsend Cottage
(They called it Homestead; it is now Romany Cottage)

Romany's Study and Bedroom opposite the Cottage
(It was here that he wrote Out with Romany by the Sea)

Chapter 21

Wilmslow

Romany's ambition had always been to retire to a remote cottage "by the side of a running stream and surrounded by gorse and heather," as he so often described it. When passing through lonely, bracken-covered moorland, he would pull up the car, and choosing a spot sheltered by grey weathered rocks, he would say to me, "This is where I'd like to build it." We had endless pleasure building these imaginary houses, but some of them were so isolated that I could not help wondering sometimes how far I should have to walk to buy a loaf of bread.

By this time, however, he had reluctantly given up all hope of his ideal, for if he was to be within easy reach of the BBC we must live within a few miles of Manchester, and the more we saw of its outskirts, the more our dream-cottage receded.

It was one afternoon in December 1938, when passing through Wilmslow, Cheshire, that we noticed a 'Houses for sale' board on a well-wooded estate almost in the centre of the village. Not only did the unspoilt surroundings appeal to us, but the architect, had shown both originality and imagination in his planning, for no two houses were exactly alike in design, giving each a certain individuality of its own. Neither high hedges nor fences hemmed in most of the gardens, it being understood that their beauty was meant for the enjoyment of the passer-by as well as the owner. Trees had been left wherever possible, showing that the builder, too, had imagination.[1]

My husband loved trees so much that I was afraid that his choice of a house would depend on whether there were any in the garden. Indeed, even now, I am not sure that it was not the fine ash tree behind the house which he eventually chose that influenced his final decision. All his life he had wanted to own trees, and I can see now his look of pride as he stood admiring it. At that moment my thoughts were on more mundane things. For the first time in our married life we were going to furnish our own home. Surely we could not buy a carpet without the permission of the Circuit Stewards? Could we really choose our own colour schemes, and be sure that the curtains matched the furnishings? Was I going to have an entirely new set of kitchen utensils that no one else had used? It all seemed too good to be true.

Meanwhile, he had disappeared, and when I found him he was sitting by the edge of one of the ponds in the fields beyond the garden, whilst Raq hopefully nosed in and out of the roots of the overhanging trees. All this may give the impression that he retired to the rural surroundings he so often depicted in his broadcasts. This was not so. Though Wilmslow is surrounded by open wooded country, the village is anything but unsophisticated. It is large, up-to-date, and boasts not only a highway[2] from Manchester to the South, but main-line trains to the great metropolis.

On our next visit we explored the village. Even in the shopping street we found a leisureliness that attracted us. To walk along the narrow pavements without being jostled was a new experience. The tradespeople, too, had time to chat and dawdle as they welcomed us, and carefully parcelled up our purchases. Everything, indeed, augured well for the future.

But when nine months later we took possession of the house, how differently it all turned out. Our August holiday was marred by rumours of war, and when we arrived in Wilmslow the first week in September, war had been declared. How ironical that it should have come that very week. I was still in the throes of unpacking when the bell rang, and I found two small evacuees on the doorstep. Would we billet them, we were asked. Surely we could have our new home to ourselves, I thought, for my husband did need quiet intervals between his public work. But one look at the faces of the two little girls, who had come from Manchester to avoid the dangers of bombing, melted us both, and though the stair-carpet was not yet down, we took them in. We were obliged to part with one of them for unmentionable reasons, but the other, a charming, gentle child, stayed with us for several months.

Not long after our arrival Romany returned from a walk one afternoon in a state of great concern. Hundreds of fine trees in one of the most attractive wooded parts of the district were being

243

cut down. How grieved he was.[3] A huge RAF. camp was being built, and it was not long before five thousand young men invaded the quietude of our village. Incidentally, it was afterwards found that a great many of these trees had been needlessly destroyed, for when the air-raids began, the camp was without camouflage.

The relatives of the new recruits then began to flock into the village. Instead of being able to saunter along the shopping street, we were now elbowed into the gutter, and proud though we were to feel that Wilmslow was not being left out of the war effort, the shopkeepers were too busy either to recognise us or care whether we patronised their shops or not. Then letters came telling of new arrivals at the camp who would be calling to see Romany, for his friends all over the country were legion, and this, together with the entertaining we shared with others, brought more than a hundred and fifty members of the forces into our house during the next two years.

There always seemed to be someone in the lounge, quietly reading or playing the piano. One afternoon I found it difficult to concentrate on my writing because of the unusual way in which the piano was being played. We were accustomed to a surfeit of modern syncopation, but this was something different. After two or three bars, there would be a pause, then a few more bars, another pause, and so it went on. I was curious, and went to investigate. The pianist, Robert Gordon, after telling me that he and his sister composed songs together, asked somewhat apologetically, "How do you like this one? We're hoping that Arthur Askey will accept it." I listened, complimented him, for he was a clever pianist, but did not tell him that I thought the words a bit inane. As his sister was responsible for these, and it was imperative that he should post the song that night, he asked if he might telephone to her. The most unusual conversation then took place as he hummed over his new ideas; she, I imagined, suggested alterations in her wording. Some time after leaving Wilmslow he wrote telling us that they were now composing Arthur Askey's 'Silly little Songs,' and he enclosed an album of them for June. He doubted if we would recognise them as the elaborate arrangements which he had often played to us, because they had been simplified to fit in with Arthur's style, and he also apologised for the latter's amusingly bad grammar.

Though Romany was able to devote some of his leisure time to entertaining these young people, he was away from home so much that it was impossible for him to join any of the voluntary war services. But as I sat in his lecture audiences and saw the harassed faces of the people around me being transformed as he took them into a new world of wonder and beauty, I knew that he was doing war-work of the highest importance. When at the close, he reassured them, "The birds will still be singing, and the woods and glens will be there for you to explore long after Hitler is forgotten," they went home smiling.

The letters he was receiving, too, were constantly telling of the refreshment his broadcasts were giving, and their calming effect was shown by a letter written to the *Radio Times* which concluded with, "How Romany's broadcasts lift one up above black-outs and war-depression." One of the best illustrations of this is given in a letter from a listener living in Gorton, Manchester: "We were bombed out of our house, and had to move our belongings ourselves on handcarts until a van was available. We went into a new district, and for the first day or so. no one came near to give us a cheery word, though we have found since that they are grand folk. For days we were too weary to put up our beds, so slept on mattresses on the floor. One afternoon we were feeling especially lost and miserable, so we put on the wireless, and it was 'Out with Romany.' When we heard his beloved voice, the sun shone once more, and we had that happy, warm feeling you have when your loved ones are with you again. We knew that the world must be a lovely place after all if people like Romany were in it, and I am not ashamed to say that I cried like a child for the joy of finding a friend again."

A story that touched my husband very much was of a little girl who was accustomed to spending her nights in a London shelter. On one occasion, during a heavy raid, her mother was obliged to leave her alone in bed, and on her return she asked the child if she had been frightened. "Oh no, Mummy," was the reply, "I've been quite happy. I've been out with Romany."

In his spare time, he was now busily engaged in building a shelter at the side of the house. Day after day he trundled his barrow backwards and forwards as he fetched every imaginable thing he could find to strengthen it. Then with infinite pains, and pleasure in using his tools again, he lined the walls, had a radiator and electric light fixed, and made it so comfortable that we not only slept there during the raids, but he used it as his special den long after they were over.

He then offered his services as an air-raid warden on the understanding that when he was away I should take his duties. "You'll go to all the committees and lectures, won t you?" he pleaded, and so we arranged matters to our satisfaction if not to that of those in control. Despite the fact that he always grabbed his tin hat and was out of the house as soon as he heard the siren, whether it was his duty night or not, he proved anything but an exemplary warden from the official point of view. The ruling was that wardens must patrol in pairs, but Romany was never to be found at the appointed place, and I was always having to think out new excuses for him at our sector meetings.

With what acute suspense he listened to the war news. He would not miss a bulletin if he could help it. "Oh, it's the same as this morning," I would say when he turned it on at lunch-time, but it had no effect. It is sad to think that most of what he heard was bad news. How he would have rejoiced in our victories today, and to have known that it was a bird, a carrier-pigeon, which brought back the first news of our successful landing in Normandy.

Though I never fully understood what they did for him, I do know that certain things had a tranquillising effect on him. One night when he was on duty, he was feeling more than a little alarmed by the menacing army of planes that roared over the village when, from a tree above him, came the unconcerned hoot of an owl, answered by the distant 'ke-vick' of its mate. Just as the serenity of the sea birds had soothed him during the violent storm on the heights of Ailsa Craig, so the unruffled behaviour of the owls had a calming influence on him. As a boy, he had often been taken out by his father to study astronomy, and though in those days his keenness, so he told me, was mainly a matter of staying up late, as he grew older one glance upwards on a moonlit night seemed to give him a sense of proportion and balance. And so it was when enemy planes passed over. He had only to stop a moment and look beyond the planes to the stars above to allay his fears. Sometimes, in our early days, as we walked home together from a church committee meeting, I would angrily denounce Mr –—— who had dared to disagree with him over a matter of business. Taking hold of my arm, he would laugh and say, "Stand still a minute, and look up at those myriad stars, and you'll see how trivial it all is." But though I stood still and tried hard to feel as he did, as we walked on, Mr —— became more odious than ever.

But I must hark back to his duties as an air-raid warden, and though I am afraid that some of my readers will skip these pages when they find that I am going to tell our bomb-story, I must include it, because it shows another side of my husband's character. It was just before midnight on Christmas Eve, 1940, that Romany, June, Raq and I were in the shelter listening to the frightening number of aeroplanes that were passing over on their way to bomb Manchester. The pilot of the last one to arrive either mistook his course, or thought our village a worthy target, for after circling very low for what seemed hours, he dropped his load almost on top of us. The ground shook, the shelter shuddered, but we were alive, and that, for the moment, was all that seemed to matter. Being fully dressed, we scrambled out of the shelter before the hum of his engine had died away. It had been pitch-black when we went inside; now it was as light as day. Our house must be on fire. No, but there was one on fire, not fifty yards away, and someone was screaming for help. "You telephone the police, and, June, get first-aid things ready," Romany cried, as he dashed across the field entirely ignoring the fact that there might be unexploded bombs in his path. Within three minutes of the crash I was at the telephone, but being an inefficient warden, I blurted out the position of the incident, and a request that all services be sent, and then ran out again, feeling distinctly proud to think that mine would be the first message received. But my pride was short-lived, for, as I guided the Rescue Party across the field, one of them said, "The house is not on fire," and I had asked for the fire service! "But with those bedroom fires alight, it may catch any minute," said another, and I breathed again. Incidentally, owing to the fact that they immediately dealt with the fires, the fire engine passed within a stone's-throw of the incident and then careered all round the village looking for my fire – but that is another story.

Meanwhile, Romany was just in time to help the occupants to scramble out through one of the windows, and to discover that the cries for help were coming from the maid who was trapped in her bedroom. By this time our good neighbour, Frank Ashworth, had arrived on the scene, and after the dishevelled family had been passed over to my care, he and Romany climbed up the wreckage and did their best to rescue the maid. Though able to reassure her that help was forthcoming, they could not manage to release her, but she was eventually brought to safety by the Rescue Party.

The irony of the whole thing was that our sector of wardens was known to be an exceptionally efficient and capable one, and the lives we had saved in imagination at our practices had been numberless; and yet, the one and only incident of the war in our sector had been dealt with by their most unbusinesslike warden, long before even those on duty arrived on the scene. We had many a laugh over it afterwards, to think that he, of all people, should have been given this opportunity of showing that he was not as unpractical as he seemed, though our methods may have been unorthodox.

Despite this unexpected invasion of our house, that Christmas stands out as a most happy one. Our war-time larder was full to overflowing, for the next morning, through the kitchen window, I saw Romany crossing the field carrying a turkey and other delicacies which he had unearthed from beneath the ruins. As they were unable to find other accommodation, this family stayed as our guests for some months. After they left us, one of them, Howard Agg, who is best known as Mabel Constanduros's collaborator in many successful plays, persuaded us to have him back again, and it was not until the summer that our house was again our own. It was a delight on more than one occasion to entertain his charming partner and I wish I could remember which one of their plays they partly wrote in our lounge.

Though the air-raid spelt disaster for this family, the demolition of their house provided endless pleasure for Romany, as he delved beneath the debris for mortar rubble for his plants, and piled up his barrow with disreputable loads of rubbish to fortify the shelter. He could not understand why June and I were none too keen to sleep out there unless there was a serious raid, and was surprised that we objected to the way in which he encouraged the field mice to scuttle in and out by feeding them. It also puzzled him that we disliked the dank, mouldy smell of the corner where he was growing mushrooms, and he was almost hurt when we hinted that Raq always chose to lie on the most comfortable bed. So contented was Raq with the shelter that as soon as he heard the siren, he ran there and staked his claim long before anyone else.

It was not long before our quietude was again disturbed by the arrival of a nice ATS. girl, who was billeted on us for many months. "Have you no marmalade?" she asked incredulously with her charming Scottish accent, for she had come from Dundee of marmalade fame. Within a few days a jar arrived from her mother. Dundee, of course, was no better off for rations than other places – her mother was merely showing her gratitude to us for our reception of her daughter.

I know that our evacuees and billetees were few compared with those of many people, but I have related these experiences to show how the war affected Romany's home-life, and how, being without a maid during these years, I found it difficult to be both a satisfactory landlady and an efficient secretary.

How he could have tolerated all these intrusions into our family life had it not been for the solace of the garden, I cannot think. As it was, he had little privacy, for our house had only six rooms, which obliged our evacuees to share our family hearth. Had he been asked what brought him most joy during his four years in Wilmslow, he would have replied unhesitatingly, "My garden." With his love of trees and flowers, it is sad to think that he was fifty-five before he had a garden of his own, and yet I believe that he derived more satisfaction from it in four years than many people experience in a lifetime.

When I first saw the rough, uncultivated wilderness behind the house, and then watched him filling reams of paper with his plans, I thought his ideas far too optimistic, but as I sit here looking out on it, I feel proud, for the wilderness has indeed "blossomed as the rose." He had but one idea in mind, to make a small rockery which would remind him of an outcrop on the Cumberland hills. First of all he spent weeks shovelling cartloads of earth to give the depth and slope he wanted. Then came the day when we went to buy his first load of Westmorland stone. To me, the rocks all looked alike, and I thought it a simple matter to choose them, but he examined them all minutely, walking round each to view it from different angles. When he found a well-weathered one, with pleasing horizontal chinks and crevices, his eyes would light up, and he and the rockery expert would talk unintelligibly of the "angle of the stratum" or the back, front or face of rock. Finally, after selecting several monsters, each weighing some hundredweight, and a variety of lesser ones, we returned home. When they arrived and he set to work to get them into position, I could not understand why he seemed to be putting most of his money into the ground, for he more than half-buried them. And no sooner had he placed several of them, as I thought, in their best positions, then he moved first one and then another. "It's not in the same stratum as the others," he would explain to me, as I sat heavily on the far end of his lever to help him to heave it out again. They spoilt many a meal, for as we sat in the dining-room window, he would notice that one of them was set out of line with the rest, and disregarding a helping of one of his favourite puddings, he would hurry out to tilt it slightly upwards so that it should be in harmony with its neighbours.

Then followed the happiness of buying his trees, shrubs and plants. Knowing that he could never resist a 'Nursery Gardens' notice-board, when travelling with him, I would try to distract his attention when I saw one looming ahead, because I knew that it would mean at least an hour's delay. But nothing escaped his keen eyes, and we would arrive home with the car loaded with bushes, and two or three trees protruding through the roof.

This zeal for his garden had its humorous side, for he would become suddenly interested in my domestic affairs, and would say, "I'm sure it's time you had the chimneys swept," and I would find that he was short of soot for his plants, or he would go out with a storm-lamp on a dark night and, armed with my best salt-sprinkler, would creep around his rockery, waging war on the slugs. His gardening sheds were always in a muddle, and when he kept adding sacks or boxes of peat, sand, lime, soot, wood-ash, mortar rubble and worst of all, every known kind of fertiliser, the odours were at times unbearable. One hot day we were motoring back from the farm when I noticed a most obnoxious smell in the car. When I expressed my disgust, he said, "Raq has probably been rolling in something." Seeing a pond ahead, I said, "Let's give him a bath," but he did not stop. When we arrived home, he un-roped a huge tin from the luggage carrier, and said casually, with a twinkle in his eye, "Oh, perhaps it was this that Joe gave me." Handkerchief to my nose, I hurried indoors, for the tin was full of a very pungent farm manure. So that was what Joe and he were laughing about as they roped it on.

What weeks of hard work he spent lifting heavy boulders and paving-flags to make those paths and stepping-stones. How the starlings enjoy splashing in and out of his miniature ponds, fringed with ferns and spongy mosses. I well remember when he made them, for everything went wrong. He called me out to help him to lift the bag of cement, but as we carried it across the wet lawn, it burst, and half of it was wasted. How feverishly he worked mixing it, and then smoothing it into the hollows. A day or so later he filled them with water, and put in his fish. Unfortunately, when he went out the next morning, both fish and water had disappeared, and he had to begin all over again.

It is difficult to put into words his garden as I see it before me. Perhaps it can best be described by saying that it is like himself, natural, unaffected and unconventional. The rockery is not a model one from an expert's point of view, but it is very satisfying to the eye. The edges of the green turf curve in and out of the paths and ponds, and merge into the rockery which almost encircles it. His was no haphazard planting. Many of the things were to him reminders of his country walks; the drifts of bluebells, foxgloves and anemones took him in imagination to cool, shady woods, and when he saw the flaming gorse, the purple heather, and caught the scent of the wild thyme, he was transported to the breezy moorlands. Of all his plants, ericas or heaths were his chief delight, and there was never a month of the year when some of them were not in bloom. I do not yet know the names of many of the creeping plants which drape the rocks nor the delicate alpines which nestle under their shadows, but I do know that his garden remains a memorial to him,[4] a thing of beauty, made with his own hands.

When the world wearies, and society ceases to satisfy, there is always the Garden.

Minnie Aumonier

Chapter 21 Notes

1   That builder was Frank Gibson, father of Romany Society member David Gibson. Even Raq's kennel was subject to careful planning:

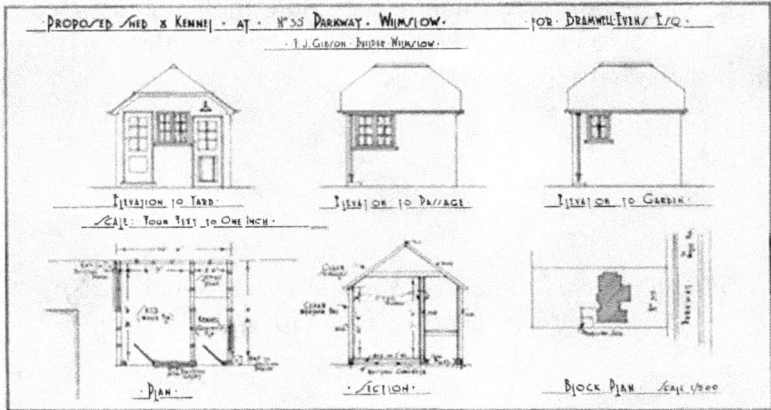

2   Today, of course, we there is the network of motorways around the Greater Manchester area. More than half the journey from Wilmslow to the City Centre is motorway.

3   Daughter Romany June recounted that, on a subsequent occasion, trees were to be felled behind Romany's garden except for a few which had been marked with white paint and were to be spared. Under cover of darkness Romany crept out and put white paint on a whole lot more trees!

4   When the house changed hands in the early 2000s the new owners no longer wished to keep Romany's rockery. Romany Society members David and Angela Gibson asked if they could have the rocks and they recreated the rockery in their own nearby garden.

The Wilmslow House
(originally 35 Parkway, now 1 Parkway)

Chapter 22

Memories Here and There

One Sunday night when on duty, my husband called at a house where the black-out was unsatisfactory. When the door was opened, the occupier, to his surprise, said to him, "It can't be you, Romany. I've just been listening to you on the wireless." It transpired that there had been a skit of some kind on my husband's programme, and as it was some time afterwards that he mentioned it to me, I concluded that it must have been the 'Itma' programme. I therefore wrote to Ted Kavanagh for details and, though I troubled him needlessly, his tribute to my husband is worth recording. "Although we made occasional references to Romany in 'Itma,' we never did a skit of any kind. When mentioning him, I always had in mind his wide appeal to children of all ages, the 'Itma' public, in fact. He was very popular with our cast, and I count myself as one of his greatest admirers."

In those days Wilfred Pickles was a familiar figure in and out of the Children's Hour Studio, and on one occasion he burlesqued the programme, calling it "Oswald, Curiel and Morris." Those who listened to the Romany broadcasts will appreciate the humour of [Wilfred's] walk in the heart of Manchester with Harold Dehn and Noel Morris, accompanied by their cat, Rake. The following is an excerpt:

M. Aren't the gas lamps looking lovely today?

O. Yes. They're just at their best. Each one has got its new spring coat. Let's creep over this Belisha crossing. Follow me....Now come along. We're right in the heart of Piccadilly. Mind that branch, Curiel.

C. Branch?

O. Yes. Branch of the Midland Bank.

(The din of traffic and motor horns then almost drowned the words.)

M. How quiet and peaceful it all is.

O. Look. A little over to the left. Can you see that red and cream box-shaped thing?

C. Yes, I can see it.

O. Well, that's what's known as a red-crested telephone kiosk.....Did you hear that?

M. Yes. What was it?

O. That was a plumber calling to its mate. He's sometimes called Great Longbill.

And so it went on, interspersed with the miaows and mis-behaviour of Rake.

This reminds me of a letter which I received from Dudley Ackroyd, with whom Romany always stayed when in Bradford. One afternoon during the Christmas of 1942, in an interval between his lectures, they went together to the Leeds Pantomime. Securing the last two available seats, they were making their way unobtrusively along the front of the orchestra stalls, when to Romany's surprise, Billy Danvers said to Evelyn Laye, the principal boy, "Do you like country walks?" "I do," she replied. "So do I," he went on, "but I like them best when I go out with Romany." Much to my husband's embarrassment the spotlight was then turned full on to him, and Mr Ackroyd writes, "The audience responded heartily to this spontaneous gag, and during the interval, your husband was besieged for autographs." As Mr Ackroyd was uncertain who the two principal artistes were, I wrote to Billy Danvers for corroboration of the incident, and he replied, "I was very fond of Romany's broadcasts, so got a great kick out of seeing him in front." His letter brought back happy memories, for it came from the old Hackney Empire, the district in which we spent our courting days.

Mr Ackroyd goes on to tell me that they had lunched previously at Schofield's, and he writes, "The restaurant was very full when we arrived, but the Manageress soon spotted him, and we were immediately shown to a table. No sooner had we sat down than children appeared from all directions for his autograph, and we were even stopped in the street afterwards on our way to the Pantomime." To him this recognition was, of course, a novelty, but my husband was so well known in most Northern towns that I was accustomed to it, and if Raq happened to be with us, it was inevitable. I would see people nudging each other as they came towards us, and then sense that they were turning round to look at him after we had passed. One summer when camping near Whitby, we left the car in one of the quaint, narrow streets near the harbour while we went fishing off the pier. On our return, we were about to drive away when a constable, with a notebook in his hand, stopped us. "This car has been standing here nearly two hours," he began. Then he looked up. "Why, it's Romany," he said, and resting his arm on the window-frame he proceeded to tell him at length how his children enjoyed the broadcasts, whilst a whole queue of cars was held up behind us, their horns blowing impatiently. Before he left, the ominous little notebook contained two of Romany's autographs.

His broadcasts must have inspired trust and confidence, too, for many were the unexpected kindnesses he received. On one occasion, a lorry-driver, seeing that he was having difficulty with his car, pulled up his vehicle on the roadside and went to his rescue. When Romany afterwards attempted to pay him, he said, "No thank you, sir, but I'd like your autograph for the missus and kids." Once when going on a long railway journey, he arrived at the booking-office with no money to pay his fare. As he stood fumbling in his pockets, to his surprise, a total stranger, seeing his predicament, came up and lent him several pounds.

His voice, too, must have been unusual, for it was extraordinary how many people who had never seen him recognised it. Harassed telephone operators would clear the line for him when they heard it, and when driving home on dark nights, if he ever stopped to ask the way, the reply would often be prefaced by, "Excuse me, but where have I heard your voice before?"

On one occasion when we were motoring through a small town in the Midlands, he pulled up the car in the market square and walked across to a tobacconist. After waiting patiently for some minutes, I thought, "He is taking a long time to get an ounce of tobacco." Five more minutes passed; then I went to investigate. There was no one in the shop, but sounds of laughter came from the room behind, so I retired as quietly as possible. It appeared that when he had asked for the tobacco, the shopkeeper had said, "I seem to know your voice, sir. Is it Romany?" and before he knew it, the whole family had flocked into the shop. But he must not go without seeing Grandma, and so, while I could have been robbing the shop till, he was being received with open arms in the kitchen.

This public recognition was, of course, gratifying to him, as it is to all public men, but there were times when he found it very exhausting. One afternoon when feeling far from well, he lectured to the combined schools of Llandudno. He had an interval of several hours before the evening lecture in the Town Hall when I hoped he would get a rest. But it was not to be; the whole way along the promenade a procession of children followed him. When he reached the hotel, a pile of books awaited his autograph, and so many people called to see him that he was kept continuously talking. Not only did I feel concerned on his account, but I was apt to resent the relentlessness with which the public were claiming so much of him.

When thinking ahead of our retirement, I had often pictured the extra leisure I should have to drive him to his engagements. But my disappointment was as nothing compared with the discomfort he suffered owing to the war-restrictions on petrol. Indeed, even now, I find it hard to forgive the authorities for granting him so little for his many journeys. Though he felt fit in other ways, his operation had left him with one weakness – an inability to stand for any length of time, and it often caused him distress to have to wait in long bus queues after a lecture which had already kept him on his feet well over an hour. As the Government made so much importance of keeping up morale, and in many cases allowed extra petrol to those who entertained the public, he undoubtedly should have come under this category. Had he joined ENSA[1] at the beginning of the war, as he was asked to do, he would have had this priority, but as it was, not until the last year or so was he able to convince the authorities that he was entitled to more than that allowed to the ordinary clergyman or minister.

Had he rested more when he was at home, it would have helped matters, but almost before the engine of his car had cooled in the garage, he had changed into his old suit and become engrossed in some strenuous hobby. In one of his books, G K Chesterton says that a real hobby is not a recreation like golf, but hard work, and the using of the other part of one's mind. How true this was of my husband. He had so many hobbies that he could not understand the mentality of those who needed outside entertainment; to him, there was never enough time to do half the things he wanted to do. But the trouble was that as his public work increased, so each hobby in turn became all-absorbing to the exclusion of everything else. If it happened to be gardening, from morning till night each day he would work at it until he was due to leave home again. It would occupy his waking thoughts, and he could not eat his breakfast quickly enough to get outside. If rain or failing light obliged him to come indoors, he would get out his gardening books and catalogues, settle himself in his armchair, light his pipe, and for the rest of the evening he was supremely happy in a world of his own. It was the same with his joinery; he would become engrossed in it with a seriousness and urgency that was difficult to understand, and then come in thoroughly exhausted and say naively, "I can't think why my legs let me down." I would tell him why, for I knew that he was working too strenuously, and living too intensely in the task of the moment. I can see now that his inclination to be by himself was in a great measure due to the abnormal life which he was leading. After spending weeks away from home, seeing multitudes of people, talking continuously, these outdoor pursuits provided him with the solitude which he needed. When he returned home it often touched me to see him drop into his armchair and say pathetically, "Thank goodness, I needn't talk any more."

And yet he had much to be thankful for. He was enjoying new health, he loved his public work, and had so many varied interests and found pleasure in such seemingly commonplace things that life was never dull. Sometimes when I was out shopping in the village I would see him sitting in the blacksmith's forge, chatting with George Mottershead and Arthur Sant as they heated their irons in the furnace and shod the waiting horses. "Aye. He's sat many an hour on that seat," said George to me yesterday when I took Raq in to see them. Or I would catch sight of him with his wheelbarrow in Kellet's yard, as he and his friend,

Arthur Timmis, laughingly hoisted on to it huge sheets of corrugated iron to make a roof for his shelter; or with rucksack on his back and the dog at his heels, getting well-meated bones from Jack Evans, or fish-bits from Sydney Thorniley or David McIntosh, for all these men saw to it that Raq did not suffer from short rations during the war. He spent many happy hours, too, with the head foremen in Brown's yard, pottering about amongst the mountains of wood with Frank Mort, or sitting in the workshop with Walker Hulme, as he admired the skill and craftsmanship of the long-experienced joiners who worked under him.

Though inclined to spend freely on his garden, his personal expenses were few, and even when he could afford to do so, he spent little more on himself than when his salary was a small one; in fact, he could not accustom himself to the idea that he could buy anything really expensive without saving up for it. "Some day I shall buy myself a really good aquarium," he would keep saying, much to our amusement, and so June and I made him a birthday present of one. But when the railway lorry drew up at the gate, and I saw two men carrying in the twenty-gallon tank which he had ordered from London, I was somewhat taken aback. However, with an effort, I kept up my birthday smile as we shuffled along under its weight from room to room, to try it first on the sideboard and then on the bookcase. Fortunately, it was too big for either, and so was finally installed on a strong table in the hall. His eyes gleamed with pleasure as he then carried in buckets of sand and stones to make the foundation, and when I left him to get my shopping done, he was busily filling the tank with the aid of the garden hose. On my return, I opened the front door, and to my dismay, found most of the twenty gallons of water on the hall floor; the aquarium was leaking, and he had gone for a walk. This was but the beginning of a series of leaks, and time after time we carried it to and from his workshop before he eventually managed to repair it and put into it his fish, aquatic plants, water-beetles and snails. However, it gave him never-ending delight, and when coloured lights were fixed behind it, it brought a constant procession of children to the door, asking, "Please may we see Romany's aquarium?"

Perhaps it was as well that his tastes were simple, for though he would not have wished to make money during the war, it affected him in many unexpected ways. As well as the common hardships of high income-tax and cost of living, lack of petrol limiting his lecture engagements, several of his newspaper columns were cancelled owing to paper-shortage, and for the same reason his books, which had only just begun to sell really well, could only be printed in small quantities. Most unfortunate still was the reduction by one-half of his BBC engagements. As ill-luck would have it, he had just reached the height of his popularity when war broke out, otherwise he might have been as financially successful as many people imagined him to be. As it was, the greatest demand for his broadcasts, lectures and books came at a time when it could not be satisfied.

It was of little interest to a man of my husband's temperament what went on behind the scenes on the administrative side of the BBC so long as it neither affected his programme nor the happy atmosphere of the studio. The time came, however, when lack of co-ordination between certain departments did touch his programme, causing him real concern.

For eleven years, owing to the unusual character of the broadcast, he and his two companions had been allowed to remain anonymous, and neither through the *Radio Times*, nor from the studio, was their identity disclosed. A J Alan, to whom Laidman Browne referred, was also allowed a similar privilege. Those who listened to the vivid personal adventures of this gifted story-teller will remember how much the mystery of his identity added to the interest of his broadcasts, and how the BBC kept his name a secret until after his death.

In the case of my husband, however, "Broadcaster" was permitted to state in the *Radio Times*, in August 1942,[2] that Doris Gambell, the singer, was Doris of the Romany programme. A writer in the *Birmingham Weekly Post*, commenting on this, said that it was "too bad of the BBC in order to round off a paragraph about an artist......to reveal the fact that she was also Doris who accompanied Muriel when out with Romany."

Broadcaster's paragraph encouraged a listener who, like thousands of others, had imagined Doris to be a child, to send the following anonymous letter to the *Radio Times*: "A paragraph in your paper reveals that the two children featured in the 'Out with Romany' programme are not children at all, but adults, one of them a well-known singer. Herbert Farjeon, the dramatic critic of *The Listener* has recently been filling his columns with raptures about the fresh, spontaneous voices of these 'children.'..... Evidently he and listeners in general have been victims of a hoax, which seems to go beyond what is permissible in broadcasting."[3]

That the *Radio Times* should have singled out this letter for publication, and drawn unnecessary attention to it by heading it "Hoax?" upset my husband even more than the views of one individual listener. The same thought must have occurred to Mr Farjeon, for, when he afterwards took up the cudgels on behalf of the Romany programme in *The Listener*, he prefaced his remarks with, "I see that the *Radio Times* has selected from its mass of correspondence a letter ....." My husband felt sure that had the Children's Hour Department been consulted, their view would have been that nothing must be done to spoil the pleasure of countless children, whose feelings mattered more than those of one critical adult. He was greatly relieved, however, that the fact that he was not broadcasting from out-of-doors had not been divulged. After all, the walk was no less enjoyable because his two companions were not children. No further correspondence followed and the matter died down.

Several weeks afterwards the BBC did the very thing that Romany hoped would not happen. Opening the *Radio Times* one morning, he was amazed to find a full column which completely 'debunked'[4] his programme by the inclusion of the words, "All these rambles take place in a studio at the BBC's Northern Head-quarters," and, as if to emphasise the ages of Muriel and Doris, their photographs appeared at the top of the column. To us it seemed incredible that they should not only have airily destroyed the out-of-door atmosphere of the walk, which had taken him so many years to perfect, but that they should have done this without consulting him beforehand; neither was the matter ever mentioned to him afterwards.

That all this had the effect of marring the programme for some listeners was shown by the following letter which then appeared in the *Radio Times*, "Why was the article on Romany's broadcasts ever published? Why were we not allowed to go on enjoying those country rambles? For me, it is 'good-bye' to one of my favourite programmes."

There seems something at fault with a system which permitted such a lack of co-ordination between its various departments, and failed to consult an artiste of such long standing on a matter which so deeply affected his programme.

During the early part of the war, his mother had been going through the worst of the Liverpool raids, and so it was a special joy to them both when we eventually bought her a small cottage on the outskirts of Wilmslow. Though they had corresponded regularly, their affection was not lessened by the fact that she had seen comparatively little of him since he left home for Colchester at the age of twenty.

She rarely left her own home and found it difficult to settle down for long away from it. When she did pay us a visit, we always knew beforehand what would happen. She would greet us affectionately, hear our news, then become restless. She would sit a few minutes, wander into the garden, come back, sit down again, then disappear, and so it would go on, until Romany, knowing the signs well, would say to her teasingly, "What train are you going home by?"

The only time when I remember her sitting still for any length of time was on a public platform. He knew how publicity of any kind pleased her, and when he called at the cottage for her on his way to a lecture, he would say jestingly, "You're like an old warhorse, Mother," for she was then over eighty. Despite her age, she was still a striking figure, with her keen, dark eyes, almost black hair and naturally dignified bearing; but as I sat in the audience and watched her, I often felt that there was something pathetic about her anxiety to recapture the thrill of being in the limelight after so many years of obscurity.

So active was she that she came to see us each week. As I sat writing, I would see her talking to my husband in the garden. When she came indoors, I knew from her worried look what she was going to say, "Why does he work so hard?" and as I watched him pick up his spade again, I knew that she had been adding her protests to mine in vain.   Perhaps it was only natural that he should have been deaf to our entreaties, for being lean of build and loose-limbed, he had the agility of a young man.   No wonder that he laughed at us.   Had he not climbed to the top of the apple tree in her cottage garden, and scrambled head-foremost through our neighbour's tiny pantry window when she had lost her door key?   How he managed this, none of us knew, for he was nineteen inches across the shoulders and the window measured seventeen by nine.

This abnormal breadth of shoulder bone was definitely inherited from his mother, for Brian Vesey Fitzgerald tells me that though the majority of Gypsy women, in all parts of Europe, are small of bone and dainty, the East Anglian Smiths are known to be exceptionally big and broad-shouldered.

As Rodney was the only member of the Smith family to be registered at birth, the age of Romany's mother, and those of the others, have been a matter of guesswork.   "If Rodney says he is eighty-five, then I must be eighty-three," she says, "and Ezekiel must be ninety."   Their father, Cornelius, lived to a greater age, for he was ninety-two when he was buried with Polly in Baldock cemetery.

When I saw him a year before he died, he was a fine-looking man, gentle and gracious, and it was easy to see that his family had inherited their charm of manner from him.   Little hard-worked Emily, who grew up to be a handsome woman, married a Gypsy who eventually became an Alderman of Hanley, and she was eighty-four when she died; in fact, with the exception of Lovinia, they all passed their eightieth birthday.   Romany, indeed, on his mother's side, came of a long-lived family.   Ezekiel and Rodney, known as Gipsy Smith, are both still engaged in religious work.[5]   Though their methods may not be generally popular today, the tens of thousands of people that Rodney, in particular, has influenced for good is beyond my telling.   As a family, in one sense, they never grew up, for not only did they retain a childlike simplicity and sincerity, but they were very susceptible to big things, especially big crowds.   This pride in the crowds which they attracted was a definite failing of theirs, and my husband always considered that, in reports in certain religious weeklies, undue emphasis was laid on the huge buildings and masses of people who attended one mission meeting after another. That this had been so was true, but to them "two or three" being gathered together did not signify success. It must have been difficult for Cornelius, too, after his 'conversion,' not to use his persuasive powers occasionally for his own ends, and it is not surprising that his children enjoyed the material benefits showered on them as a result of their Missions. Their critics would do well to compare the advantages of their own upbringing with those of this Gypsy family, whose background of poverty was poor preparation for sudden success.

When I think, too, of how much the younger generation, including my husband, managed to accomplish for their fellow-men, I doubt if there ever has been a family which has done so much to reveal God, both through religion and nature, as have the descendants of Cornelius Smith, who was a nomad roaming the lanes of this country less than a hundred years ago.

There's a divinity that shapes our ends
Rough-hew them how we will.

Shakespeare

Chapter 22 Notes

1   ENSA (Entertainments National Service Association) was an organisation established in 1939 by Basil Dean and Leslie Henson to provide entertainment for British armed forces personnel during World War II.

2   This article was actually published in August 1943, not 1942.

3   The 'hoax' letter was published in September 1943, not 1942

4   The article completely 'debunking' the programmes, which Eunice implies was also 1942, was published on 29th September 1943.

   Tragically, Romany died on 20th November 1943 just over three weeks after that article which had distressed him so much. Was Eunice's alteration of the date simply a mistake or might she have deliberately wished to disassociate his death from this major upset, just weeks before he died? (See note 1 on page 175)

5   Gipsy Smith lived until 1947. Margaret Bell (formerly Potter, Alan's wife) recollected that, through Romany, Gipsy Smith came to the newly built Lazonby Village Hall (not far from Old Parks Farm). There was a service in the afternoon, and in the evening an open-air meeting to which 3000 people came

   David Lazell has written a biography of Gipsy Smith – *Gypsy from the Forest.* (1997)

Bram and Myself, 1930

Photo: Walter Scott

Chapter 23

Last Days

My husband died very suddenly on the twentieth of November, 1943. He went into the garden that morning as soon as he had finished breakfast, and I caught sight of him several times as he shovelled into his wheelbarrow the leaf-mould for his precious plants, and chatted with John Gore, the 'farmer,' and then with five- and seven-year-old Sonia and Christopher Shelmerdine. I like to think that it was with children that he was last seen. Then he came indoors and complained of a pain similar to one which he had experienced a few weeks before. Though he needed no persuasion to go upstairs and rest, it did not occur to either of us that it was serious enough to justify sending for our doctor, and when he seemed more at ease, I left him and came downstairs. Half an hour later, when I went up to see how he was, he had gone. It was incredible that he, of all people, who was so vitally alive, should be taken from this world; he, who had such a capacity for absorbing its wonder and loveliness. All that Dr Bruce, his medical adviser and friend, could say, after expressing his sympathy, was, "I often told him not to work so hard in his leisure hours."

He had lectured twice at Rochdale on the previous Saturday; he felt at home there, for it was his eighth visit. On the Sunday he preached twice at the Cavendish Street Congregational Church, Manchester. Those who heard him tell me that there was something very simple, yet strong and virile, about his talk, as he spoke on one of his favourite subjects – the grace of hospitality and neighbourliness, as illustrated by the story of the Shunammite woman. I had often heard this sermon – if my husband's intimate, friendly talks could be called sermons – for he usually spoke without notes of any kind, and yet each time he took us into fresh bypaths of thought and beauty.

He came home on the Sunday evening in the highest spirits. "Six full days in my garden," he kept exclaiming joyfully, for this was to be one of his periodical rests from public work. Each day that week he pottered about outside until dusk fell, when he came in and settled down to the writing of his book. On the Friday evening, I decided to join my sister at the cinema. On my way I called in at his den. "I suppose you won't come," I said, for having so many other interests, he only went on very rare occasions. To my astonishment, he replied, "Yes. I will. I've just finished the last chapter of my book."[1] How relieved and light-hearted he was that it was finished at last, and how strange, as I have already said, that he should have told me some months previously that this was the last book of the series that he intended to write. I did not feel entirely happy about his coming with us, because I recalled more than one occasion when he had fidgeted restlessly, and then apologetically walked out in the middle of a second-rate picture. However, this one turned out to be a pleasing, harmless romance, and he sat it through to the end.

On the Saturday morning as he left the breakfast table I said, "Go easy today. You've a lecture at Hurst to-night." As usual, he smiled tolerantly, and said nothing. Fortunately, there were those about me that afternoon who remembered that an audience would be assembling at Hurst in a few hours' time, and perhaps the predicament in which the tragic news placed the Rev Thomas Entwistle is best told in his own words. "I shall never forget that Saturday night. We had sold hundreds of tickets for the lecture. There was nothing we could do but let the people come to the schoolroom. At seven o'clock the place was crowded, waiting for Romany's arrival. When I went up on the platform, I was so overcome that I could not utter a word. The effect on the audience when I managed to pull myself together and told them was most moving and, before they dispersed, they stood a moment in silent sympathy." This was but one of many scores of disappointed audiences during the year that followed, for my husband had engagements booked until 1946, showing how confidently he was looking forward to years of public life.

More than a year has passed since that day, and some of the countless letters which I then received have a fuller meaning for me today. A doctor friend of his, Dr Fairweather of Clitheroe, wrote, "How glad he would have been had he known in advance that his passing was to be so peaceful, and that he was to be spared a life of inactivity and failing powers. I cannot but feel there was mercy in the manner of his going."

My brother-in-law, John Parsons, wrote, "Well done, Bram. He has made his exit as he made his walks from one field to another with hardly a sound. How true to nature. It is just what his birds and animals do when their time is up, and it must be the envy of us all. Would that we could all creep silently away. It is a truly aesthetic achievement."

And a letter from the Rev Harold Darby touched me deeply, in which he said, "He strode over a stile out of the field of wind and sunshine into the shades and mysteries of a wood. I am sure that he is now exploring it."

How strange it was that in my husband's wallet I should have found a scrap of paper on which he had scribbled, "Nobody grows old merely by living a number of years. Years wrinkle the skin, but to give up one's enthusiasm wrinkles the soul." He, indeed, never lost his enthusiasm for living. Nevertheless, it is sad to think that he might have prolonged his life had he not resumed his work and his strenuous hobbies so soon after his operation. But knowing him as I did, I feel sure that had he been curbed in any way, he would have been most unhappy. To be told that he must no longer use his tools to make a rustic seat for his garden or climb the ghylls where the ravens nested would have depressed him, and had he been given the choice of life as it was, or a longer life with limitations, he would most certainly have chosen the former.

On our last visit to the farm, we had spent most of the afternoon seated in a field by the side of one of his favourite woods, which slopes steeply down to Daleraven beck. He was quite content, listening to the soft cooing of the wood-pigeons in the trees above, and the music of the waters far below, and laughingly watching Raq's vain attempts to catch even the baby rabbits as they dashed into their burrows. Then he got up and, climbing to the top of one of the small, grassy hillocks in the undulating field, he stood awhile drinking in the beauty of the scene. "This will do for me," he said, and then added, "When I die, I'd like you to scatter my ashes up here." In my embarrassment I laughed, and hastened to assure him that he was so strong and vigorous that he would most certainly outlive me.

Memorial marking the spot where Romany's
ashes were scattered.

Within a few months I returned there alone, and carried out his wishes.[2] As Raq and I wandered over the fields, each tree and hedge had hallowed memories. Sauntering through the stillness of Bluebell Wood, with its overgrown, untrodden paths, I knew that his feet had made the track we were following, for no one loved that wood as he did. There was the field where he had settled down in his hiding-tent one morning to photograph the curlew's nest when, looking through one of the spyholes, to his alarm, he suddenly saw the white shorthorn bull charging towards him. Grabbing his camera, he took to his heels and jumped the gate just as the bull stampeded towards him with the hiding-tent impaled on its horns. There was the cornfield where he had saved the lives of several little wild creatures whose sanctuary, to their dismay, was growing mysteriously smaller as the noisy, relentless binder rattled round and round the field. Each time that he saw a small brown head peeping furtively through the stems, he would distract the attention of Willie Bird, the gamekeeper, hoping that the bewildered creature would reach the safety of the hedge before he could raise his gun.

Along the beck-side I strolled, past our favourite bathing-pool, and the quiet backwater where he had caught the nine trout. Was Raq going to do what had always made us laugh so much? Yes. In his eagerness to scent out the moorhens on the opposite bank, he dashed pell-mell across the narrow, slippery tree-trunk and fell plop into the icy water. That finished my walk, for remembering the warmth of the rag hearthrug in the kitchen, he was already half-way up the slope leading to the farm. After trying in vain to skirt the ankle-deep mud round the gate, churned up by the waiting cows, I climbed the wall on which he had sat so often as he watched Laddie cleverly rounding up the sheep for Joe; past the barn where I had heard him laughing, and had found him sitting beneath the wisps of hay which tumbled untidily through the roof. He had been watching one of the cats as it sat by the corn-bin, patiently waiting for an unwary mouse, when Raq had dashed in unexpectedly and caused pandemonium.

In spite of Sallie's hug of welcome when I passed through the kitchen, so many things brought back memories. There hung his old brown overcoat in the hall, and on the dining-room mantelpiece the pipe that he always left in Joe's pipe-rack; when we gathered round the fire after the evening meal, we were very conscious of his presence.

Notwithstanding the kindness of old friends, my subsequent visit to Carlisle was a sorrowful one. No one greeted me as I walked along English Street, and when I turned up Howard Place, intending to ask if I might see our old home again where June had been born, and the garden where we had buried Raq, I could not face it. Walking along Lowther Street, it saddened me to find that dear old John Rubb's shop[3] was no longer there, for he, too, has passed on. If heaven is a place of rivers and streams, as described by one of the old prophets, I am sure that my husband has met John. Over Eden bridges I went, and as I sat for a while by one of his favourite pools, I could see his long, lean figure standing on the bank. I recalled the time when, hearing the scream of his reel, and seeing the upward flick of his rod, I ran along the bank, knowing that he had hooked a fish. Unfortunately, he had left his landing-net at home, and so I offered to fetch it. But there was the danger of his losing his prize whilst I was gone, so I took off my shoes and stockings and waded in to the rescue, almost enveloping the slippery sea-trout in my new frock as we landed it.

My stay was brightened by one unexpected incident. For some time I had not been feeling well, and during my visit I asked my hostess if she would make an appointment for me with her doctor. During the consultation she did not know who I was, but the following day I received a letter from her, returning the fee I had given her – "In gratitude for many happy memories of listening to Romany."

I should perhaps have told before this of the great concern caused to his many friends by the announcement of his death on the six and nine o'clock news. Many children were so inconsolable that BBC officials worked overtime answering the telephone enquiries of distracted mothers whose children were crying themselves to sleep, not only because they had lost their Romany, but because many of them believed that Raq had been left alone in the caravan. This, unfortunately, was emphasised by a full-sized photograph of Raq which appeared in a Sunday paper, above the caption, "Romany's dog is wandering about looking for his master."

Incidentally, I should like to record my indebtedness to the BBC, and to Nan Macdonald in particular, for the way in which the many hundreds of letters of condolence which were sent to Muriel and Doris were dealt with. Each one was individually answered with a sympathetic understanding which one does not usually connect with officialdom. These, together with those which I received, all expressed a sense of deep personal loss, even by those who had never seen my husband. "Children's Hour will never be quite the same to my family." "I shall never walk in God's good green world without thinking of him, and of his smile and his merry eyes." "His passing has robbed thousands of the only breath of nature they have ever experienced in their lives."

The sad reading of these letters was lightened by the gratitude expressed to Muriel and Doris for the part they had played in the broadcasts, by the children who wrote to the BBC asking if they might have Raq, by the tiny boy who wrote that he had "cried real tears," and the Frenchman who wrote, "Messieurs, the BBC – Oh Sirs, what in the world are we going to do without our much-loved Romany? The way I shovelled my work aside on those magic Tuesdays was scandalous. That delightful half-laughing personality can never be replaced, though I could mention several broadcasters who, like the man in 'The Mikado,' would never be missed."

It was relieved, too, by the original way in which some listeners addressed their envelopes, and the ingeniousness shown by the Post Office officials in delivering them here – "Romany's home, Cheshire," "Anyone at Wilmslow connected with Romany," and "The caravan where Romany lived, near Fletcher's Farm, Cheshire."

The effect on some of the children when they went to school on the following Monday wrought havoc with their lessons. A Durham schoolmistress wrote, "I have never seen such signs of grief amongst my children. When the time came for prayers, I asked them what they should pray about, and one small child said, 'Let's say thank-you for Romany.'" Doris was telling me that a music teacher in a certain school was obliged to give up her lessons for the day as one pupil after another dissolved into tears. She also told me that in some areas, lessons became so impossible that the Education Authorities were asked if certain schools might be closed for the day.

Many letters told of the acts of homage paid to my husband by the congregations of churches of various denominations, and as I feel that it will be of special interest to my Methodist readers, I am including extracts from a few of the many letters from his fellow-ministers, amongst whom were numbered some of his dearest friends.

"To know him was to love him, not only for his genius but for his rich humanity. He was so friendly and lovable, and I count it a great honour to have known such a dear man." (Rev W Bardsley Brash)

"He was one of the people God sends to open the eyes of the blind and unstop the ears of the deaf. The mould of that kind of soul must, with Divine fitness, be unique. We shall never see his like again." (Rev Harold S. Darby)

"He clearly discerned 'the mystic heaven and earth within, plain as the sea and sky .... and taught his hearers to use their eyes and other God-given faculties." (Rev Arthur Phillips.)

To quote more than two of the appreciations which appeared in the various newspapers, would be repetition, and those I have chosen are from the BBC press because he was known to the greatest number of people as a broadcaster. Before doing so, however, I should like to include a sentence from a letter which I value from W L Andrews, the editor of the *Yorkshire Post*: "Your husband gave us all the purest kind of pleasure, and I am proud to have been one of his editors."

The *Radio Times* said: "The sudden death of Romany, one of the most gifted and beloved of broadcasters, will have saddened not only the children today, but thousands of those who were children at any time during the last twelve years, to say nothing of the more mature listeners who are never too grown up to listen and learn from the Children's Hour. There must be many young men and women in their twenties, now possibly serving with the Forces, or pulling their weight in factories, who owe their present delight in the English countryside in great part to their memories of Romany. He established himself as one of the great personalities of radio, a man who made millions of friends by his genius for being just himself. He was as individual in his way as were Walford Davies or John Hilton in theirs; and the loss is equally irreparable. No radio rambles along the country lanes can ever have again the same exhilarating flavour."

Herbert Farjeon wrote in *The Listener*, "The death of Romany bereaves the Children's Hour of its happiest and most distinguished feature. We have lost a friend who will be irreplaceable. But his influence, so simple, direct, unvulgar and unvain, remains." The following May, when reviewing his first year's work as a Radio Critic, he said, "Perhaps the rarest and most abiding memory of the year, and of many years previous, was furnished by the childhood-echoing rambles of Romany, Muriel and Doris – never to be heard again, but never to be forgotten."

My husband left a lasting influence on the BBC staff, judging from the letter which I received from the North Regional Director. "I am writing to express the sincere sympathy of all the staff here. To us, your husband's death is a personal grief. We knew him well and admired him deeply, and we shall always miss him. It is impossible to praise his work for the BBC too highly. It was unique, and with him something good and rich goes out of our life."

A great number of the letters received by the BBC contained requests that recordings of the Romany programme should be put on from time to time, and that his listeners should raise some memorial to him. Neither of these could be answered satisfactorily. Only one recording of the programme had been made, and the BBC, of course, is unable to sponsor memorial funds to individual broadcasters. It happened, however, that Derek McCullough was making his Annual Children's Hour Christmas appeal a few weeks later. As the North Region had in mind the endowment of a cot in memory of Romany, listeners who wrote expressing a wish for a national memorial were asked to subscribe to this fund. £12,000.00 came in as a result of this appeal, against £4,000.00 the previous year. Of this £500 was set aside for the endowment of a cot at the Cripples' Hospital at Leasowe, near Birkenhead. The ceremony, which was preceded by the one recorded programme, took place on the anniversary of my husband's death, and some of us will not forget the feeling expressed by Muriel and Doris as they unveiled the tablet and read the inscription – "From the BBC Children's Hour in memory of Romany. 'He loved birds and green places and the wind on the heath, and saw the brightness of the skirts of God.'"

Raq also took part in the ceremony, and not only delighted the children by jumping up and down their beds while the press photographers struggled to get him to sit for his photograph, but he also enlivened the journey for June and me. The North Regional Director kindly took us there in his car, and his happy recollections of the impression that the broadcasts had made on all classes of people we remember gratefully. One of the things which Mr Coatman told us was, that he had found that even among Oxford Dons, some of world-wide repute, there were those who would not dream of missing a Romany broadcast. When we reached Leasowe, we stopped to ask the way of two constables who stood chatting at the crossroads. A glance at the BBC label on the windscreen was sufficient to ensure their interest, but when they caught sight of the dog and one of them asked, "Is that Raq, sir?" their faces lit up, for they, too, had been Romany listeners. How proud it made me feel that he had been able to hold the interest of both professor and policeman.

I could tell many interesting stories showing the wideness of my husband's appeal, and of the varied and unexpected people who were his listeners. When travelling to and from her home in Staffordshire, Muriel told me that she had frequent chats with a porter on one of the small stations through which she passed. What happened to the trains between five-thirty and six o'clock on the day of the broadcast, I do not know, for he told her that he never missed a Romany broadcast. Not long ago, June and another Wren were given a lift in a car by someone whom she described as a "successful middle-aged business man." When they were passing through wooded country near Oxford, three cock pheasants flew across the road. To quote her letter, "To my astonishment, he turned to me and said, 'Did you ever listen to Romany?' When I told him that he was my father, he was so overcome that he couldn't speak, and when I gave him my photo of Daddy with Raq, he broke down completely. Wasn't it strange? Instead of going to Worcester as he intended, he took me all the way to Cheltenham."

To keep his memory alive listeners have formed a Romany Society,[3] and another memorial takes the form of a tablet placed in the X-ray room of the Ilford Dispensary for Sick Animals, a branch of the Society for which he collected so much money; the donations which the Society have since received in his memory now bring the total of the Romany Fund well over £700.00.

Perhaps the one which has brought me most pleasure is the one inaugurated by this village, which has already been the means of bringing thousands of people to see my husband's caravan. It was a happy thought of my friend, Anne Geake, that I should present it to the Romany Memorial Committee of the Wilmslow Urban District Council[4] so that his friends might visit it. Though it was with sorrow that I parted with it, the joy I have already experienced in meeting his listeners has more than compensated me for this. It was officially opened by Muriel and Doris last October, and it was an impressive sight to see the crowd, many of whom had travelled long distances, queueing up on that chilly autumn afternoon to see the *vardo*, in which, in imagination, they had spent so many happy afternoons. The very disorderliness of the rough wooded glade, with its half-tints of bronze and gold, seemed to enhance the setting of the caravan, its roof brushed with the feathery branches of a lofty larch. As Muriel and Doris stood on its steps and told of all that Romany had meant to them, I could see by the expressions on the up-turned faces of their listeners how grateful they were for the great part they had played in the broadcasts. This public recognition meant far more to them than most people knew. Unlike my husband, whose lectures gave him continuous opportunities of meeting his listeners, the fact that they had unselfishly remained anonymous had debarred them from this pleasure, and they had little conception of the place which they held in the hearts of their admirers.

Muriel wrote to me recently telling me that she had been speaking at a BBC War Exhibition, and she added, "The audience rose at me, and there were tears in my eyes when I realised their real affection for us all. Romany still lives, dear, and always will." In another way, Doris, too, is now realising it. As she travels about the country fulfilling her concert engagements, the announcement of her name immediately warms the hearts of many of the members of her audiences, and the rest of her fellow-artistes know that a friendly atmosphere is assured if she is there. She described to me how she went with a CEMA[5] Concert Party to tour some of the remote villages in the Trough of Bowland. In one place several hundred people were assembled in a hayloft, lit by paraffin lamps, and as soon as her identity became known, her reception was a royal one. When she went into the farmhouse, the farmer's wife hugged her and said, "I never thought I should have this honour," and as she described to me the big, homely, raftered kitchen, she said sadly, "I felt as though I was back with Romany in Mrs Fletcher's kitchen." They are now having visible proof of the widespread appeal of the programme again shown by the result of a ballot of War Radio Favourites taken recently by the *Sunday Chronicle*: Announcer – Alvar Lidell;   Woman Announcer – Joan Grifliths;   Comedian – Tommy Handley; Comedienne – Suzette Tarri;   Singer   – Webster Booth; Speaker – Winston Churchill; War Reporter – Richard Dimbleby; Radio Actor – James McKechnie;   Radio Actress – Gladys Young; Children's Hour favourite – Romany.

But I must return to the queue slowly filing into Romany's *vardo*. Did the inside of it come up to their expectations? I think it did.   Betty, the gamekeeper's wife, and Mrs Johnson, the farmer's wife, were both there to welcome them, and they told me afterwards how deeply affected many of them were to see his bed, crockery, pipe-rack, aquarium, fishing-rod and his favourite old mackintosh and sou'wester. Lining the walls they saw many of his photographs of wildlife of which he was so justly proud, and several of his early water-colours. In a special corner were some of the poems composed by his friends, the most deeply moving of these being the one by Geoffrey Dearmer, of the London Children's Hour, which was read at the BBC Memorial broadcast, and which appears at the end of this book.

But the old weather-beaten caravan, which has rumbled along the Yorkshire moorlands, and listened to the music of the Cumberland streams, has not yet reached its last resting-place. The Memorial Committee have a delightful idea in mind, for when the war is over they intend to make a Romany Walk in some rough parkland nearby. What could be more fitting than that his *vardo* should come to rest amongst the trees and shrubs planted by those who loved him, and nearby one of his favourite ponds. How thrilled he would have been to know that as Raq and I walked round it yesterday, a beautiful heron rose up from the tangle of rushes and, with a harsh protest, flapped its huge grey wings and flew awkwardly away. How worried he would have been, too, to know that it was scarcity of food, due to hard frost, that made this shy bird visit a pond so close to human habitation.

I shall always be grateful to Mrs S B L Jacks and Mr J F Roe, because the Memorial scheme was due to their initiative, and the money which they collected from the children of this village is now being augmented by a larger circle of listeners. One dear woman sent her full week's Old Age Pension, a small boy his month's pocket-money, and a Lincolnshire family sent a generous gift, "In memory of Laura, our parrot, who always shouted 'Hurrah' as soon as she heard Romany's voice."

Muriel and Doris at the Opening of the Vardo
7th October, 1944[6]

Photo: Sunday Express

Comparatively few will be able to visit the caravan, the Leasowe cot or the X-ray room at Ilford, but I like to think that there are many who have planted trees in their own gardens and elsewhere in his memory. "Can you tell me which was Romany's favourite tree?" writes a little girl who is planting one. How pleased he would have been to know this, for in one of his last weekly articles he wrote, "It saddens me to see the devastation of trees caused by the war. How I wish that I could persuade every child to plant a sapling once a year as a birthday comes round." Had he a favourite tree, I wonder? Though entranced by the emerald-tufted larch in springtime, the coppery-red beech in mid-autumn sunshine, or the symmetry of a shapely ash in winter, he had but one choice all the year round, and that was the Lady of the Woods, the dainty silver birch.

"May we see his garden?" some of the caravan visitors ask. As we walk round it together, I am always conscious of a feeling of helplessness, for it was he who made it, in more senses than one. The very tone of affection in his voice as he pointed out the delicate blooms of one of his favourite gentians, not only enhanced their beauty but seemed to deepen the azure-blue of their petals, and made his crimson maples glow like burning bushes. That he should not have been here to discover the first touches of early spring was beyond understanding. Across the snow-covered field he would stride carrying armfuls of what looked like dead twigs, and within a short time the sticky chestnut buds had blossomed out into green foliage which filled every vase in the house. Or while I was bustling around, I would hear a tap at the window, and his beaming face and beckoning finger would entice me out into the cold to see the first brave snowdrop, the fragrant pink blossoms of a daphne, or a deep purple primula. "Listen," he would call, as I hurried indoors to the warmth. "The bellman of spring," and I would be just in time to see a flash of yellow and black as a great-tit flew to a higher branch to continue its attempts at a song.

He should have been here, too, in the summer to see how the magenta foxgloves, which he planted under the ash tree, grew tall and stately, just in the position that he wanted them; to see the way that the honeysuckle, which he brought from Daleraven

281

beck-side, climbed almost to the roof of the house. So heavy with blossom and murmurous with bees was it, that as I sat writing by the open window, its intoxicating scent almost overpowered me too, as, from time to time, I wrestled with the straying inebriates which flew in and out. I should also like him to have known that the oak tree in the field, which he smeared with tar when the woodman felled it in error, did survive the winter frosts after all, and that the mallards which the children scared away from the pond came back again this year and nested there.

Should this book prove worthy to be included amongst the memorials to my husband, what I am now going to relate may not be out-of-place in this chapter. It was over a year ago that Mr Herbert Knott first cycled along to see me. I had known him as the father of a friend of mine, a much-respected magistrate, and a tireless worker for charitable objects. "I hear that you are going to write your husband's life," he said. "Could I help you with the typing of it?" I was astounded, for, vigorous as I knew him to be, he was in his eighty-ninth year. I thanked him, but more to please him than for the help that I imagined he would be, I handed him the first few pages of my almost unintelligible manuscript. Within two days he brought his copies, neatly and correctly done. Since then, allowing for my numerous alterations and corrections, he has typed well over a hundred and fifty thousand words. What an achievement. How anxious he has been to get it finished. "How far have we got now?" he would continually ask, and then add, "If anything happens to me, you'll find your manuscript in the top drawer of my bureau." His real reward will be that he may live to see it published. Not only am I grateful to him, but also to others whose suggestions have helped me in the writing of this book – my friend Phillipa Fletcher, my sister Margery Thomas, and especially my sister Kitty Parsons, whose interest in it has never flagged. At times I have written with a great sense of urgency. Will my husband be forgotten by his listeners before I have finished it, I wonder? Then have come interruptions in my work, but what welcome ones they have been. Through my window I see a family approaching his caravan, the children running eagerly ahead. "Come on, Raq," I call as I fetch the keys, and when he hears their familiar jingle, he needs no telling; off he dashes across the road to greet them. Or perhaps Doris comes over to see me, and as we sit by the fireside recalling happier days, the doorbell rings. Raq, who has been curled up at our feet, gets up reluctantly, with an 'I-expect-it's-me-they-want' look on his face. But no. "Is Auntie Doris here?" asks a small boy. "Would she give me her autograph?" And as he fondles Raq and looks up at Doris, I know that Romany still lives.

Spring is unchanged, although you cannot see
A halo spreading round our chestnut tree.
Spring cannot change, and in my heart I know
You who loved life so much would have it so."

B R Gibbs

Chapter 23 Notes

1   That book was *Out with Romany by Moor and Dale.*

2   A stone birdbath was subsequently erected on the hillock and is still visited and remains tended by members of the Romany Society. See illustration on page 271.

3   The first Romany Society, formed in 1946, ran until 1965. For information about the current Romany Society, begun in 1965, visit: **www.romanysociety.org.uk**

4   The Council, through its subsequent organisational changes, continued to own the *vardo* and display it at Wilmslow until in 2013, following a major restoration, Cheshire East Council donated it to the Bradford Industrial Museum where it is now displayed under cover.   (Bradford Industrial Museum, Moorside Road, Bradford BD2 3HP: telephone 01274 435900)

5   CEMA was the wartime Council for the Encouragement of Music and the Arts.

6   The boy sitting on the *vardo* steps is Bobby Ashworth, the son of farmer's wife, Mrs Johnson (Winifred Ashworth) who, with Betty (Clara Growther) the gamekeeper's wife, was often present to welcome visitors to the *vardo*.

Appreciations

GEOFFREY DEARMER LVO (1893 –1996)
wrote this Poem when Romany died:

FAREWELL TO ROMANY

Goodbye, dear friend. If we no more shall roam
Fresh woods with you, nor fields your voice made cool;
Nor find the fieldmouse in his harvest home,
The brown trout in the pool;
Nor with hands made more gentle at your words,
Pick up the shrew mouse or the trembling hare;
Nor, with ears wiser, name the singing birds
In trees no longer bare.
If we no more with you shall do these things,
Let us, at least, say sometimes when the clear
Spring skies are full of song and woods with wings,
"I wish that he was here."
Then shall we keep your memory green and true;
Then shall the lovely world more lovely grow,
And you, dear Romany, I think that you
Would wish to have it so.

An article from the
RADIO TIMES
3rd December, 1943

★ BOTH SIDES *of the* MICROPHONE ★

The sudden death of 'Romany,' one of the most gifted and beloved of Children's Hour broadcasters, will have saddened not only the children of today but thousands of those who were children at any time during the last twelve years, to say nothing of the more mature listeners, parents and others, who are never too grown-up to listen and learn from the Children's Hour. There must be many young men and women in their twenties, now possibly serving with the Forces or pulling their full weight in factories, who owe their present delight in the English countryside in great part to their memories of 'Romany' and his vivid way in his broadcasts and his books of directing young eyes towards all its wonders and beauty. He established himself as one of the great personalities of radio, a man who made millions of friends by his genius for being just himself.

Journalist, writer and friend of Romany
HERBERT LESLIE GEE (1901-1977),
known as 'HL,' wrote (1949):

It is impossible to imprison Romany's rare and elusive spirit between the covers of a book. The man himself, with his amazing knowledge of the outdoor world, his humour and friendliness, and above all his genius for enjoying life, was revealed in much that can never be recaptured. It was not only what he said but how he said it that gave us glimpses of his mind and heart; and we loved him for whimsical thoughts that never found their way into cold print, for his boyish smile, his deep and utterly charming voice, that sudden lighting up of the swarthy face – the dark eyes twinkling mischievously – and for the sheer dynamic of his engaging personality. Most at home when out of doors, Romany was happiest when alone with his friends, the birds and animals. He had a profound (and often ill-disguised) contempt for starched collars and drawing-room formality; but how he delighted in a ragged suit, an old pipe, a country lane, the life of the farm, the companionship of Raq his spaniel, and the friendship of anglers, gamekeepers, tramps, and boys and girls. As a broadcaster Romany was unique, educating while entertaining, and for no less than twelve years maintaining his fascinating *Out With Romany* programme, the most popular of its kind ever devised. As preacher and lecturer he drew large congregations and audiences, and in the pulpit as on the platform he remained informal and wholly irresistible. Unorthodox in his methods he undoubtedly was, but he touched many hearts and influenced many lives for good.

Edited LH – from HL's Foreword to his book *The Spirit of Romany*.

Former Patron of the Romany Society
TERRY WAITE, CBE writes:

My father was a village policeman and so I was brought up in small rural community in the heart of the countryside. Policemen were not well paid in those days so there was little or no money to spend on extras such as books. I delivered newspapers and saved up enough money to buy several volumes at the local 'bring and buy' sales. This is where I came across my first Romany books. It was later that I discovered that Romany's Caravan (*Vardo*) was just a few miles away in Wilmslow, and it was not until sixty years later that I discovered that the lady who typed Romany's manuscripts for his publisher was a bridesmaid at my parents wedding!

Romany might well be described as the first BBC Naturalist as his programmes on Children's Hour informed a whole generation of young (and not so young) people about the wonders of the countryside. His many books, of which I have many signed copies, are collectors' items. I hope the publication of this volume will introduce a whole new generation of young people to Romany and his companions, and, through them, to the delights of the British Countryside.

————————————

Editor: I remember having heard Terry say that, whilst in captivity he would relive in his mind episodes from the *Out with Romany* books. LH

————————————

Broadcaster and writer
ERIC ROBSON OBE writes:

I first came across Romany thanks to a lovely lady at Carlisle library. I was about six and she was trying to wean me off my preferred diet of cowboys and Indians. Romany was an instant hit as indeed was Raq. I didn't have a dog at home so Raq became my pet substitute.

Weekend family outings became Romany rambles. I pretended to fish using a five-foot garden cane as my high-tech fishing rod. The Romany of my imagination seemed to catch a sea trout with every cast.

The joy of the countryside that Romany generated in his books and broadcasts lives with me still as does his delight at gently breaking the rules. One of my favourite Romany tales is of Romany the preacher noticing out of the corner of his eye a hand belonging to one of his angling pals easing through the door at the back of the hall and silently undulating. He was reporting that the salmon were running through the pools in the River Eden half a mile away. No meeting ever finished so quickly. Romany was changed into fishing gear and on the road to the riverbank before his audience could escape the hall.

Matching the boundless pleasure that he gave to his thousands of loyal readers and listeners was his delight in exploring the wild Debatable Lands that hugged the England/Scotland border. These I can share with him having been born in Newcastleton on Liddel Water and sharing a fondness for nearby Penton Linns. When I made my television documentary *A Romany in Cumberland* it was to these riverbanks that we brought the horse-drawn *vardo* – the wooden caravan that would have been his rustic headquarters.

We tried our hardest to be true to the spirit of Romany, reflecting his passion for and knowledge of the natural world but some things would invariably change. His cocker spaniel Raq had gone to the kennel in the sky but in his stead was my Raq, a rather bolshie border terrier. I'm sure Romany would have approved.

I never met Romany – he died a few years before I was born – but if you doubt his influence you don't have to take my word for it. I'm just a jobbing broadcaster but both David Attenborough and David Bellamy credit Romany with inspiring their love of the natural world.

———————————

*Romany's Grandson and President of
the Romany Society*
SIMON BAIN, writes:

I was twenty-one before I was curious enough to read this amazing book for the first time. Quite apart from learning more about my famous grandfather, I was overwhelmed by the insights into the past life of my grandmother Eunice, known to me as 'Nunu,' who doted on me, her first grandchild. She was then in her eighties, and her little flat downstairs from us was austere excepting every December when strings would be hung with dozens upon dozens of cards - which had always puzzled me. Now I understood why, decades after his passing, Romany was still so loved by so many who had known him and my grandma. It was the Romany books, I guess, that enabled her to book places at a top school for me, and then my brothers, at birth, enabling me to get to Cambridge. And it was, I believe, his unseen legacy which inspired me a few years later to begin working with Traveller families, living in caravans, and realising I would always be drawn to the outdoors.

My second encounter with Romany came when, married to a Mancunian, I first visited the *vardo* at nearby Wilmslow. Here, in a little garden, still cared for, open to passing visitors and pilgrims alike, was the base camp of all those years ago. Across the road was the home, fated to be his last, where I was taken once as a baby.

But I never saw inside the *vardo* until, a year or two ago, I took my grown-up kids on two visits to the Bradford Industrial Museum where it is now housed. To see the little photos of my mum and grandma on the wall, and to sit with my family where he sat with his family a hundred years earlier, was deeply moving. The *vardo* was his little chapel in the great cathedral of Nature, and, inspiring in others the love of it was his true and lasting ministry. _____

FAMILY DATES

George Moysey Evens – *Romany's Father*   1860-1920
Mathilda (Tilly) Smith/Evens – *Romany's Mother*   1862- 1945
George Bramwell Evens – (*Romany)*   1884-1943
Eunice Thomas/Evens – *Romany's Wife*   1887-1976
Glyn Kinnaird Bramwell – *Romany's Son*   1912-1977
Romany June Evens/ Bain/Watt – *Romany's Daughter*   1924-2015

———————————

BOOKS by ROMANY   OP denotes out of print

A Romany in the Fields OP	Epworth Press 1929
A Romany and Raq OP	Epworth Press 1930
A Romany in the Country OP	Epworth Press 1932
A Romany on the Trail OP	Epworth Press 1934
Broadcast Echoes – Walks with Romany OP	E J Arnold & Sons 1937? 1941?
Out with Romany OP	London University Press 1937
Out with Romany Again OP	London University Press 1938
Out with Romany Once More OP	London University Press 1940
Out with Romany by the Sea OP	London University Press 1941
Out with Romany by Meadow and Stream OP	London University Press 1942
Out with Romany by Moor and Dale OP	London University Press 1944
Walks with Romany (New edition with illustrations by Leonard Hollands)	Lamorna Publications 2014

Other BOOKS about ROMANY

Romany, Muriel and Doris – G K Evens OP	London University Press 1939
Romany Turns Detective – G K Evens OP	London University Press 1949
The Spirit of Romany – H L Gee OP	St Hugh's Press 1949
Romany on the Farm – G K Evens OP	Epworth Press 1952
Romany's Caravan Returns – G K Evens OP	Epworth Press 1953
Romany Returns – Guy Loveridge	Douglas Loveridge Publications 1995
Romany in the Lanes – Phil Shelley	Lamorna Publications 2007
Romany on the Fells – Phil Shelley/Leonard Hollands	Lamorna Publications 2011
Reading Romany – David Barnaby	Bookcase 2018

Index

Lamorna Publications

Lamorna Publications is a private non-commercial specialist publisher offering books which might not be readily accepted by mainstream publishing houses. We are based in the beautiful Marshwood Vale in West Dorset.

Set up in 2007 we do not have an extensive book list, but more volumes are in the course of preparation.

Our areas of interest include Theology, Romani Gypsies, Wildlife, Art etc.

BOOK LIST

THEOLOGY

An Introduction to the Celtic Orthodox Church   *Fr Leonard Hollands*

The Little Celtic Prayer Book   *Fr Leonard Hollands ed*

Celtic Orthodox Prayer Book   *Fr Leonard Hollands ed*

St Gwenn's Daily Office Book   *Fr Leonard Hollands ed*

Divine Liturgy of the Celtic Orthodox Church   *Fr Leonard Hollands ed*

Celtic Orthodox Holy Week and Pascha   *Fr Leonard Hollands ed*

Celtic Orthodox Liturgical Calendar (Annually)   *Fr Leonard Hollands ed*

ROMANY/GYPSY INTEREST

Green Lanes & Kettle Cranes   *Dominic Reeve*

The Tarmac and the Trees   *Dominic Reeve*

Romany Road   *Beshlie*

Wayfarers All   *Beshlie*

Beshlie's Romany Road Sketch Book   *Beshlie, ed Hollands*

Settela   *Aad Wagenaar, translated Eliot*

The Gypsy Piano Tuner   *Janna Eliot*

Gypsy Guise and Disguise   *Juliet Jefferey*

ROMANY [G Bramwell Evens]

Romany in the Lanes   *Phil Shelley*

Romany on the Fells   *Shelley/Hollands*

Walks with Romany   *G B Evens*

WILDLIFE ART and ART

A Passion for Bird Art   *Leonard Hollands*

My Sea Eagle Odyssey   *Leonard Hollands*

Bird Drawings of Brendon Hollands   *Leonard Hollands ed*

Compelled to Paint   *Leonard Hollands ed*

Leonard's Landscapes   *Leonard Hollands ed*

MISCELLANEOUS

Contemplations   *Sally Davies/Leonard Hollands*

Schoolboy Soldier   *Bertram Armitage*

IN PREPARATION

Lavengro/Romany Rye – A concise edition containing both books
        George Borrow ed Peter Ansell

_____

www.lamornapublications.co.uk

Please do not submit any manuscripts without prior agreement. We cannot undertake to read or return unsolicited material.